Britain and Latin America:
a changing relationship

Contents

Contents

Contributors

David Atkinson, Adviser, Latin American Region, Developing Countries Division, Midland Bank

Peter Beck, Reader in International History, Kingston Polytechnic

Leslie Bethell, Professor of Latin American History and Director of the Institute of Latin American Studies, University of London

Victor Bulmer-Thomas, Reader in Economics of Latin America, Queen Mary College, University of London

Malcolm Deas, Fellow of St Antony's College, Oxford

Robert Graham, Latin American Editor, *The Financial Times*

Stephany Griffith-Jones, Reader in Economics, Institute of Development Studies, University of Sussex

Gerald Martin, Professor of Hispanic and Latin American Studies, Portsmouth Polytechnic

George Philip, Reader in Latin American Politics, London School of Economics and Institute of Latin American Studies, University of London

David Thomas, Former Assistant Under-Secretary of State for the Americas, Foreign and Commonwealth Office

David Webb-Carter (Brigadier), Former Commander British Forces, Belize

Laurence Whitehead, Official Fellow of Nuffield College, Oxford

Preface

British relations with Latin America have fallen badly into disrepair. The deterioration in the relationship was brought home in spectacular fashion by the war between Britain and Argentina in 1982 over the Falklands/Malvinas, although the decline had begun many years earlier. Even before the First World War, it was becoming clear that Britain's exceptional influence in the nineteenth century – based on trade and investment – could not be sustained and the two world wars, together with the intervening depression, left the United States as the undisputed hegemonic power. Since 1945, British preoccupations with decolonisation on the one hand and the rise of Western Europe on the other have pushed Latin America even further towards the margin of official interest.

The reduction in British influence in Latin America was, of course, inevitable. British hegemony in the nineteenth century was based on the absence of commercial rivals able to provide the capital and goods needed by the newly independent republics. With the emergence of other capital-exporting countries before the First World War (notably France, Germany and the United States), the British monopoly declined and commercial competition led to a diversification of Latin America's trade and investment links. British influence remained strongest in the Southern Cone of Latin America (Argentina, Chile, Uruguay), but this position was further undermined by the debt defaults of the 1930s and the wave of nationalisations (including that of the Argentine railways) in the late 1940s.

From their low point at the end of the 1940s, British relations with Latin America have declined still further. This has not, generally speaking, been the result of conscious decisions by British or Latin American policy-makers. On the contrary, official pronouncements on both sides continue to speak of the need to maintain and, if possible, strengthen the existing relationship, while interest in Latin America on the part of the British public appears to be greater now than for several decades. Thus, the decline in the relationship raises several important questions: why did it occur, has it gone too far and will it be reversed in the 1990s?

These questions were addressed by the Latin American Study Group (LASG) at the Royal Institute of International Affairs (Chatham House) throughout the academic year 1987/8. The Study Group, formed in 1982, brings together specialists on Latin America from the fields of higher education, journalism, commerce and finance; in addition, the Study Group enjoys a close relationship with the Foreign and Commonwealth Office (FCO), as well as other government departments, giving it insights into official thinking and recognition of the problems faced by policy-makers in the real world. The LASG provides one of the few opportunities in Britain for specialists from different disciplines and backgrounds to meet to focus on problems of common interest and it was therefore felt to be the ideal forum for a study of British relations with Latin America. In addition to the core group (of approximately twenty members), other specialists were invited to the monthly seminars according to the issue under consideration. Thus, over the year some fifty people participated in the work of the Study Group, giving rise to a useful exchange of ideas and information.

The Study Group's first task was to define Latin America. Following decolonisation in the Caribbean, several English-speaking former colonies (for example, Guyana, Jamaica and Trinidad and Tobago) have joined regional institutions such as the Organization of American States and the Inter-American Development Bank, breaking down traditional barriers with Latin America and leading to the adoption of common positions on a number of issues of regional concern. It became clear, however, following a seminar on this subject to the Study Group given by Roberto Espindola (of Bradford University), that this trend was not yet sufficiently strong to justify treating these independent countries as part of Latin America; at the same time, the continuation of their close economic, political and cultural ties with Britain (even stronger in the case of the remaining dependent territories) did not appear to provide a source of friction with Latin America. Thus, the Study Group concluded that the English-speaking Caribbean does not as yet have any significant impact on British relations with Latin America and the same was true *a fortiori* of the Dutch-speaking countries and the French *départements d'outremer*. The Study Group therefore worked with a traditional definition of Latin America, involving all the mainland republics together with Cuba, the Dominican Republic and Haiti, although in our analysis of territorial disputes and the trade in illegal drugs it has obviously been necessary to consider a number of English-speaking Caribbean states. Puerto Rico, because of its special relationship with the United States, was also excluded.

The Study Group also faced a problem of what time-horizon to adopt. All members agreed that a primary concern should be the evolution of British relations with Latin America in the 1990s. At the same time, it was recognised that it was not possible to write intelligently about the future without a clear understanding of the past. Generally, contributors interpreted 'the past' as post-1945, although in some cases it was possible to begin the story much later. The first chapter (by Leslie Bethell) has also been devoted to an overview of British relations with Latin America from the time of the struggle for independence in the early nineteenth century to the end of the Second World War.

Thus, the book examines the changing relationship between Britain and Latin America with much of the emphasis on future prospects.

In relations between states or groups of states, there are bound to be sources of friction and British–Latin American relations are no exception. The Falklands/Malvinas dispute has become the bone of contention with the highest profile in recent years and the Study Group could not fail to address it. The traffic in illegal drugs, however, is also a potential source of friction of great concern to government officials and ministers, many of whom have no special interest in Latin America; the overlapping claims to sovereignty of Britain, Chile and Argentina in Antarctica warranted the attention of the Study Group in view of the outcome of other territorial disputes in the South Atlantic. These three issues – Falklands/Malvinas, drugs, Antarctica – have been brought together in Part III of the book under the heading 'Sources of friction'. Trade disputes – increasingly important – are discussed in the economics chapters (Part II) and the Conclusions (Part IV). The border disputes involving former British colonies (Belize with Guatemala and Guyana with Venezuela) are no longer major problems in British relations with Latin America; they are discussed at several points in the book, but the Study Group did not feel they warranted special treatment.

Environmental questions have also grown in importance in recent years and could become a source of friction in the 1990s. At present, the issues (such as the destruction of tropical rain forests in Amazonia) are primarily of concern to Nongovernmental Organisations (NGOs), but public interest is such that the British government may feel compelled to give the environment a higher priority in its relations with certain Latin American states in the future. Environmental questions are discussed at a number of points in the book, particularly in chapters 3 and 10.

The Study Group explored several areas which were believed *ex ante* to be of importance, but which turned out *ex post* to be of only limited interest. One area was Britain's role as an international centre for commodity trading, which was explored by Carlos Fortín of the Institute of Development Studies at the University of Sussex; Latin American involvement in the London commodity markets is rather minor and Carlos Fortín concluded that 'involvement in futures markets follows the path of physical trading, and here the general trend is one of Latin American commodity export markets continuing to shift from Britain and Europe generally towards the United States, Japan and the newly industrialising countries'. Another area examined was that of British communities in Latin America, among which the best known is the Anglo-Argentine. Eduardo Crawley (editor of the *Latin American Newsletters*) was forced to conclude, however, that these communities did not offer much immediate prospect for improved relations between Britain and Latin America, although he did feel that the 'second generation' – assimilated offspring of the old local British community – could eventually act as 'aides or mediators in the construction of new, more mature links across the Atlantic'.

Preface

The Study Group gratefully acknowledges financial support from the Inter-American Development Bank, whose representative in the UK, Hector Luisi, has consistently encouraged the Group and stimulated its debates over the years. The Study Group has also received excellent support from Chatham House, where Lucy MacDermot organised all the meetings and acted as rapporteur. As convenor of the Latin American Study Group and editor of the present volume, I would like to express my gratitude to the chairman of LASG, David Thomas, whose premature retirement as Assistant Under-Secretary of State for the Americas at the FCO has been their loss and our gain.

VICTOR BULMER-THOMAS

1 Britain and Latin America in historical perspective

Leslie Bethell

There can be no field of enterprise so magnificent in promise, so well calculated to raise sanguine hopes, so congenial to the most generous sympathies, so consistent with the best and highest interests of England as the vast continent of South America.

Henry Brougham, House of Commons, 13 March 1817

For more than a century – from the Napoleonic Wars and, more especially, from the dramatic events of 1807–8 in the Iberian Peninsula which eventually led to the breakup of the American empires of both Spain and Portugal – Britain was the dominant external actor in the economic and, to a lesser extent, the political affairs of Latin America. The foundations of British commercial and financial pre-eminence in Latin America were firmly laid at the time of the formation of the independent Latin American states during the second and third decades of the nineteenth century. Throughout the century which followed, until the outbreak of the First World War in 1914, Britain supplied more of the manufactured and capital goods imported into Latin America, more of the loans given to the new Latin American governments and more of the capital invested in Latin American infrastructure (above all, railways), agriculture and mining than any other nation. British merchant houses and, from the 1860s, British banks played a central role in the Latin American economies. British ships carried the bulk of the produce exported from Latin America and Britain was itself a major market for Latin American food and raw materials. The nineteenth century was the 'British century' in Latin America.

During the first half of the twentieth century, and especially after 1914, the United States replaced Britain, first as Latin America's leading trading partner and then as Latin America's main source of capital. By 1945 the United States had also established its political – and in many cases cultural – hegemony throughout the subcontinent (except in Argentina). Britain nevertheless maintained a considerable financial and commercial presence in South America, and indeed retained a dominant position in Argentina (then the leading Latin American republic), until the Second World War. Even in the years immediately after 1945 Britain remained second (albeit a poor second) to the United States among the outside powers with an interest in the region. It was only in the second half of the twentieth century that Britain finally abandoned its role as a significant actor in the economic and political affairs of Latin America.

British interest in Latin America goes back to the late sixteenth century when, like other maritime powers, England first cast envious eyes on the immense and mineral-rich empire that Spain had acquired in the New World and the colonial trade it was attempting to monopolise. Hawkins, Drake and Raleigh became Elizabethan heroes as a result of their attacks on Spanish fleets and on Spanish possessions in Central America and the Caribbean. During the seventeenth and eighteenth centuries, however, with a few exceptions like the (permanent) capture of Jamaica in 1655 and the (temporary) seizure of Havana in 1761, the English concentrated on developing an extensive contraband trade with Spanish America (and with the Portuguese colony of Brazil). In the late eighteenth and early nineteenth centuries, and especially during the Napoleonic Wars when European markets were largely closed to British manufactured goods, a powerful lobby of politicians, merchants and manufacturers, naval and military officers brought pressure to bear on successive British governments in favour of conquest in Spanish America. There were plans for conquest as there were indeed for liberation. The only serious attempt, however, to annex any part of the Spanish empire – the British invasion of the Río de la Plata in 1806–7 – was, at least in its inception, entirely unauthorised.

'By an express which we have just received from Portsmouth', reported *The Times* on 13 September 1806, 'we have to congratulate the Public on one of the most important events of the present war … *Buenos Aires at this moment forms a part of the British Empire.*' On 27 June some 1,600 British troops had captured the second-largest city in Spanish South America and capital of a vast region, the Viceroyalty of the Río de la Plata, which stretched from the Atlantic to the Andes and from Patagonia in the far south to the borders of modern Peru. The idea of capturing Buenos Aires had originated in the fertile mind of Sir Home Riggs Popham, commander of the English fleet that had taken Cape Town from the Dutch earlier in the year. Nevertheless the British government, with the enthusiastic support of commercial and manufacturing interests, decided to back the invasion. Additional forces were dispatched to the River Plate (and plans were prepared for major expeditions to Venezuela and Mexico). In the meantime, however, the British troops had suffered a bloody and humiliating defeat. After less than seven weeks they had been driven out of Buenos Aires. On 3 February 1807, after reinforcements had begun to arrive, the British captured Montevideo. On 28 June 9,000 troops began a second assault on Buenos Aires. It was a disastrous failure (401 dead, 649 wounded and 1,924 taken prisoner). With the evacuation of Montevideo on 9 September 1807, Britain's short-lived empire in southern South America came to an inglorious end.

There were in fact only three outposts of the British Empire in Latin America which survived into the twentieth century: British Guiana and the settlement of Belize (British Honduras) on the mainland and the Falkland Islands 300 miles offshore. Essequibo, Demerara and Berbice on the 'wild coast' of northern South America between the Orinoco and the Amazon were first seized from the Dutch in 1796 and formally ceded to Britain by treaty in 1814–15. In 1831 they were united in the Crown colony of British Guiana which became a major producer of sugar. The boundaries were not clearly defined, however, and British claims based on the surveys of the German naturalist Robert Schomburgk in the 1830s and 1840s were disputed by British Guiana's Latin American neighbour, Venezuela. British logwood cutters had first established themselves at the mouth of the Belize river on the western shore of the Bay of Honduras on the Caribbean coast of Central America in the middle of the seventeenth century. By the end of the eighteenth century Spain had reluctantly come to recognise limited British rights there although Spain never renounced sovereignty. During the first half of the nineteenth century the Belize Settlement expanded to twice the area of the old Spanish concession and became a major producer of mahogany and the principal entrepôt for independent Central America, which lacked deep-water ports. In the meantime Britain had attempted to strengthen its position in Belize's 'dependencies'. In 1839 Roatán and neighbouring islands, strategically situated off the northern coast of Honduras and only 120 miles from Belize, were seized and in 1852 became the Crown colony of the Bay Islands. In 1842, after a lapse of half a century, a protectorate was re-established over the Mosquito Shore, an ill-defined area several hundred miles long on the Caribbean coasts of Honduras and Nicaragua. However, the Bay Islands were ceded to Honduras in 1859 and Britain withdrew from the Mosquito Shore in 1860. Only the Belize Settlement remained of Britain's Central American possessions. In 1862 it became the Crown colony of British Honduras – its territorial limits, like those of British Guiana, to be disputed by a Latin American neighbour (in this case Guatemala).

The Falkland Islands (Islas Malvinas), 'discovered' by the ships of several nations in the sixteenth century, had been first settled in the 1760s by France (1764–7) and then by Spain (1767–1811), in the case of East Falkland, and by Britain (1765–74), in the case of West Falkland. The newly independent state of the United Provinces of the Río de la Plata (Argentina) occupied the Islands in 1816, began their settlement in 1820, established a political and military command there in 1829, but was expelled by Britain in 1833. In 1841 the Falklands became a Crown colony and ten years later had been settled by 287 British subjects. By the end of the century the Falkland Islands, still claimed by Argentina, were occupied by some 2,000 people and 800,000 sheep.

With few political or military obligations of empire Britain's interests in Latin America during the first three-quarters of the nineteenth century were primarily, indeed almost exclusively, commercial. Only five months after the Buenos Aires débâcle an early opportunity had arisen to expand British trade – and extend British political influence – throughout much of South America. In November 1807 the British navy escorted the Portuguese court, fleeing Napoleon's armies, across the Atlantic to Brazil, where the following January the

Prince Regent opened Brazilian ports to the trade of friendly nations, that is to say, Britain. Not only was Brazil an important market in itself for British manufactured goods, especially textiles and ironware; it was a convenient back door to the Río de la Plata and the Pacific coast of Spanish America. British exports to Brazil in 1808 were valued at over £2 million (8 per cent of total British exports). At the same time, in the wake of Napoleon's overthrow of the monarchy in Spain, rebellions (which eventually became revolutions for independence) broke out in the Río de la Plata and many other parts of Spanish America and the resulting new regimes, like the Portuguese government in Rio de Janeiro, were eager to open their ports to British trade. In some years before the end of the European war in 1815 Latin America absorbed as much as a third of British exports.

Although officially neutral in the wars for independence, Britain made it clear that it would never allow Spain to reimpose its commercial monopoly in Spanish America and insisted that the region must remain open to British trade. With the Royal Navy in complete command of the Atlantic, Britain was also able to guarantee that no other European power intervened in Spanish America on behalf of Spain. Meanwhile, unofficially, 6,000 British officers and men fought alongside the insurgents, especially in Venezuela and Colombia, Peru and Bolivia. In December 1824, George Canning, the British Foreign Secretary, was able to write in a famous and much-quoted letter to his friend Lord Granville, British ambassador in Paris, 'Spanish America [including by this time Mexico and Central America] is free and if we do not mismanage our affairs sadly, she is English', and in a similar vein, a year later, 'Behold! the New World established and, if we do not throw it away, ours!'[1] Commercial treaties were imposed on Mexico, Colombia, Argentina and other independent Spanish American republics (with little possibility of negotiation) as a precondition for much-sought-after recognition by Britain, the world's leading power. These guaranteed most-favoured-nation treatment for British trade and protection for the lives, liberties and properties of British subjects. Exceptionally, the treaty of 1827 with Brazil, which in 1822 had separated itself from Portugal to become an independent Empire, included preferential duties on imported British manufactured goods (while Britain continued to discriminate against Brazil's major exports, sugar and coffee, in favour of colonial produce) and extraterritorial rights and privileges (including special courts) for British merchants in Brazil.

By the late 1820s there were sizeable British communities in all the major coastal towns of Latin America, especially Rio de Janeiro, Montevideo, Valparaíso (the principal port of entry and entrepôt for the west coast of South America) and Buenos Aires, where 3,000–4,000 British subjects had their own church, chapel, cemetery and library. In the lower depths of these communities could be found what Henry Stephen Fox, the British minister in Buenos Aires, in 1832 described as 'persons ... of the most foul and disreputable character ... all under the impression that this is a British colony, to be governed by British laws of which I am to be the administrator'. Fox, who in 1835 had moved to the British legation in Rio, claimed that he had never seen, or read of, or heard described 'so vile a community as the English scrapings now settled in South America'.[2] Yet there were also respectable cabinetmakers, tailors, physicians, apothecaries, upholsterers, blacksmiths, bootmakers, hatters, watchmakers and saddlers. At the head of these British communities were the representatives – some transient, some becoming permanent residents – of more than 200 major London and Liverpool merchant houses. Over half of these establishments were in Rio de Janeiro, a third in Buenos Aires and Montevideo, but there were many also in Valparaíso, Santiago and Lima (for example, Antony Gibbs, Duncan Fox, Balfour Williamson, Graham Rowe), in Caracas and La Guaira (above all, the House of Boulton) and even in San Blas on the Pacific Coast of Mexico (Barron Forbes).

The merchant house, which has been called the predominent institutional expression of British business in Latin America in the nineteenth century, existed primarily, of course, to import and distribute British goods: mainly textiles (cottons, woollens, linens and so forth), but also other manufactured consumer goods (such as ironware, cutlery, porcelain, glass, pianos, furniture, hats, stockings) and some capital goods and raw materials, especially coal. The size of the Latin American market had been grossly exaggerated at the time of Independence and hence quickly overstocked. Nevertheless in the early 1840s Brazil was receiving half its imports from Britain, worth £2–3 million per annum. This represented 5–7 per cent of total British exports – a decline from the 15 per cent of the 1820s, but still making Brazil Britain's third-largest market after the United States and Germany. British goods worth another £2 million (5 per cent of total British exports) were exported to Spanish America (more than half going to the River Plate and Chile). By the early 1870s £25 million worth of British goods (10 per cent of total British exports) were being imported annually into Latin America (a third into Brazil).[3]

At the same time British merchant houses handled the export of many local primary products: Brazilian coffee (here the firm of Edward Johnston and Co. played a key role, although the main market was the United States); Argentine hides and wool; Chilean silver and wheat; above all, Peruvian guano (natural fertiliser). The profitable trade in guano to Britain, the most important of the European markets, was largely in the hands of Antony Gibbs and Sons during the 1840s and 1850s (hence the verse well known in the City of London, 'Antony Gibbs / made his dibs / selling the turds / of foreign birds').

In general, however, most of Latin America's exports stagnated during the second and, to a lesser extent, the third quarter of the nineteenth century, which produced a marked imbalance in trade. In some sectors, particularly in mining, but also in agriculture, exports fell well below the level of the late-colonial period as a result of physical destruction and flight of capital during the wars for independence, political instability in the aftermath of Independence and lack of investment in the modernisation and expansion of production. Not much capital was accumulated locally; indeed, there was an outflow of precious metals to pay

Leslie Bethell

for excessive imports of British consumer goods. Furthermore, neither the British, nor other foreigners, invested in Latin America on a major scale for several decades after the financial and economic failures of the 1820s.

Several loans to the new Latin American states, many in excess of £1 million, had been floated on the London capital market during the years 1822–5. By 1828 every state except Brazil had defaulted on at least the interest payments, bringing into existence a host of committees of anxious and angry British bondholders. At the same time, taking advantage of the stock exchange boom of 1823–5 numerous joint-stock companies had been created to explore the legendary mineral wealth of Mexico, Peru, Bolivia, Colombia and Chile. Only a few Mexican mining companies, like Real del Monte, survived the crash which followed. None were profitable.

During the period after Independence the great British merchant houses invested modestly in internal commerce, land, food processing, even mining, and also provided valuable financial services for British and local clients. Only in the late 1850s and the 1860s, however, was a significant financial connection re-established between Latin America and Europe, especially Britain. Barings, for example, floated a loan of £1.5 million for Chile in 1858, a loan of £1 million for Venezuela in 1862 and loans of £1.25 million in 1866 and £1.95 million in 1868–9 for Argentina during the Paraguayan War.[4] Brazil and Peru, however, were the major borrowers, accounting for at least 50 per cent of total British portfolio investment in Latin America before the investment boom of the 1870s and 1880s. The first joint-stock enterprises, a new type of business concern with headquarters in the metropolis, invested in early railway development (in Brazil, Argentina, Mexico and elsewhere), in public utilities (for example, gas companies in all the major cities of Brazil), in land (in Argentina, Uruguay and Paraguay) and in mining (in Chile). Significantly, perhaps, the first British commercial banks – the London and Brazilian Bank (1862), the London and River Plate Bank (1863), the London Bank of Mexico and South America (1863–4), the English Bank of Rio de Janeiro (1863), the London and Venezuela Bank (1864) – suddenly appeared on the Latin American scene and their business expanded rapidly.[5] By 1865 £80 million and by 1875 £175 million was invested in Latin America, 10 per cent of total British investment abroad, most of it in government bonds and, to a lesser extent, railways.[6]

In the economic history of Latin America the third quarter of the nineteenth century represents a transitional period between the immediate post-Independence period, which was generally characterised by poor export performances (with exceptions like coffee in Brazil, guano in Peru, sugar in Cuba) and consequent economic stagnation, and the 'Golden Age' of export-led growth (*desarrollo hacia afuera*) from the 1870s and 1880s to the 1920s. The impetus for the often spectacular growth of the Latin American export sectors in the late nineteenth and early twentieth centuries came primarily from international (including British) demand for Latin American foodstuffs and raw materials. It was made possible by the British-led revolution in communications

6

and transportation, especially railways and transoceanic steam navigation and cables, and by a massive inflow of (mainly British) capital into infrastructure and, to some extent, production. This in turn was facilitated by a much improved business climate in Latin America, as the political instability in most countries after Independence gave way to stability in the form of both constitutional and representative regimes (for example, in Argentina and Uruguay) and dictator-ships (as in Venezuela and Mexico) – all of which encouraged foreign invest-ment. These changes did much to increase the flow of British capital to Latin America after 1880, although there were occasional disruptions such as that caused by the Baring Crisis (1890–1), after which new investment in Argentina (and elsewhere) dried up for a period.

The measurement of foreign investment in Latin America in the nineteenth century is a historical minefield. However, it would be generally agreed that British investment in Latin America grew from under £200 million in 1880 to around £1,000 million in 1913[7] – a third in Argentina (which in some years, for example 1889, had absorbed 40–50 per cent of all British capital invested abroad),[8] a quarter in Brazil and a sixth in Mexico. This represented 20–25 per cent of total British overseas investment and almost 60 per cent of all foreign investment in Latin America.

A large proportion of British investment in Latin America in the thirty to forty years before the First World War was portfolio investment (government bonds and minority holdings in foreign-controlled companies), although direct invest-ment increased from a quarter in 1880 to almost half in 1914. The British investor in Latin America put more than a third of his money into government (federal, state and municipal) bonds. Barings remained the principal bankers of Argentina and a number of other Spanish American republics. (Between 1902 and 1914, for example, they were directly responsible for thirteen issues for Argentina or Buenos Aires totalling £27 million.)[9] For Brazil it was Rothschilds. They financed, for example, the funding loan of £10 million in 1898, although Schroders led the consortium which raised the loan to the state of São Paulo in 1906 in order to finance valorisation, the price-support programme for coffee. Not only a large part of portfolio investment but also half of direct British investment went to finance railway construction – especially in Argentina, but also in Brazil, Peru, Uruguay, Chile and Venezuela. Throughout Latin America, besides passengers and imports, exports were moved rapidly and cheaply to the seaports by railways financed, built and run by the British – the Central Argentine Railway, the Buenos Ayres Great Southern Railway, the Argentine Great Western Railway, the Central Uruguay Railway, the San Paulo Railway which linked São Paulo to the port of Santos (one of the greatest – and most profitable – achievements of Victorian engineering), the Tarapacá Railway, the Peruvian Corporation's Central Railway, the La Guaira–Caracas Railway, the Mexican Southern Railway, the Tehuantepec Railway and the Western Railway of Havana. The rail networks of Argentina and Brazil, in particular, expanded from less than 500 miles each in 1870 to 21,000 and 15,000 miles respectively in

1914. In 1900 British-owned companies accounted for almost 90 per cent of aggregate railway investment in Argentina and some 15 per cent of Argentina's total capital stock.[10]

The British also invested in banking and insurance; in shipping; in harbours and port works (Rio de Janeiro, Santos, Buenos Aires, La Guaira, Vera Cruz); in river transport; in telegraph and cables ('All the earth is caught up in the net of English telegraph lines ...', wrote Eduardo Prado in Brazil, 'powerful invisible nerves ... connecting the most remote regions to the brain of the world, London');[11] in sheep farms in Patagonia and cattle *estancias* in Buenos Aires province and in the mesopotamian and littoral provinces of Argentina (in 1913 10 per cent of British direct investment in Argentina was in land)[12] as well as in Uruguay, Paraguay and Southern Brazil; in meat-packing plants like George Drabble's River Plate Fresh Meat Co. (1882), flour mills (Rio Flour Mills and Granaries, established 1886, was the most successful British manufacturing investment in Brazil), sugar refineries, breweries and textile mills (J. & P. Coats in Brazil); in nitrate mines (the British owned 70 per cent of the Chilean nitrate industry in 1890), silver mines in Mexico, Chile and Peru, copper mines in Chile, Peru and Venezuela, gold mines in Brazil (the St John del Rey Mining Co. in Minas Gerais) and oil fields in Peru, Ecuador and, most successfully, Mexico (El Aguila); and finally, almost rivalling railways in importance in the decade before the First World War, in urban public utilities. Urban growth accompanied export-sector growth and the British financed and managed urban transport companies, waterworks, sewage and drainage systems, gas and later electricity companies throughout Latin America – especially in Argentina, Brazil, Uruguay, Chile and Peru. The Anglo-Argentine Tramways Co. (1869) is a notable example: it had acquired by 1910, through a series of amalgamations and mergers, a network of 430 miles in Buenos Aires (75 per cent of the most extensive system in the world)[13] and in 1913 it opened the city's (and Latin America's) first underground railway. Montevideo, perhaps even more than Buenos Aires, was a city almost totally dominated by British capital. As early as 1881 the British minister was able to declare that 'all the industrial enterprises ... which are of any importance are in English hands. Railways, Tramways, Banks, Docks, Gas and Water supplies have been established by English capital and are managed by Englishmen.' In 1890 the President of the Republic compared his position to that of 'the manager of a great ranch, whose board of directors is in London'.[14]

To the enterprising British entrepreneur, Latin America now offered opportunities without parallel. Two outstanding examples of many who were tempted are John Thomas North and Weetman Pearson (who became Lord Cowdray in 1910).[15] North first went to Peru in 1869 at the age of twenty-seven as the representative of Fowlers, a Leeds engineering firm exporting nitrate-extracting machinery. Within a few years he owned his own nitrate *oficina* near the coastal town of Iquique. After the War of the Pacific (1879–83) and the transfer of the rich nitrate provinces of the Atacama desert from Peru and Bolivia to Chile,

North acquired the title deeds to the richest nitrate fields. Operating mainly from London, he also controlled the water supply, gas, coal and provisions supply companies of the key province of Tarapacá, as well as the railway linking the most important *oficinas* to the port of Iquique. In 1889, with the nitrate market showing signs of weakness and the Chilean government threatening to impose controls on foreign monopolies, the 'Nitrate King', who was by now a leading figure in English society, made an extensive tour of his 'kingdom'; he was accompanied by a number of distinguished journalists, including W. H. Russell of *The Times* who discovered, for example, that the Tarapacá Railway was not, as had been reported, 'a tramway ending in a marsh' but a network of 'stations, sidings, platforms, locomotive sheds ... worthy of any city in Europe'. North, who met President Balmaceda three times, left Chile having successfully restored confidence in the industry and in his companies. The nitrate boom was over, however, and before his death in 1896 North, who had in his own words risen from 'mechanic to millionaire' through his activities in Peru and Chile, had quietly diverted his capital from Tarapacá to collieries in England, factories in France, cement works in Belgium, tramways in Egypt and gold mines in Australia.

Pearson first visited Mexico in 1889 at the age of thirty-three and during the next twenty years spent several months of almost every year in Mexico City. He became an intimate friend of the dictator Porfirio Díaz and, as Liberal MP for Colchester, was generally known in England as 'the Member for Mexico'. His major achievements in Mexico included the draining of Mexico City and the valley of Mexico by means of a 30-mile-long Gran Canal – a task that had baffled engineers for three centuries; the construction at Vera Cruz, on Mexico's Caribbean coast, of a deep-water port with three giant breakwaters, a half-mile jetty for ocean liners, wharves, warehouses, a railway station, pure water supply and electricity; and the construction of a railway across the Isthmus of Tehuantepec, connecting the Atlantic and Pacific Oceans, with a modern, well-equipped port at each end – Salina Cruz on the Pacific, Coatzacoalcos on the Gulf. In 1910, on the eve of the Mexican Revolution, after almost a decade of failure and competition from a subsidiary of Standard Oil of New Jersey, the Pearson Trust's Mexican Eagle Co. (El Aguila) finally struck oil – the great Potrero Four well – and became immediately by far the largest oil producer in Mexico. Cowdray rode the storm of the Revolution, but began to pull out after the First World War and in 1919 sold his oil interests to Royal Dutch Shell.

During the period from 1880 to 1914 a dramatic expansion in trade between Latin America and Britain accompanied the massive increase in British investment. Although many Latin American foodstuffs (such as coffee, cacao, sugar and fruit) still could not compete with British colonial produce and were exported (often by British merchant houses and shipping companies) to France, Germany and the United States, Latin American exports to Britain quadrupled. In 1913 Britain imported primary produce worth £76 million from Latin America, which represented 10 per cent of total British imports and 25–35 per cent of the exports of Brazil, Argentina, Uruguay, Chile and Peru. Much of the increase after 1880 was accounted for by minerals (Chilean nitrates until the 1890s, copper from Peru and Chile, Mexican oil after 1910), Brazilian rubber, and wool, cereals and – above all – chilled, frozen and canned meat from Argentina and Uruguay. Imports from Argentina alone amounted to £42 million, 6 per cent of British imports. Britain was not only Argentina's main market, but Argentina was also one of the main half-dozen suppliers to the British market and the second most important source of food for Britain after the United States.

At the same time Latin America in 1913 absorbed £58 million worth of British goods. This represented 25–30 per cent of the imports of most of the major Latin American republics – Argentina, Brazil, Uruguay, Chile, Peru – and 10 per cent of total British exports. Textiles (especially cotton goods) remained the largest single element in this trade, but intermediate and capital goods – iron and steel, coal, rolling stock, agricultural and industrial machinery, telegraph equipment and above all metallurgical and engineering products for railway construction – made an increasingly important contribution. In 1899 Argentina had become Britain's major Latin American market, overtaking Brazil which had held that position since 1808. By 1913 Argentina alone absorbed almost half of Britain's exports to Latin America. Only the United States outside the Empire was a more important market.

The British communities in the major cities and ports of Latin America – Buenos Aires, Montevideo, Rio de Janeiro, São Paulo, Valparaíso, Santiago, Lima – now included (besides merchants) the managers and office staff of British-owned railways, public utilities, banks, shipping and insurance companies, landed estates, mines and even factories. (Charles Miller, the agent of the Royal Mail lines in São Paulo, is said to have introduced soccer into Brazil in 1886.) 'The Englishman in Latin America', wrote C. Reginald Enock in *The Republics of Central and South America* (1913), 'is still to a certain extent a "milord" ... generally not falling below a certain standard of education ... He comes for great enterprises, his pockets are overflowing with silver, which he is supposed to dispense liberally ... The lower class Briton is rarely encountered.' Scattered throughout the subcontinent were small groups of skilled workers – anything from 50 to 300 men and their families – under contract to British-owned concerns: engine drivers, plate layers and fitters on the railways and in the railway workshops of Argentina; miners in the Chilean copper, Brazilian gold and Mexican silver mines; machinists at J. & P. Coats' thread factory in São Paulo; millers at the Rio Flour Mills; engineers, carpenters, moulders and fitters in the Pacific Steam Navigation Company repair works and factory at Callao in Peru. In general wages were high, hours relatively short and conditions good. However, the vast majority of poor working people emigrating from Britain in the nineteenth and early twentieth centuries were directed by the Government Emigration Commissioners not to Latin America, but to the United States and, within the Empire, to Canada, Australia, New Zealand and South Africa. After the Famine in 1846 several thousand Irish settled in the province of Buenos

Aires, mostly in sheepfarming, and at the end of the century land-hungry Scots – and Falkland Islanders – took over large areas of Patagonia, where they continue to play an important role. Yet the several attempts, both private and state-financed, to establish British agricultural colonies in Latin America – in the 1870s, for example, Alexandra (Santa Fé, Argentina), the 'Lincolnshire Farmers' scheme in Paraguay, Cananea (São Paulo) which attracted 500 emigrants and Assunguy (sixty miles from Curitiba, Paraná) which attracted over 1,000 – almost all ended in disaster.[16]

The only successful agricultural colony was that of the Welsh in Argentina. The Welsh Emigration Society had for some time been looking for an isolated spot where Welsh language, culture and religious Nonconformity could be preserved. After rejecting California, British Columbia and Australia, the Society alighted upon Chubut in north-east Patagonia, 800 miles south of Buenos Aires. The first 150 colonists landed, singing hymns, in July 1865. Y Wladfa survived the first difficult years, partly because of the spirit and determination of the colonists, but mainly because of the support given by the British community in Buenos Aires and by the Argentinian government which was anxious to settle the area. In 1889 the Welsh were sufficiently well established to form a second colony – Cwm Hyfryd – in the foothills of the Andes. In 1902, now 3,000 strong, the Welsh unsuccessfully petitioned the Colonial Office in London for the annexation by Britain of Patagonia and several hundred colonists subsequently emigrated to Canada. Only a small proportion of the population of Chubut is now of Welsh descent, but the province still retains traces of its original Welsh character.

The number of British subjects resident in Latin America in the nineteenth century therefore remained small. In the 1890s, for example, the British numbered 2,500 in Montevideo, 1,500 in Rio de Janeiro and a few hundred in São Paulo. In Chile, however, there were already 4,000 in the 1860s and 11,000 by 1900 if first-generation Anglo-Chileans are included. In Argentina, furthermore, the British and Anglo-Argentinian community, already 5,000-strong in the 1830s, had by 1914 expanded to 40,000 – the largest British community outside the Empire. Several thousand lived on the pampa and in Patagonia, but the majority were concentrated in Buenos Aires. Here there were clear social divisions within the British community. The working class lived mostly in the south of the city (around, for example, the railway workshops), the middle and upper-middle class in the northern garden suburbs like Hurlingham, thirty-five minutes by train from the city centre. There they had their own schools (which were also attended by the children of many prominent Argentine families), hospital, churches, sports and social clubs: Hurlingham boasted not only cricket and polo grounds, but also a race course. They were served by two daily newspapers, the *Standard* and the *Buenos Aires Herald*. Many employed British lawyers, doctors and architects. They shopped at the local branch of Harrods and ate at the Victoria Tea and Luncheon Rooms. They frequently took their holidays in hotels owned and staffed by British railway companies. Some of the

British in Argentina, who had bought and developed cattle *estancias*, introducing improved livestock and new breeding methods, had accumulated immense wealth. Sir David Kelly, who was a young secretary in the British legation in Buenos Aires just after the First World War, recalls being shown a private list of between ten and twenty individual British fortunes in land and capital running into millions of pounds.[17]

Considering the extent of Britain's economic supremacy – and British naval supremacy – British governments exercised considerable restraint in their dealings with Latin America. A good deal of political arm-twisting took place behind the scenes; individual diplomats on the spot – for example, Frederick Chatfield, the British representative in Central America during the period 1834–54 – were often inclined to act in a high-handed 'imperialistic' manner; coercive measures – especially naval demonstrations – were undertaken to protect the lives and properties of British subjects or to preserve existing trade on 'fair and equal' terms; and on a few occasions – for example, the Anglo-French blockade of the Río de la Plata in the 1840s, the Anglo-French-Spanish intervention in Mexico in 1861, the Anglo-German-Italian blockade of Venezuela in 1902–3 – Britain (with other powers) resorted to gunboat diplomacy for the promotion of trade or the collection of debts. On the whole, however, British governments pursued a policy of influence rather than outright intervention in the internal affairs of the sovereign states of Latin America. The one notable exception was the long, but eventually successful, British campaign for the abolition of the transatlantic slave trade. In the case of Brazil, the chief offender, the issue dominated political relations between the two countries for almost fifty years. In the end, in 1850–1, the British navy was sent into Brazilian territorial waters to stop, search and destroy vessels suspected of trading in slaves and Brazil was finally forced to suppress the trade.[18] In general, however, relations between Britain and Latin America were good and this was especially the case after 1870. Outright intervention, much less coercion, was unnecessary. The Latin American political and economic elites on the whole welcomed British economic 'penetration' and pursued enthusiastically the 'model' of capitalist modernisation by means of foreign loans, direct foreign investment, export-sector growth, free trade and integration into world markets.

Latin America, though relatively peripheral, did not entirely avoid the Great-Power rivalry of the late nineteenth century. There was, however, no scramble for Latin America, no partition. Britain's position as the dominant external power, though challenged by both Germany and – especially in Mexico, Central America and the Caribbean – by the United States, was not seriously threatened in the nineteenth century, and Britain, as we have seen, had few colonial ambitions in Latin America. The United States, which since the Monroe Doctrine (1823) had made claims to some vague sort of political pre-eminence in Latin America, had itself – once Mexico had been deprived of half its territory (1846–8) – only limited imperial ambitions, except in the Caribbean. Latin America remained the only area of the globe largely free of imperialism in the nineteenth century. The extent to which Latin America could be said to have been part of Britain's 'informal empire', with Argentina becoming virtually a 'Sixth Dominion', and whether this relationship was detrimental to Latin America's long-term development are different and broader issues which still divide historians and which cannot be properly discussed here.

On the eve of the First World War Britain remained economically pre-eminent in Latin America: it was the principal holder of the Latin American public debt, the principal investor in Latin America and Latin America's principal trading partner. Yet Britain's position, much stronger in absolute terms, was *relatively* weaker than it had been in, say, 1890. Other industrial powers – France, Belgium, and especially Germany and the United States – had been increasing their economic stake in Latin America much faster than Britain during the previous twenty-five to thirty years.

From the late 1880s the *South American Journal* regularly warned that the Germans, rivals for world markets in the period before the First World War, were putting more effort into their commercial relations with Latin America than the British. Germany's trade with South America increased from under 1 per cent of its total trade in 1881 to 7.6 per cent in 1913, when Germany supplied 16.5 per cent of South America's imports as well as 10.5 per cent of its foreign capital.[19] Starting from scratch in 1891, the German banking system in Latin America had grown to half the size of the British by 1914. Moreover, at the outbreak of the war, German advisors were restructuring and organising a number of Latin American armies, including those of Argentina and Chile, while there were large communities of German immigrants and their descendants throughout Central and South America.

The commercial, financial – and political – challenge to British pre-eminence in Latin America posed by the United States was even more serious. For more than half a century following the promulgation of the Monroe Doctrine the United States lacked the means, economic or political, to make effective its aspiration to remove European influence from the western hemisphere, although under the Clayton–Bulwer treaty (1850) Britain agreed to share 'dominion' over Central America with the United States. In the 1890s and 1900s the United States began to play a more assertive role further south, as for example in the Anglo-Venezuelan dispute over the borders of British Guiana (1895), when Secretary of State Olney made the exaggerated claim that 'today the United States is practically sovereign on this continent', in the war with Spain (1898), from which it acquired an empire in the Caribbean, and in the Roosevelt corollary to the Monroe Doctrine (1905). Britain's failure directly to challenge US pretensions in the region – on the contrary, to welcome, as did Balfour, the British Prime Minister, in 1903, 'any increase of the influence of the United States of America upon the great Western Hemisphere'[20] – had profound long-term consequences, particularly in view of the advances being made at this time by US trade and investment.

The United States had always been an important market for Latin American exports – for example in 1900 43 per cent of Brazil's exports (mainly coffee, rubber and sugar) went to the United States, only 18 per cent to Britain[21] – but the United States had exported relatively little to Latin America. With industrialisation, however, came a search for markets abroad and a greater share of world trade. Between 1860 and 1914 US exports grew sevenfold and Latin America's share increased from 7 per cent in the early 1890s to 30 per cent in 1913. On the eve of the First World War the United States had already supplanted Britain as the main supplier of manufactured and capital goods to Mexico (50 per cent of total imports), the Central American and Caribbean republics (45–65 per cent), Venezuela (40 per cent), Colombia and, marginally, Peru (25–30 per cent). The United States had, however, only a 15 per cent share of the three major South American markets – Argentina, Chile and Brazil.[22] From the late 1890s US capital was for the first time transferred to Latin America on a significant scale. Some of this took the form of portfolio investment in government bonds, national railways and public utilities, but US investment in Latin America was overwhelmingly direct and employed in mining, agriculture and manufacturing: copper in Chile, Peru and Mexico, oil in Peru and Mexico; sugar in Cuba; bananas in Colombia and Central America; and, from 1907, even meat-packing in Argentina and Uruguay. In 1900, however, 80 per cent of US direct investment in Latin America was in two countries only, two-thirds in Mexico (the only country in the world where the United States 'outinvested' Britain) and one-third in Cuba; in 1914, almost 90 per cent of US direct investment was still accounted for by only four countries – Mexico, Cuba, Peru and Chile. On the eve of the war the United States had nominal capital of only $173 million in the ten republics of South America ($50 million in Brazil, $40 million in Argentina, $35 million in Peru) compared with Britain's $3,835 million ($1,162 million in Brazil, $1,861 million in Argentina, $133 million in Peru).[23] France as well as Germany had a bigger stake in South America. Furthermore, nationally chartered US banks were forbidden by law until 1914 to establish branches abroad, whereas in 1913 Britain had banks like the London and River Plate Bank with assets of £32 million, the London and Brazilian and the Anglo South American with £22 million and £20 million respectively and British banks in Brazil held 30 per cent of the total assets of all banks and 57 per cent of the assets of all foreign banks.[24]

The First World War, which in so many other ways brought an end to the nineteenth-century international political and economic order, produced a major shift in Latin America's external relations.[25] It accelerated Britain's relative decline, virtually destroyed the growing influence of Germany and considerably strengthened the economic presence of the United States in Latin America. In imposing blockades and blacklisting hundreds of 'enemy' firms, Britain and the United States were concerned not only with a more effective prosecution of the war against Germany, but also with the elimination of Germany as an economic competitor in Latin America in the post-war period. In this they were almost entirely successful. Apart from a brief period between the Nazi seizure of power in 1933 and the outbreak of the Second World War in 1939, which saw a revival of German trade with Latin America, Germany did not re-establish significant economic links with Latin America until the 1960s. The two remaining powers may have been allies in the war against Germany, but they had conflicting economic as well as political interests in Latin America; inevitably, given the geographical factor and the very different impact of the war on the two economies, it was the United States which dramatically gained ground during the war – mostly at the expense of Germany, but also to some extent at Britain's expense. On the one hand, lack of goods available for export – and lack of shipping (the tonnage of British ships entering Brazilian ports fell from 9.9 million in 1913 to 2.2 million in 1917)[26] – led to a further decline in Britain's share of the Latin American market during the war, especially in Brazil and even in Argentina. On the other hand the United States, which already absorbed almost three-quarters of the exports of Mexico, Central America and the Caribbean republics, not only consolidated its position as Latin America's main market by increasing its share of South American exports from 16.8 per cent to 34.8 per cent between 1913 and 1918, but also increased its share of goods imported into Mexico, Central America and the Caribbean republics from 53.2 per cent to 75 per cent, and, even more significantly, into South America from 16.2 per cent to 25.9 per cent.[27] At the same time the United States established regular shipping services to South America (making use of the newly opened Panama Canal in the case of the West Coast republics) and, with the opening of direct lines to Brazil in 1917 and Argentina in 1919, broke the British monopoly of cable communication.

It was also during the First World War that US banks entered Latin America and began to compete with the well-established British banks. The First National City Bank of New York opened its first branch – and in Buenos Aires – in 1914. (Its representative John H. Allen, in the opinion of the Barings' agent, was 'not a gentleman, simply a common North American bounder-bully, entirely unscrupulous'.)[28] By 1919 it had forty-two branches in nine countries and, whereas Britain was forced during the war to reduce new overseas investment (by 16 per cent world-wide) and liquidate some of its assets, the United States increased its lending to Latin American governments and its direct investment in Latin America, preparing the way for the investment boom of the 1920s.

During the 1920s British exports to Latin America recovered to some extent in absolute terms, but at the end of the decade Britain's share of the market had declined to around 5 per cent in Mexico and Cuba, 5–15 per cent in the other Central American and Caribbean republics, around 15 per cent in Venezuela, Peru, Uruguay, 18 per cent in Chile and 21 per cent in Brazil and Argentina. Only in Argentina, where the proportion of its exports sold to Britain actually increased (26.1 per cent in 1911–13, 32.5 per cent in 1928–30), did Britain have the largest share of the market for imports, and there only marginally. Even before the war the growth of manufacturing industry had reached the point where countries like, for example, Brazil could themselves produce many of the goods (especially textiles) which had dominated Britain's export trade for more than a century. Furthermore, Britain simply could not compete with the United States (or for that matter Germany before 1914) in producing – and selling – the goods for which Latin American demand was rising most rapidly: modern agricultural and industrial machinery, office equipment, electrical machinery, household electrical goods, chemicals, proprietary drugs and automobiles (especially to Argentina which experienced a 'car fever' in the 1920s). The Report of the D'Abernon trade mission to Argentina, Brazil and Uruguay (August–September 1929), recognising that British exports had lost further ground in South America since the war, blamed

> our apparent incapacity to accommodate ourselves to local circumstances ... inadaptibility ... persistent adherence to what Great Britain thinks good, to the exclusion of what South America wants. Typical of this, to take only those of major importance, are the motor trade, [and] agricultural machinery – harvesters, ploughs, tractors, windmills ... In the first six months of 1929 Argentina alone imported 51,067 motor vehicles valued at £5,000,000, and her agricultural machinery requirements are on a corresponding scale. Our failure to capture even a small proportion of these trades may be attributed to inability to produce on a sufficiently large scale, insufficient finance, high prices, unsuitability to South American needs, defective salesmanship – including inadequate advertisement, inadequate service, inadequate show-rooms, inadequate range of choice. Moreover, South America is not one market but several, and each requires separate study and special organisation for sales.[29]

The United States had secured the largest share, often overwhelmingly the largest share, of the market everywhere in Latin America except in Argentina: 70–75 per cent in Mexico, 50–80 per cent in Central America and the Caribbean republics, 40–45 per cent in Venezuela, Colombia and Peru, 30 per cent in Brazil, Uruguay and Chile. Even Argentina now took 20 per cent of its imports from the United States. In 1929 the United States could be said to have definitively displaced Britain as Latin America's principal trading partner.

British investment in Latin America did not decline in the 1920s, but – with a ban on new overseas investment in force until 1925 – it increased only modestly; according to one estimate, from a little under £1.2 billion to £1.3 billion.[30] British capital was invested in land and meat-processing in the Southern Cone (by such companies as Liebigs and Vesteys) and oil in Venezuela and Mexico (by Royal Dutch Shell) as well as, for the first time, in manufacturing industry other than textiles (by ICI, Pilkingtons, Lever Brothers, Glaxo, among others). It was still to a large extent, however, concentrated in railway and public utility companies, which faced mounting opposition from the urban middle class over reserved jobs for British subjects and over the cost and quality of the services provided and from workers over wages, conditions of work and the rights of organised labour. This had been evident in, for example, Uruguay even before the First World War. It was generally true after the war. In Argentina, for example, as early as 1919, British-owned public utilities faced 'an ever growing cold war of niggling and obstruction'.[31] Nevertheless in 1930 investment in Latin America still represented a third of British investment overseas and in South America at least Britain remained the principal investor with $4,485 million ($2,140 million in Argentina, $1,414 million in Brazil and $390 million in Chile).

In contrast, in the so-called 'dance of the millions' in the 1920s, Latin America received a massive injection of new capital, portfolio and direct, from the United States.[32] (In the years 1924–8 the flow of US investment in Latin America is said to have exceeded the flow of British investment in the boom years 1904–13.) The most dramatic advance had come in South America where US direct investment had risen from only $173 million in 1913 to $2,293 million in 1929 ($661 million in Argentina, $476 million in Brazil and $396 million in Chile). In 1929 more than one-third of US capital invested abroad was invested in Latin America (over $5 billion). Mexico still absorbed a fifth and Cuba another fifth of investment in Latin America, but the United States was also rapidly closing the gap on Britain in South America. Overall the United States had probably replaced Britain as Latin America's main source of capital.

In 1929 – in, for example, the D'Abernon Report – there remained some optimism that the relative decline in Britain's commercial relations with Latin America since the First World War could still be reversed, at least in South America. 'We look forward to the rapid development of commercial possibilities in South America', D'Abernon wrote, 'with greater confidence than in any other part of the world',[33] but then came the world depression, the contraction of world trade and the rise of rival trading blocs. During the 1930s Britain turned away from the rest of the world, including Latin America, towards the Empire – especially India and the colonies of white settlement (Australia, New Zealand, Canada, South Africa). The one exception was Argentina, which was regarded 'almost as part of the Empire'.[34] Against all the trends, trade with Argentina under the Roca–Runciman Pact (1933) grew during the 1930s. In 1938 Britain still received 17 per cent of Latin American exports (of which a high proportion consisted of Argentinian chilled and frozen meat and cereals), though it now supplied only 12 per cent of Latin American imports.[35] Meanwhile, capital flows to Latin America had largely dried up in the aftermath of the Wall Street Crash and there was relatively little new investment in Latin America – British or US – during the 1930s. Widespread defaults on existing loans in the 1930s had a profound effect on British bondholders. (By 1934 only Argentina, Honduras, Haiti and the Dominican Republic maintained the servicing of the external national debt, although oil-rich Venezuela had repaid all principal by 1932.) Latin American exchange controls also affected the remittance of profits on direct investment. Then came the dramatic nationalisation of US and British oil companies in Mexico in 1938.

The Second World War dealt an even more crushing blow to British–Latin American trade and British investment in Latin America than the First World War. Britain's export trade as a whole collapsed due to shipping shortages and the exigencies of war-time production. By 1944 exports to Latin America had fallen to only 25–30 per cent of their 1937 level.[36] Even exports to Argentina fell from £23 million to £5 million (a figure lower than in the 1880s). Britain, however, still bought 40 per cent of its imported meat, essential for both the civilian population and the armed forces, from Argentina which was the second most important non-Empire supplier to the British market after the United States. New investment overseas was prohibited during the war. Instead the withdrawal of British capital from Latin America, begun during the 1930s, gathered pace. Globally, Britain liquidated over £1,000 million of its overseas assets of around £3,000 million to pay for war-time imports. In Latin America, Britain liquidated £100 million of its total investment of £800 million[37].

In sharp contrast the Second World War brought the United States and the Latin American republics, which apart from Argentina lined up with the Allies against the Axis powers, closer together in every way. Military ties – bases, technical co-operation, Lend Lease – were extended and economic links were consolidated. Latin America supplied the strategic minerals and raw materials required by the United States and the US supplied loans and technical assistance to Latin America, including a limited amount of co-operation in Latin America's industrial development; a number of US trade missions visited Latin America and US exports to Latin America expanded from $700 million in 1942 to $1,000 million in 1944.[38] Moreover, political and cultural ties were enormously strengthened as a result of the efforts of Nelson Rockefeller's Office of the Coordinator of Inter-American Affairs (OCIAA). By the end of the war the United States had created and expected to maintain a 'closed hemisphere in an open world'. Eric Johnston, President of the United States Chamber of Commerce and Chairman of the United States section of the Inter-American Development Commission, had no doubt that 'just as the last century in Latin America was a "British century", the next would be an American century'.[39]

During the Second World War Britain was obliged, with varying degrees of reluctance at different levels of government, largely to concede hegemony in Latin America to the United States, even finally in Argentina where a particularly interesting struggle for supremacy between the two Allies occurred, similar to that in Mexico during the First World War.[40] In Buenos Aires Sir David Kelly, the British ambassador, tried to warn London of what was at stake and to resist the expansion of US influence in Argentina. In this he played a similar role to that of Sir Lionel Carden in Mexico City almost thirty years earlier. Carden it was who expressed the view (to the German minister) that

> very few people in England grasp the real goal of American policy ... It is not Mexico but the entire continent which is at stake. The United States may have told them that they want to stop at the Panama Canal; they will never do so. Once they have gotten that far, they will of necessity take Colombia ... then comes Brazil ... and from there it's on to Cape Horn.[41]

In the immediate aftermath of the Second World War there were great commercial opportunities in Latin America. Demand was high as a result of the war-time disruption of imports, and substantial foreign exchange reserves had been accumulated as a result of generally strong export performances during the war. This was particularly true of Argentina, still the prize Latin American market, and Argentina had also built up large sterling balances. Britain, with its massive balance of payments deficit, desperately needed to export, but had no exports (except armaments) until industry returned to peacetime purposes. There was in any case, in view of the experience of the inter-war years, a doubt whether Britain could provide the consumer goods, capital goods and industrial raw materials the major countries of Latin America now required and whether, apart from Argentina, the Latin American market was regarded as a high priority in Britain. There were to be no commercial missions to Latin America in 1945 similar to the Maurice de Bunsen mission in 1918 which had played an important role in the partial recovery of British trade with Latin America at the end of the First World War.

As for British investment, the Treasury ruled out any substantial export of capital to Latin America in the immediate post-war period. After five years of total war, in which it has been calculated Britain lost a quarter of its wealth and from which Britain emerged with external liabilities of £3,000 million, the country faced, in Keynes' dramatic phrase, a 'financial Dunkirk'. The post-war problems of sterling led in 1947 to exchange controls designed to deter British companies from investing in the dollar area (including Latin America). On the contrary, there was an acceleration of the pre-war and war-time disinvestment and, in particular, the selling of British-owned railways and public utilities to Latin American governments.

In Argentina, where one-third of British capital in Latin America was still invested and where, in particular, the sixth-largest railway network in the world was 57 per cent British-owned, the anglophile political elite with its economic interests in the export sector and close ties to British capital had been finally overthrown in 1943 and replaced by the nationalist, anti-British regime of Perón in 1946. After protracted negotiations, in March 1948 Argentina used the bulk of its reserves and its blocked sterling balances to purchase for £150 million the British-owned railways. Railways and utilities in Brazil, Uruguay and elsewhere were also sold. The Bank of England estimated that Britain's nominal overseas investment had declined by 45 per cent between 1938 and 1948 – in Argentina by 86 per cent, Mexico by 55 per cent, Brazil by 50 per cent.[42] Argentina, which alone had accounted for 10.4 per cent of total British capital overseas in 1938, accounted for only 2.6 per cent in 1948.

As Britain retreated on so many fronts in Latin America in the course of the first half of the twentieth century, especially after 1914, British investments in Argentina and in particular in Argentina's railways – Britain's single most important investment in Latin America – had come to acquire an enormous symbolic importance. As Malcolm Robertson, the British ambassador in Buenos

Aires, had said in 1929, 'I look upon them [the railways] as the mainstay, the backbone of our whole position out here. If they go, we all go.'[43] The nationalisation of the British railways in Argentina in 1948 can thus be taken to mark the end of an era. However, this is not the end of the story of the decline of Britain's position in Latin America. In 1950, Latin America (above all, Brazil and Argentina) still absorbed 7.1 per cent of British exports and Britain had a 7 per cent share of the Latin American market although these figures were under half the level of 1938. Latin America also supplied 7.8 per cent of Britain's imports, although this figure was only as high as it was because of Argentina. Britain had £250 million invested in Latin America, although this was now below 10 per cent of Britain's greatly reduced investment overseas. There was still some way to fall before the low levels of the 1970s and 1980s were reached: by that time less than 2 per cent of UK trade was with Latin America and British investment in Latin America was only 3–5 per cent of total British investment overseas (see chapter 6, below).

British pre-eminence in Latin America in the nineteenth century is not difficult to explain. Britain, the 'first industrial nation', was the 'workshop of the world'; the City of London was the world's major source of capital for export; Britain had more than half the world's merchant shipping as well as the Royal Navy. Britain exercised an unchallenged global hegemony from 1815 until 1860 or 1870 and a somewhat less secure global supremacy until 1914. Moreover, Britain, having been 'present at the creation' of the independent Latin American states, had established with them from the beginning a close relationship – commercial, financial, political – which some historians have seen as one of 'informal empire'. In the nineteenth-century international division of labour the British economy and the Latin American economies were complementary, Britain supplying manufactured goods and capital to Latin America, Latin America supplying Britain with foodstuffs and raw materials.

The decline of British pre-eminence in Latin America in the first half of the twentieth century, first relative, then absolute, is a more complex issue. In large part it was, of course, a consequence of Britain's overall decline. The balance of world forces, economic as well as political/naval/military, had begun to change after 1870. Other European nations, especially Germany, and the United States industrialised. Britain's share of manufacturing output and of world trade inevitably fell, but British industry also failed to remain competitive; it was no longer at the forefront of technological change. Restrictions were increasingly imposed on the movement of British capital and New York replaced London as the world's main capital market. Above all, the damaging effects of two world wars on the British economy cannot be overestimated. At the same time, Britain increasingly strengthened its commercial and financial ties with the Empire, and especially with the Dominions, at the expense of Latin America (with the exception of Argentina until the years immediately after the Second World War).

The decline of Britain's position in Latin America was also a consequence of changing economic and, to a lesser extent, social and political structures in Latin America itself. The major republics began to develop their manufacturing industries after 1880 and the shift from export-led growth to import-substituting industrialisation gathered momentum in the inter-war years, especially during the depression of the 1930s. Britain was a prisoner of its nineteenth-century past and had great difficulty adapting long-established patterns of trade and investment to the changing needs of Latin America. With the incorporation of the urban middle class and, in some countries, the urban working class into the Latin American political systems British capital, concentrated as it was in such highly visible and politically sensitive sectors as railways, public utilities and oil, became for the first time a symbol of foreign economic domination and an easy target for nationalist propaganda.

Finally, Britain faced a powerful competitor for pre-eminence in Latin America. As the United States overtook Britain as the world's leading industrial and creditor nation it steadily increased its trade with, and investment in, its Latin American neighbours. The United States replaced Britain as the dominant economic power first (even before the First World War) in Mexico and in the Central American and Caribbean republics, then in the northern republics of South America, the West Coast republics and Brazil, and finally after the Second World War in Argentina. Moreover, unlike Britain, the United States had an hegemonic project in Latin America which Britain, in view of its declining economic and military power, world-wide commitments, different priorities and, not least, 'special relationship' with the United States, chose not to resist – except to some extent in Argentina. Lord Palmerston said it all in 1857 at the time of an early US challenge to British ascendency in Central America:

> These Yankees are most disagreeable fellows to have to do with about any American Question. They are on the spot, strong, deeply interested in the matter ... and determined somehow or other to carry their point. We are far away, weak from distance, controlled by the indifference of the nation as to the Question discussed, and by its strong ... interest in maintaining peace with the United States.

Nevertheless, in 1950 Britain still had significant commercial and financial interests in Latin America and there was still considerable Latin American goodwill towards Britain. Britain remained the second most important external actor in Latin America and, despite Britain's severe post-war economic problems, the opportunity was there possibly to reverse, certainly to slow down, the secular decline in Britain's position in Latin America since the First World War, not least because ironically the United States, which now had global and not merely hemispheric interests and responsibilities, appeared to be neglecting Latin America and its long-term development needs. There was, however, no longer any great interest in Latin America, official or unofficial, no political will to strengthen Britain's relations with Latin America, no consistent policy – economic, political or cultural – pursued by any British government towards Latin America (see chapter 3, below). As a result, Britain's position in Latin

Leslie Bethell

America, already relatively weak in the years immediately after the Second World War, was allowed to decline still further from the 1950s to the 1980s. Britain to a large extent withdrew from Latin America during the second half of the twentieth century.

Notes

I would like to thank Oliver Marshall for research assistance in the preparation of this chapter. I am also grateful to my colleague Dr Colin Lewis for allowing me to read drafts of chapters for a volume on British business in Latin America which he and Dr Rory Miller of the University of Liverpool are currently editing. It promises to be a valuable addition to D. C. M. Platt (ed.), *Business Imperialism 1840–1930* (Oxford: Oxford University Press, 1977).

1 Quoted in R. A. Humphreys, 'Anglo-American rivalries and Spanish American emancipation', in his *Tradition and Revolt in Latin America* (New York: Columbia University Press, 1969), pp. 148, 153. The literature on Britain's role in the independence of Latin America is immense. For a recent synthesis, see D. A. G. Waddell, 'International politics and Latin American Independence', in Leslie Bethell (ed.), *The Cambridge History of Latin America*, vol. III (Cambridge: Cambridge University Press, 1985).

2 Fox to Charles Stuart, private, 25 September 1832, Buenos Aires, and 15 December 1835, Rio de Janeiro, Stuart papers, Archivo Histórico do Itamaraty, Rio de Janeiro.

3 Figures for British trade with Latin America throughout this chapter are taken from D. C. M. Platt, *Latin America and British Trade, 1806–1914* (London: A. and C. Black, 1972), Appendix I, 'Exports of produce and manufactures of the United Kingdom to Latin America, 1850–1913', and Appendix II, 'Imports of Latin American produce into the United Kingdom, 1854–1913', and from B. R. Mitchell, *Abstract of British Historical Statistics* (Cambridge: Cambridge University Press, 1962), 'United Kingdom trade with Central and South America, 1881 to 1938', pp. 322–3, and, for Argentina alone, pp. 325–6.

4 Philip Ziegler, *The Sixth Great Power. Barings 1762–1929* (London: Collins, 1988), pp. 230, 234.

5 On British banking in Latin America, see David Joslin, *A Century of Banking in Latin America* (Oxford: Oxford University Press, 1963).

6 Bill Albert, *South America and the World Economy from Independence to 1930* (London: Macmillan, 1983), p. 29, Table I, based on I. Stone, 'British long term investment in Latin America 1865–1913', *Business History Review*, 42:3 (1968).

7 Albert, *South America and the World Economy*, p. 34, Table 4; Stone, 'British long term investment'; and, for South America only, Rosemary Thorp, 'Latin America and the international economy from the First World War to the World Depression', in Leslie Bethell (ed.), *The Cambridge History of Latin America*, vol. IV (Cambridge: Cambridge University Press, 1986), p. 64, Table 3. Some economic historians have put British investment in Latin America in 1913 below £1,000 million.

8 H. S. Ferns, *Britain and Argentina in the Nineteenth Century* (Oxford: Oxford University Press, 1960), p. 397.

9 Ziegler, *The Sixth Great Power*, p. 306.

10 Colin M. Lewis, *British Railways in Argentina, 1857–1914* (London: Athlone Press, 1983), p. 219.

11 Quoted in Richard Graham, *Britain and the Onset of Modernization in Brazil 1850–1914* (Cambridge: Cambridge University Press, 1968), p. 303.

12 On British land ownership in Argentina, see Eduardo José Míguez, *Las Tierras de los Ingleses en la Argentina (1870–1914)* (Buenos Aires: Belgrano, 1985).

13 I am grateful to Dr Colin Lewis for this information.

14 Quoted in Peter Winn, 'British informal empire in Uruguay in the nineteenth century', *Past and Present*, 73 (1976), p. 112.

15 On North, see Harold Blakemore, *British Nitrates and Chilean Politics. 1886–1893: Balmaceda and North* (London: Athlone Press, 1974); on Pearson, see Desmond Young, *Member for Mexico. A biography of Weetman Pearson, First Viscount Cowdray* (London, 1966).

16 On British agricultural colonisation in the nineteenth century, see two articles by D. C. M. Platt, 'British agricultural colonisation in Latin America', *Inter-American Economic Affairs*, 18 and 19 (1964/5). The last British colonisation scheme was the Colonia Victoria, in Misiones, Argentina in 1932. See Oliver Marshall, 'Peasants to planters? British pioneers on Argentina's tropical frontier', in Alistair Hennessy and John King (eds.), *The Land that England Lost: Essays in British–Argentine Relations*, (London: Lester Crook Academic, 1989).

17 Sir David Kelly, *The Ruling Few* (London, 1952), p. 116.

18 On this extraordinary episode in Anglo-Brazilian relations, see Leslie Bethell, *The Abolition of the Brazilian Slave Trade* (Cambridge: Cambridge University Press, 1970).

19 Holger H. Herwig, *Germany's Vision of Empire in Venezuela 1871–1914* (Princeton: Princeton University Press, 1986), pp. 14–15.

20 Quoted in R. A. Humphreys, 'Anglo–American rivalries and the Venezuelan crisis of 1895', in *Tradition and Revolt in Latin America*, p. 215.

21 Graham, *Britain and the Onset of Modernization*, p. 76.

22 Thorp, 'Latin America and the international economy', p. 66, Table 4.

23 *Ibid.*, p. 64, Table 3.

24 Joslin, *A Century of Banking*, p. 109; Graham, *Britain and the Onset of Modernization*, p. 96.

25 On Great-Power rivalry in Latin America during the First World War, see, for Mexico, Friedrich Katz, *The Secret War in Mexico. Europe, the United States and the Mexican Revolution* (Chicago: University of Chicago Press, 1981) and, for Brazil, Argentina, Chile and Peru, Bill Albert, *South America and the First World War* (Cambridge: Cambridge University Press, 1988). Also of interest is Joseph Tulchin, *The Aftermath of War. World War I and US Policy towards Latin America* (New York: New York University Press, 1971).

26 Graham, *Britain and the Onset of Modernization*, p. 316.

27 Thorp, 'Latin America and the international economy', p. 60, Table 1.

28 Ziegler, *The Sixth Great Power*, p. 325.

29 Department of Overseas Trade, *Report of the British Economic Mission to Argentina, Brazil and Uruguay* (1930), p. 6.

30 Albert, *South America and the World Economy*, p. 34, Table 4.

31 Kelly, *The Ruling Few*, p. 115. On growing friction between British public utility companies and local governments, see Linda and Charles Jones and Robert Greenhill, 'Public utility companies', in Platt (ed.), *Business Imperialism*.

32 Barbara Stallings, *Bankers to the Third World. US Portfolio Investment in Latin America 1900–1986* (Berkeley: University of California Press, 1987), pp. 67–75; Thorp, 'Latin America and the international economy'.

33 Department of Overseas Trade, *Report of the British Economic Mission*, p. 5.

34 Sir Malcolm Robertson, British ambassador in Buenos Aires, quoted in Roger Gravil, *The Anglo-Argentine Connection, 1900–1939* (Boulder, Col.: Westview, 1985), p. 180.

35 R. A. Humphreys, *Latin America and the Second World War, 1939–1942* (London: Athlone Press, 1981), p. 7. During the period 1910–40, indeed until the 1970s, UK imports from Latin America generally had twice the value of UK exports to Latin America. See Laurence Whitehead, 'El comercio de Gran Bretaña con América Latina', *Foro Internacional*, 17.3 (1977), p. 383.

36 R. A. Humphreys, *Latin America and the Second World War, 1942–1945* (London: Athlone Press, 1982), pp. 222–3.

37 Laurence Whitehead, 'Britain's economic relations with Latin America', in J. Grunwald (ed.), *Latin America and the World Economy* (Washington, D.C.: Brookings Institute, 1978), p. 91.

38 Humphreys, *Latin America and the Second World War, 1942–1945*, p. 268, n.85.

39 Quoted in Michael Grow, *The Good Neighbor Policy and Authoritarianism in Paraguay: United States Economic Expansion and Great Power Rivalry in Latin America during World War II* (Lawrence, Kan.: Regents Press of Kansas, 1981), p. 90.

40 There is an immense literature on Anglo–American–Argentine relations during and immediately after the Second World War. See, for example, most recently Mario Rapoport, *Gran Bretaña, Estados Unidos y las Clases Dirigentes Argentinas 1940–5* (Buenos Aires: Belgrano, 1981); R. A. Humphreys, *Latin America and the Second World War 1942–45*, chapters 6 and 7; Carlos Escudé, *Gran Bretaña, Estados Unidos y la Declinación Argentina 1942–49* (Buenos Aires: Belgrano, 1983); C. A. Macdonald, 'The politics of intervention. The United States and Argentina 1941–6', *Journal of Latin American Studies*, 12:2 (1980), and 'The United States, Britain and Argentina in the years immediately after the Second World War', in G. di Tella and D. C. M. Platt (eds.), *The Political Economy of Argentina 1880–1946* (London: Macmillan, 1986). On Anglo-Argentine bilateral relations, see Noel Fursman, 'The decline of the Anglo-Argentine economic connection in the years immediately after the Second World War: a British perspective' (unpublished D.Phil. thesis, Oxford University, 1988).

41 Quoted in Katz, *The Secret War in Mexico*, p. 189.

42 Bank of England, *UK Overseas Investment, 1938 to 1948* (1950), p. 5. I am grateful to Dr Colin Lewis for drawing my attention to this source.

43 Quoted in Roger Gravil, 'Anglo-US trade rivalry in Argentina and the D'Abernon mission of 1929', in David Rock (ed.), *Argentina in the Twentieth Century* (London: Duckworth, 1975), p. 51.

Part I
Cultural and political relations

2 Britain's cultural relations with Latin America

Gerald Martin

This chapter will operate between two poles of concern: (1) the wider perspective – the British approach to cultural relations generally and to national self-presentation through cultural diplomacy (it is impossible to consider the Latin American case without examining this wider context); and (2) the more narrow focus – Britain's cultural relationship with Latin America through history to the present day, with particular reference to the recent and contemporary period and to the formulation of policy.[1]

Of course this second, specifically Latin American, focus is only narrow in relative terms: it is a vast subject. Yet I may as well start by declaring that in the light of my own experience of educational and cultural relations, and of visits to Latin America and elsewhere, I began this inquiry with a certain amount of scepticism as to the effectiveness of the national effort in this direction and have ended it with something close to dismay, if not despair. Admittedly, much depends on one's understanding of culture and its current and possible functions, on the one hand, and on the other on one's understanding of Britain today, the British national interest and the objectives of cultural diplomacy. What is not in doubt, however, is that the subject of cultural diplomacy has been aired in the past four years as never before in post-war British history.

Equally beyond doubt is the assertion that, in theory at least, few if any nations, with the possible exception of France, ought to be better placed than Britain to develop a modest, but mutually beneficial, relationship with Latin America. One could mention three facilitating circumstances by way of background.

First, Britain dominated the first century after Independence in Latin America, but never incurred the weight of odium accumulated by either Spain in the colonial period or the United States in the twentieth century. Admittedly, those who nostalgically remember us tend to be associated with conservative, or even backward-looking, sectors of Latin America and those in Britain who most vigorously pursue this old-style relationship sometimes occupy similar positions here: the familiar 'long ago and far away' syndrome. Since we are often admired, like the BBC, for our 'gentlemanly' image, sense of 'fair play' and apparent 'disinterestedness', it can sometimes be difficult to exploit respect based on such qualities. This needs to be understood in order to use it to best advantage, instead of allowing it to become a stumbling-block.

Secondly, we have the inestimable advantage of a world population of more than 300 million native speakers of English, another 300 million for whom it is a second language and 100 million who speak it as a foreign language. In short, we speak the twentieth century's *lingua franca* – indeed, it is *our* language – but we are not the United States and we have the cultural prestige of our European background and the strategic advantages of our membership of the European Community (EC).

Thirdly, we have, and used to value, a relationship with a large number of other Third World or developing areas, and could perhaps, with a change of mentality, have used this relationship as a means of rapprochement with Latin America rather than as an excuse to ignore it. This implies dealing with a whole range of political and ideological strata of Latin American society (whilst always remembering that only in specific circumstances do even radical Latin Americans take kindly to being identified with the Third World) and not just the traditional elites – all of which requires intimacy, knowledge and subtlety, not inactivity masquerading as such.

There are many other themes that one could develop, but I believe that enough has been said thus far to suggest that no country is better placed to practise positive diplomacy world-wide than Britain and that Latin America could be very much a part of an enlarged diplomatic effort (though on any view, other than the short-term, a redistribution of interest in favour of Latin America would seem to be desirable in any case). I have come to the conclusion, however, that we need a different model of diplomacy from that which has characterised us historically and that a hard-nosed analysis of quite a different kind from the ultra-tough approach of the past few years is necessary if we are to be successful. I believe that, historically, our diplomatic effort towards Latin America has been fundamentally – culturally, intellectually and politically – lazy, passive, reactive, neglectful and often patronising.[2] This is not, however, intended as a criticism of the Foreign and Commonwealth Office (FCO) *per se*: in this regard its perspective accurately reflects not only that of successive governments, but of British society as a whole, except that the FCO is at the sharp end where attitude slides into policy.

Britain's cultural relationship with Latin America

On the whole the British do not care much for culture, perhaps in part because we do not understand it. We are really quite good at doing it, but unfortunately not at either thinking about it or communicating it to others.[3] The syndrome goes back hundreds of years and may even derive from that liberal instinct expressed in Elizabeth I's refusal to 'make windows in men's minds'. Regrettably, however, our 'analogues', the Germans and to a much greater extent the French, do care for culture. Since both spend more than twice as much as Britain does on cultural diplomacy, and since both sell more than twice as much to Latin America, a crude calculation suggests that this connection needs looking into. Admittedly, there is no giant French-speaking or German-speaking superpower above our European rivals, but this reality is one that cuts both ways and can be turned to advantage. The French always think deeply about cultural policy (the famous *mission civilisatrice*) – which is, I am certain, an astonishingly cost-effective, but unfortunately unquantifiable, investment – and always purport to be doing something positive and imaginative even when they are not; they recognise that cultural work is a thoroughly worthwhile activity, valuable for its own sake, and invaluable in the absence of other instruments. But of course it has to be done well.

Moreover, one has to work hard these days just to keep pace and even harder when you are behind in the race, as Britain is in Latin America. The British attitude seems to be that if trade with a certain region is insubstantial, it is probably not worth bothering with. Yet consider how much advertising is done by industry to retain market share or by politicians to win elections. As Simon Jenkins noted in *The Economist*: 'The private sector knows how elusive are the factors which condition the way a marketing message is received. The messages of nations are no different.'[4] We live in an era of political propaganda, packaging of politicians, ghosting of speeches, ubiquitous admen and PR specialists, yet that world appears to me to have had very little really profound impact on the presentation and marketing of 'UK plc'. The British unfortunately cling tight to their innocence.

The fact is that people do not live by trade alone and do not wish to talk about business all the time, preferring to pretend that they are not really in perpetual cut-throat competition and that they have other things in common with one another. This is particularly important in regard to Latin America, since the Latin Americans themselves care about culture to a degree inconceivable in this country, for well-known historical and sociological reasons, most important of which are aspects of the quest for national and continental identity and compensation in the cultural arena for disadvantages in the political and economic spheres. This is a reality that simply has to be recognised, and in one sense it is, given the FCO's quite reasonable protestations that the ratio of effort to results in Latin America is at least twice as great as in the rest of the world.[5] Nevertheless our approach always seems to involve the perfidious ambiguity evident in the following statement by Alison Peers when the Hispanic and Luso-Brazilian Council (Canning House) was set up in 1943: 'Our great hope consists in combining the commercial with the cultural in getting the belief across that Spanish is as well worth studying for its own sake as any other modern language. Whatever we think, we must appear to be interested in Spanish as much for educational as for commercial reasons.'[6] Peers, of course, was an academic, not a diplomat!

Latin America, it must be remembered, is one of our historical failures, a wistful symbol of our decline, the place where the United States began to supplant us and, finally, to frighten us off. As to recent events, it has become clear that there is considerable resentment in Britain at the problem of debt and we need to remind ourselves that it was debt defaulting which alienated us from Latin America half a century ago. This resentment, of course, makes it all the more astonishing that British banks should have lent the region – including some fairly ferocious military regimes – so much in the 1970s and 1980s and history, compounded by the desperado drug image, may be on the point of repeating itself. It prompts me to say that I have been surprised by the extent to which we remain uninterested in the views of Latin Americans themselves on these matters. Why has no one ever seriously surveyed Latin American perceptions and opinions of Britain and our relationship with the region?[7] The Falklands conflict looks set to become a permanent symbol of the 'very little England' mentality, but this is not inevitable and the saga is by no means over. One great consolation is that it may have damaged Latin American perceptions of Britain less than might have been imagined, simply because it is so closely identified, rightly or wrongly, with the person and character of the present Prime Minister. That is why, in my own opinion, it is essential to prepare for a post-Thatcher era in British–Latin American relations and for all sections of Britain's cultural-diplomatic machinery to be ready to move with speed when the moment comes.

It is impossible to survey all the cultural links, both formal and informal, which currently exist between Britain and Latin America, though I shall refer to some of these as the need arises. The emphasis here is on policy formulation, and most of these links are too diffuse to be able to think about them in this way (though of course education at one end and diplomacy at the other can take note of them, encourage them as and when appropriate and make use of them). Suffice it to say that there are more such contacts now than at any time in history, but that this is not as hopeful as it may seem, since international communication and cultural relations are proliferating everywhere and in all directions at an unparalleled and still accelerating rate of change. We have to work harder just to stay in the same place, which is precisely what Britain failed to do in the 1920s, for example.

Recent times

'Otra vez nos descubren' was the rather weary title of an article in the magazine *Visión* in 1965, in response to the now-celebrated special number of *Encounter* in September of that year.[8] Rediscoveries of Latin America are a periodical, if unpredictable, tidal occurrence in the affairs of Britain (usually 'merely an eddy off the main current of British relations with Washington', according to D. C. M. Platt).[9]

At the risk of exaggerating the importance of events in the educational system, I think there can be little doubt that 1965 really was the year when we first rediscovered Latin America in the post-war era and the one which effectively sets the time-scale for our contemporary cultural relationship with the region. It was the moment of that famous special number of *Encounter*, but above all of the Parry Report, which provided for the first time a comprehensive review of Latin

American Studies in British universities, with proposals for future developments.

The mid-1960s also saw the so-called 'boom' of the new Latin American novel, still with us today and probably the single most important factor in giving Latin America a positive image in the last quarter of a century. It hardly needs stressing that this too arose out of a complex sequence of factors, but was certainly not unconnected to the socio-economic condition of Latin America itself, the Cuban Revolution, Alliance for Progress, guerrilla movements and military coups and other such upheavals. To concentrate on Britain, though, I believe that the 1960s did see a brief opening out to the world, both in a readjustment of the relationship with the old Empire through the new Commonwealth, and, given the implications of that, in a resurgence of interest in other parts of the globe such as Latin America. That same decade was the era of comprehensive education, the Robbins Report, the birth of the new universities and of the polytechnics, the publication of the Parry Report itself, the consequent creation of five Latin American Centres in Britain and a new era for Latin American studies in this country. Clearly, however, the excitement of those early years, like so much else in the sixties, dissolved into the crises of the 1970s, both in this country and in Latin America itself. There events in Chile, and later in Central America, created a quite new focus of interest among new sectors of British society, as well as significantly increasing the number of Latin Americans resident here, whilst for Britain herself the economic difficulties of the 1970s, despite or because of entry to the EC, initiated waves of cuts by successive governments which have made it difficult in most fields, including Latin American studies, to do better than keep pace in the face of negative circumstances.

It is just over a decade since the establishment of the Latin American Bureau (LAB) in March 1977, a nongovernmental organisation supported by voluntary development agencies and church bodies, which aims 'through research, documentation and publicity to raise public awareness on social, economic, political and human rights issues in Latin America, especially in relation to British involvement in the region'. Writing in one of the Bureau's first publications, *Britain and Latin America: An Annual Review of British–Latin American Relations* (1978), Hugh O'Shaughnessy and Juan Rada argued, just as the D'Abernon Report had in 1929,[10] and just as I am today, that it was possible to construct a new and 'advantageous relationship with Latin America' if Britain 'cared to look further than its year-end balance of payments with the region and committed itself to being an active partner in the democratic development process'.[11] It was conceded that the scenario was not at first sight encouraging. Trade was declining, aid packages were small; old-style investments in land, mines, utilities and oil had passed into Latin American control, sometimes dramatically as with Cárdenas in Mexico in 1938 and Perón in Argentina in 1948, and Britain's most visible presence in the region lay in such anachronisms as Belize, the Falklands and a number of Anglo-communities still looking backwards to the nineteenth century. Nevertheless, those writers argued, popular interest in Latin America had been increasing throughout the 1970s and it was possible for Britain to seize the initiative and transform her own, and indeed the EC's, attitudes towards Latin America.

The evidence of the companion chapters in this volume suggests only too starkly, I think, that if there really were opportunities, then they have been missed. ('Dismissed' may be a better word: I vividly recall attending a meeting shortly after the general election of 1979 when an Overseas Development Administration (ODA) official informed the participants unequivocally that Latin America would not be an area of interest under the new administration. So it proved, though little did we know how costly that could turn out to be.) It is perhaps typical of initiatives relating to Latin America that LAB's own annual review of British–Latin American relations from which I have just quoted appeared only once more, though in other respects LAB's energy and ability to deliver has been undeniable. LAB's short-lived annual review had been preceded by similar ventures by other organisations, such as the *Economist para América Latina* (1967–70), the *Latin American Review of Books* (1973), and the Pelican Latin American Library (1971–3).[12] Our current ineffectiveness in the region makes all this seem part of the natural order of things and we may even be inclined to see the failure of most of our initiatives as somehow Latin America's fault, a reflection of that subcontinent of solitude and frustrated aspirations condemned always to exist largely in the future (to paraphrase Anthony Eden on Brazil). Viewed in historical perspective, however, our neglect is doubly surprising, as we shall see. It was in part concern for British interests in Latin America, given Britain's 'disastrous export performance' and the 'extreme feebleness of most British responses to the North American advance',[13] and particularly following the D'Abernon Mission in 1929 and the interest the then Prince of Wales took in its findings, that led to the establishment in the 1930s of our two principal instruments for cultural communication with the world, the British Council in 1935 and the BBC External Services in 1938. We shall return to them below.

The work of the Latin American Bureau has largely coincided with the period of the current government and began, as mentioned above, and like so many organisations before it, with high hopes for a transformed relationship with Latin America. With more time and space, one could sketch in such cultural currents as the strong influence of British popular music in Latin America since the 1960s and the recent reciprocation through the influence of reggae and salsa; the very important relationship in terms of the multi-class sport of association football[14] and the upper-class networks of polo; the proliferation of British television programmes about Latin America, especially since the arrival of Channel 4, which has forced the BBC to move on from flights of the condor to flights of capital and refugees; important film seasons at the National Film Theatre and exhibitions at the Hayward Gallery and elsewhere;[15] hugely increased interest on the part of the British press, particularly *The Financial*

Times and of course the excellent *Latin American Newsletter* and its companion publications; an astonishing growth in the 1980s in travel guides to the region, though none seems likely to supplant the classic *South American Handbook*;[16] and an equally remarkable growth in the market for translations of Latin American fiction on a scale never experienced before. Institutions like the Hispanic and Luso-Brazilian Council at Canning House (founded in 1943, for 'the advancement of knowledge in the British Commonwealth and in the countries of Latin America, Spain and Portugal, of the culture, languages, literatures and economies of those countries and closer relations between them') and the Society for Latin American Studies (founded in 1964) continue to play their full part. One might also mention the work of the Latin American embassies in London (though it must be said that they seem far less active here than in Paris or Washington), and the contribution of the various Anglo-Latin American societies in close individual communication with them.

There is nevertheless, in my opinion, a peculiarly unsatisfactory and possibly even damaging disjuncture in our existing cultural relationship with Latin America. The old elite groups who had interests, and thus used to take an interest, have been distanced by all that has happened since 1945 and the sectors which have developed a new and indeed unparalleled interest in the region – out of all proportion to Britain's material stake in that part of the world, though probably no greater than France's interest in the 1920s and 1930s – are on the whole out of sympathy with current government policy and concerned at one and the same time with political and cultural developments. In education, publishing, the media, the cinema and the art world, there has been an extraordinary, unexpected and in some respects inexplicable growth in coverage of and interest in Latin America and its affairs. This is mainly among the younger age groups and it is curious to think that we are quite unconsciously developing a 'successor generation' in this country which will be interested in Latin America throughout its next half-century whilst neglecting to foster a British-oriented counterpart in Latin America itself. In addition to this wider public, there are now innumerable sub-systems which grew mainly in the 1970s and arose out of the various solidarity campaigns, human rights committees, missionary and aid organisations, links between trade unions and their Latin American counterparts, twinning of towns like London and Managua, Oxford and León, and so on. Add to this a renewed interest in Portugal since 1974 and Spain since 1975, and the prospect of a massive increase in Hispanic population and culture in the United States, and it seems clear that we need a really flexible and vigorous diplomatic counterpart to the academic infrastructure which has existed since the late 1960s following publication of the Parry Report. Yet all the signs have been pointing in the opposite direction, even for higher education itself. It is to education that I now turn.

The education system

The present government is firmly committed to the concept of an 'enterprise culture'. Unfortunately discussions of the question have tended to concentrate on enterprise, and much less on culture and how to encourage or manipulate it. On the whole, our way of proceeding is to lurch from one policy extreme to another: thus, if we want enterprise, we shall have to cut culture. However, even influential business voices have become increasingly alarmed at this way of carrying on. A few years ago a Board of Trade report under the aegis of the Duke of Kent expressed concern at the failure of British business to acquire and use foreign language skills and the situation has deteriorated since then. In 1986 Sir Peter Parker's report on scarce languages declared that with our 'post-imperial hangover' we are 'consigning whole areas of the world to a linguistic and informational vacuum'; yet the entire system of teaching languages and area studies has been 'eroded piecemeal'. He went on: 'What is more, knowledge of a language has increasingly become a necessary but not sufficient condition of success abroad: sensitivity to cultural background and history is becoming a vital factor in dealings with executives and politicians alike.'[17] In May 1988 the Secretary of State for Trade told Hampshire businessmen to 'brush up their languages' in readiness for the formation in 1992 of a European Domestic Market (EDM), whilst confessing that he himself spoke only English.[18] In June the FCO admitted to the House of Commons Foreign Affairs Committee (FAC) that the training situation in regard to both management skills and languages is 'deplorable'.[19] At this point I should probably add that academics are not immune from criticism even on this score. Most Latin American specialists in this country can boast no more than passable Spanish, very few speak Portuguese and few indeed would be able to write an academic article in either language.

Perhaps the most striking intervention, however, in this sorry debate is that of Sir John Harvey-Jones, formerly chairman of ICI and probably Britain's best-known executive of recent years, whose book *Making it Happen* appeared in January 1988. He urges that business in the new multinational and multicultural era 'requires much greater sensitivity to national differences than we are accustomed to having'.[20] He notes that our command of language skills is far behind that of major rivals and, showing an acute awareness of the complexity of human interaction, emphasises that the problem of linguistic and cultural difference applies almost equally even to our dealings with the United States. In short, what is required, if the enterprise culture is to become more than a slogan, is a major cultural – and in the first place educational – transformation of Britain.

The reality is that the number of sixth-formers taking A-level languages declined by 33 per cent between 1983 and 1988 and applications for Postgraduate Certificate of Education places in languages fell by almost 60 per cent, with a further 20 per cent drop expected in 1989. Despite the fact that several million Britons visit Spain each year, Spanish is in decline in a quarter of the schools where it is taught (though the independent sector is maintaining provision) and there are fewer pupils taking A level now than there were in 1970 (the median annual figure has been about 2,500).[21] The teaching of Portuguese in schools continues to be negligible. It remains to be seen what effects the new core curriculum will have, but it would seem unlikely that it will arrest the decline in Spanish. Meaningful figures for higher education language teaching are difficult to come by, given the variety of courses and vagaries of definition, but the position would appear to be reasonably stable at present, with some 250 graduates in Hispanic Studies from universities each year (as against 170 in 1962–3), 50 or 60 from polytechnics and colleges, plus another 200 from the same sector taking Spanish with another language. Whether this will continue with the decline in the study of the languages in schools, and whether these are in any case the kinds of language graduates we need, are other matters entirely, though beyond the scope of this chapter.

Schools have been gradually increasing Latin American content in their curricula (though there was a time when a certain newspaper was urging parents to boycott secondary schools with Latin America-related items on their notice-boards). In 1970 the Leverhulme Trust gave five years' funding for school-teacher fellowships in Latin American Studies at the Institute of Latin American Studies in London.[22] In this connection one should certainly mention the outstanding educational and informational role played by the Education Department of the Hispanic and Luso-Brazilian Council at Canning House, though it can only be truly effective in schools where Spanish or Portuguese are taught. In general my impression is that schools have really only been increasing their interest in line with general trends.

As for higher education, the inevitable point of reference is the report of the committee set up in October 1962 under the chairmanship of Professor J. H. Parry 'to review development in the Universities in the field of Latin American Studies and to consider and advise on proposals for future developments'.[23] The committee reported in August 1964 and the Parry Report was published in 1965. It concluded that 'the state of Latin American studies in British universities entirely fails to reflect the economic, political and cultural importance of Latin America. It reflects, instead, a lack of interest in, and a general ignorance about, this great area in Great Britain' (p. 1). The Report recommended the setting up of five centres for Latin American studies, the creation of forty-five teaching and research posts in those centres and thirty in other universities, twenty specific postgraduate awards per year for ten years, increases in travel, libraries, and visits from Latin American scholars and a campaign to expand Spanish and Portuguese teaching in schools. Oxford set up a Centre based on St Antony's College, with Ford Foundation assistance, as early as 1964. The Institute at London was established in 1965 (under Professor R. A. Humphreys, with a coordinating national role), the Cambridge and Liverpool Centres in 1966 and Glasgow in 1967. Subsequently the new University of Essex set up what was effectively a sixth Latin American Centre in 1968, with the assistance of the

Nuffield Foundation. Portsmouth Polytechnic launched Britain's first under-graduate languages and area studies degree in Latin American Studies in 1971 and the University of Warwick began a Comparative American Studies pro-gramme in 1973, later reinforced by a Centre for Caribbean Studies in 1985. Ford's aid to Oxford ended in 1973 and Nuffield's to Essex in 1976. 'Parry'-earmarked funds for the five official centres came to an end in 1977. Neverthe-less all the universities concerned continued to support the centres, though expansion effectively ceased in the mid-1970s, and the system envisaged by Parry is still effectively in place.[24]

Almost a quarter of a century later, then, the situation in higher education has been transformed, even if there has been some contraction since cutbacks began in 1981. The five centres still exist, however precariously in some cases, and each runs its own postgraduate Master's degree. Whereas between 1920 and 1948 there had been twelve doctoral dissertations on Latin America in history or social sciences, and a further twenty-seven between 1948 and 1966, there were 117 students registered for dissertations at the MA and PhD level, including languages and literature, in 1966–7, 282 in 1973–4, and 403 in 1984–5, although this had fallen back to below 300 by 1987–8.[25] No doubt these figures should be divided by four for likely annual completions, but this is still a very healthy picture in terms of commitment, enthusiasm and contributions to knowledge – leaving aside the increasing difficulties of actually pursuing research and the impossibility of more than a few of those involved ever acquiring academic posts. Whether the situation will be quite as healthy when the next set of figures is compiled may be doubted, given the really quite savage cuts in support for postgraduate work in recent years. Nevertheless, in the area of postgraduate research, Parry's objectives would seem to have been more than adequately met and there has been a massive shift (in proportional terms) away from literary studies and, to a lesser extent, from history towards the social sciences.

The same general picture is true of specialist research and publications. Without invoking the newly fashionable science of bibliometric analysis, it seems clear that the volume and quality of research and publication on Latin America by British higher education staff since 1965 is remarkably high and stands comparison with that from any comparable country. There seems little doubt that by the end of the century Latin American Studies will have matched the already outstanding achievements which British Hispanism has made in his-torical and literary studies of Spain and Portugal (particularly for earlier periods in the case of literary specialists). Academic publishing ventures such as the outstanding Cambridge Latin American Series launched in 1967, the *Journal of Latin American Studies* (London, 1969–) and *Bulletin of Latin American Research* (Oxford, 1981–), the *Cambridge History of Latin America* (1985–) edited by Leslie Bethell, and numerous other initiatives give additional weight to what is, I am sure, a picture more satisfactory than the members of the Parry Committee might have dreamed. Nevertheless, one must also admit that these publications appear to have impressed our academic peers far more than the public at large.[26] As in other areas of research, what we are not good at is application.

There have also been failures and disappointments, however, some of which can be traced back to the fact that as usual in this country affairs were placed in the hands of those who represented the system as it already was and who were coming to the end of their professional careers. Only now is the first post-Parry era drawing to a close. Considering the surprising enthusiasm for Latin American culture among the general public today, one feels that not enough has been done by Latin Americanists to participate in a more general education process outside of their own academic milieu. There has been a trickle-down effect but not much more. Equally, no one can be satisfied with the state of the relationship between British higher education specialists in Latin American Studies and the government, public agencies and the media. (Up to now, of course, government and higher education have effectively left each other alone, and I have not troubled to touch on the question of academic freedom. This looks set to become yet another highly controversial issue in the years to come.) Above all, I think it is fair to say that there has been a failure to establish links with British business and commerce, or to establish businesslike links with Latin American agencies, institutions and individuals. I would certainly not wish to suggest that this is the fault of the academics alone, but just as they maintain within their institutions a divorce between the two cultures of science and technology and humanities and social sciences, so there remains a great cultural divide between higher education and the rest of British life. On this I suppose most of us would agree with much of what the government has been saying (providing it is also applied to its own institutional and managerial practices), but academics have come to fear that all such concessions these days lead not to genuine rethinking but to summary decapitation or ejection of babies with bathwater. This at any rate is another area where the example of Canning House (founded in 1943) might have been followed, in its efforts to unite all areas, all disciplines and all walks of life. The Royal Institute of International Affairs at Chatham House (founded in 1920) also deserves mention in this regard, although its orientation is naturally much wider in perspective, if narrower in target audience.

In a number of respects, then, and despite the generally positive picture of Latin American Studies at the postgraduate and research level, Parry has failed to deliver the required transformation in British knowledge of, and concrete links with, Latin America. It is almost a classic case of the British inability to apply theory to practice. Were these not times when only cuts follow reviews, one would suggest that it was time for a second Parry Report, like Hayter's 1961 follow-up to the 1947 Scarborough Report on Oriental, Slavonic, East European and African Studies, except that it would need to be more broadly based than any of these and to look at the whole question of Britain's actual and desired relationship with the region.[27]

Finally, while I am on the subject of education and diplomacy, a now notorious example of short-sightedness is the 1979 decision to charge 'full-cost' fees to overseas students, in a situation where our European competitors charge little (Germany £40) or nothing (France). This decision has since been attenuated by the rather desperate injection of 'Pym' money and the FCO scheme for 5,000 targeted scholarships. This has not prevented the number of overseas students plunging from 93,000 in 1978–9 to under 60,000 in 1985–6, a fall of 38 per cent when the overall pool had risen by 19 per cent with Britain's share of the total falling from 11 per cent in 1978–9 to 5½ per cent in 1984–5. There has been a slight recovery in the last three years, but in 1987 there were still only 64,434 foreign students in Britain compared with 72,242 in West Germany, over 100,000 in the USSR, 133,848 in France and 342,113 in the USA. Japan is aiming for 100,000 by the end of the century.[28] Detailed statistics for Latin American students studying in higher and further education institutions in Britain are not always readily available. There were 119 Latin Americans out of 14,020 foreign students in Britain in 1962/3, 392 out of 16,154 in 1968/9, and 1,358 out of 50,708 in 1982/3, a figure of 2.67 per cent of the total. The vast majority of these students came from Brazil (424), Mexico (369) and Venezuela (256). Central Bureau for Educational Visits and Exchanges (CBEVE) figures show that the number of language assistants going in either direction is extremely small (38 British in Latin America and 32 Latin American in Britain in 1987/8), though it has more than doubled in the past four years.[29]

The D'Abernon Report in 1929 had noted that Latin Americans were no longer sending their children to study in Britain, and argued: 'To make this country a training ground for the foreign student cannot but be of advantage to our export trade.'[30] In 1985 a survey of seventy heads of state who had studied abroad revealed that twenty-seven had been educated in the UK, fourteen in France, thirteen in the USA and four in the USSR,[31] while a number of leading Latin American politicians have studied in Britain. Yet by the end of the century, on current policies, the situation and the figures outlined above will no doubt look very different.

Cultural diplomacy

There is by now a vast amount of material on this – to British ears – alien-sounding activity, though most of it is dispersed in press and magazine articles, and relatively little exists in books or official reports.[32] The subject can be debated endlessly, but regretfully I have come to the conclusion that it is almost impossible to persuade those who do not wish to be persuaded of its value. That appears to include most inhabitants of this country. Early in this century the concept of selling Britain to the world was considered demeaning and needing to do so out of the question. Everyone knew what an Englishman stood for and there are numerous celebrated quotations to this effect, particularly that of the British official in 1919 who said that 'to promote an image of oneself in time of peace is not cricket'.[33] The unspoken corollary of this is the view that if the economic return on cultural diplomacy cannot be costed, then it does not exist. France and West Germany seem to find middle ways between these two positions and give generous support to the Alliance Française and Goethe Institut respectively, but Britain on the whole does not and organisations such as the British Council are often forced to take up an apologetic posture inconceivable in other countries. To quote John Mitchell:

> In the lack of any comprehensive statement of government policy on cultural relations, there has never been a rationale for justifying them except in terms of political and trade advantage. On top of this there is the current compulsion – positive, in many respects – to justify public expenditure on the coolest assessment of returns to national interest. But as a study of Britain's parsimony and myopia in external cultural policy between the wars will reveal, this is nothing new. Whereas France still largely sees the value of its cultural role in the world, dominant as it was for centuries, in terms of national prestige, Britain has never succeeded in detaching itself from the expectation of tangible returns, either in minds won over to our cause or in pounds, shillings and pence.[34]

Talleyrand exhorted French diplomats departing from Paris for service abroad to 'make them love France'. The more sober British version of this is Dr Johnson's famous dictum that 'a man's friendships should be kept in good repair'. Many chastening experiences later, in his lecture at Chatham House on the occasion of the British Council's fiftieth anniversary in 1984, Sir Anthony Parsons expanded on the theme:

> If you are thoroughly familiar with someone else's language and literature, if you know and love his country, its cities, its arts, its people, you will be instinctively disposed, all other things being equal or nearly equal, to buy goods from him rather than from a less well-known and well-liked source; to support him actively when you consider him to be right and to avoid punishing him too fiercely when you regard him as being in the wrong.[35]

Much lip-service is paid to these sentiments, until it comes to cash and its priorities. Wherever the blame lies in this century-old, but newly controversial debate, most parties now agree that, whatever cultural diplomacy is, it has become 'hydra-headed' and 'is no longer confined to political chanceries and foreign ministries, but rather occurs increasingly through a complex web of commercial, economic, educational and cultural contacts'.[36] There is an uneasy feeling that whatever the game is – surely not cricket – Britain is well behind in it, but then we always were.

For our purposes the most chilling version of the incantation came in 1929 in the Report of the D'Abernon Trade Mission to South America. Simon Jenkins sets the scene as follows: 'In 1929 the French were devoting £500,000 to promoting their culture overseas, the Germans and Italians slightly less. The British were spending nothing, in the implicit belief that the British Empire and English language would suffice.'[37] The final chapter of the D'Abernon Report was entitled 'The Commercial Importance of Cultural Influence'. The authors

Gerald Martin

concluded that Britain had simply not understood 'the direct relation between culture and trade', and pointed out that France, Germany, Italy and the United States had all seen the link only too clearly. As Frances Donaldson says in her controversial book on the British Council, much of the Report 'might have been written yesterday'.[38] It was in the wake of D'Abernon that the Ibero-American Institute (1932–8), the British Council and, eventually, the BBC External Services were established, in the face of foreign, and particularly Fascist, competition, only for their operations to be scaled down as and when emergencies once more subsided. Again, Simon Jenkins has encapsulated the process:

> Since the D'Abernon Report in 1929, Germany, Italy, France and the United States have devoted large sums to cultural and educational missions to Latin America. D'Abernon predicted that Britain's neglect of this activity would result in trade being deflected away from British firms. This has happened: in 1958 Britain sold twice as much as France to Latin America and 60% as much as Germany. Today France sells twice as much as Britain, and Germany more than twice as much. Some attribute this to the poor quality of British goods, some to bad British salesmanship. But cultural projection is cheap, and Britain's competitors were in no doubt of its value. Britain casually left public relations in much of Latin America to local Anglophile societies.[39]

Reliable comparative figures are difficult to come by, but best estimates for 1983 would suggest that the United Kingdom spent £71.5 million on cultural diplomacy, Italy £80.8 million, Japan £95 million, the United States £173.7 million, West Germany £253 million and France £287 million; that in 1985 the United Kingdom spent £89.6 million, the US £246.7 million, West Germany £263.5 million and France £300.9 million; and that in 1986–7 the United Kingdom spent £216 million (unlike the previous figures, this now includes ODA aid and training schemes, much the greater part of the overall budget), West Germany £568 million and France £739 million (the figures for these countries now including schools abroad).[40] It is difficult to see any justification for this huge disparity.

These arguments cut little ice with the British Government, do not seem to weigh heavily upon FCO thinking and I have little doubt that their resistance would be echoed by the population at large. I fear that only a long-term transformation of our culture, which at present seems unlikely, could bring about the change in attitude that seems to be required. I say this because, as I have mentioned above, the question of cultural diplomacy has been aired more thoroughly in the last four years than at any time in the last half-century, culminating in a major report by the Foreign Affairs Committee (FAC) of the House of Commons in the summer of 1987. One could quite easily devote this entire chapter to that very interesting and important document. During the course of 1986 and 1987 it received submissions and heard evidence from the FCO and the major cultural agencies it controls or influences, such as the Central Office of Information, the British Council and the BBC External Services; and from other interested parties such as the Arts Council, the British

Museum and the Publishers Association. The Report makes depressing reading for anyone concerned with Britain's willingness and ability to promote a positive national image and foster mutually beneficial relationships with other cultures. For those concerned specifically with Latin America, however, the depression is especially severe, since the subcontinent is only really mentioned to note how low it is on the list of FCO priorities.

After the British Council had set the pinball rolling with a series of sober memoranda (CD/4 to CD/7) on the importance and complexity of cultural relations and cultural diplomacy, the first Foreign Office statement opened with a sentence that may go down in the annals: 'Cultural diplomacy is a Humpty Dumpty term. It can mean more or less what one wants it to mean. It has never been satisfactorily defined.'[41] (As the *Times Higher Education Supplement* commented at the time, 'For Humpty Dumpty, read Mickey Mouse'.) Following this it offered a rough and ready definition of what the government and the FCO choose to understand by the term and then showed how their activities and those of their agencies reflect this in policy terms. Finally, in a most defensive annex, beginning with an 'important' quotation taken totally out of context from J. M. Mitchell's excellent book on *International Cultural Relations*, it asserted that it is impossible to compare national statistics on expenditure under this heading and implied that in any case Britain has no need to spend as much as our unfortunate competitors (pp. 60–1). When asked by the FAC to justify Britain's low spending on cultural diplomacy, Mr Tim Eggar, Parliamentary Under-Secretary of State with responsibility for Latin America, replied, along the lines of so many before him, that 'one has to ask oneself whether, in fact, a good performance by Britain economically does more for Britain's image abroad than additional expenditure on cultural activities' (p. 237); and when invited to explain why it was that France and Germany were spending considerably more on such activities, he replied that it was necessary to promote French and German in a way that English did not require and that in any case these were more prosperous societies (p. 239).

In a second FCO memorandum submitted to the Committee in March 1987, on its policies for the British Council, top priority in cultural relations was reserved for Europe. Latin America was an area where 'Britain values her long established links and ties of friendship and would not want to see any decline in the general level of activity' (p. 233). This sounds all right, but as we all know, this level of activity is already extremely low, and in reality the diplomatic language cloaks what is actually one of the most lukewarm statements in the document. Astonishingly, there is no cultural representation whatsoever in the Caribbean, from which a large section of our multicultural society comes; such representation could provide us with a stepping-stone to the rest of the region, which is apparently being abandoned to the influence of the United States, as in the case of Grenada (though the FCO 'is of the view that there is a strong case for strengthening cultural links in the region', p. 234). Since the Falklands/Malvinas conflict, understandably enough, Britain has no representative in

Gerald Martin

Argentina, where there are 100 French centres swamping the English 'Culturas', which continue to operate, nor, inexplicably, in Uruguay – a country obsessed, for good or ill, by culture (and football), and where French has recently replaced English as the compulsory element in the secondary-school curriculum. We have no representatives in Central America, Cuba, Paraguay or Bolivia. What there is elsewhere is more likely to be reduced than expanded.

The British Council singled out the Americas as an area where more resources were needed to counteract successful competition from our rivals. Britain compared very unfavourably with both France and Germany, which spent respectively three times and twice as much as the UK on cultural diplomacy, as far as comparisons could be made. The British Council submission to the Foreign Affairs committee notes that Latin America is a top geographical priority for France, 'with particular efforts being made to develop links with newly established or fragile democracies' (p. 9). By contrast the Council's own position was as follows:

In the Americas the council is insufficiently represented, particularly in comparison to the French and Germans. As a matter of policy the French are cultivating North and South America; they view Latin America as an emerging economic force where democracy is fragile and needs supporting. They have a strong Alliance Française presence in every country including the main Caribbean islands, with nearly 200 associations in the USA and over 100 in Argentina. (p. 7)

Mr Roderick Cavaliero, Deputy Director General of the British Council, told the Committee that

we have always felt uncertain about the Americas. One of the things we have said to the FCO is that it would be good to get a long-term perspective of how important British interests are. Is this America's backyard, is there a great future for British trade and political interests in Latin America, or is it a lost continent? It is very hard to get more than an empirical judgment at any stage in this more than peristaltic development. (p. 46)

Sir John Burgh, the Director General, had already appealed to the Committee: 'We need to spend more, because our reputation abroad in so many fields is declining, and the task of cultural relations is to try and counteract the depressing and declining picture of Britain which one sees overseas time and again if one travels abroad' (p. 35). Yet when asked if the British Council was planning to 'open up the Americas to British Council influence more directly', Sir John replied:

The answer to that very briefly is no. One always comes back to the question of priorities within the particular resources we have and the only way in which we could open up our offices in South America, open further offices, would be by taking the resources from elsewhere. The priorities and evidence from the FCO or our own experience is at the moment we should not do that. (p. 47)

The evidence from the British Council, which receives most of its budget direct from government through the FCO and ODA, demonstrates the intense pressures now exerted on cultural institutions to measure up in narrow economic

42

terms. Subjected to twenty-one reviews in its first fifty years, asked to concentrate on the Commonwealth from 1959, then on Europe from 1973 and effectively recommended for liquidation in the Berrill Report of 1977 ('The authors of this report are sceptical about the value of cultural influences in international relations . . .'), the Council was unsurprisingly defensive, pessimistic and almost defeatist in much of its evidence. There was good reason for this pessimism. Sir David Orr, the British Council Chairman, told the FAC that even an extra £5–£10 million would 'make an enormous difference to what we do' (p. 147). But they were not to get it. When Burgh made his last report before retirement in July 1987, as the FAC report appeared, he announced that without the extra £10 million the Council would have to withdraw from another eight countries before 1991 and drastically cut back in ten more. Latin America would certainly be one of these areas affected.[42] In the previous eight years the Council's disposable income ('mixed money') had been reduced by 21 per cent despite the growth in the volume of its work as an administrator of ODA schemes. (In 1987–8 the basic grant was £74 million from the FCO, plus £126 million from the ODA and £58 million earned from English-teaching operations.) With a sharply declining revenue for cultural activities, it found itself almost alone in trying to counteract what the FAC itself described as 'the adverse image of Britain as a static, class-ridden society in economic decline' (p. 1). F. Baveystock, writing in 1987, noted that despite the realities of decline, 'the British Council seems to be up against a deep-seated complacency about Britain's world-wide standing that permeates much of our national thinking'.[43] The Council struggles to maintain representatives in eighty-one countries and to administer aid projects, educational programmes, student exchanges and library centres, as well as the arts and cultural visits activities – a mere 7 per cent of the total budget – which have evoked jibes and provoked philistine hostility from Beaverbrook in the 1930s to the present day. In 1986–7 the seven countries of Latin America, with British Council representatives, consumed a budget of £9.6 million out of a total of £224 million for eighty-one countries, with the Brazilian office receiving £3.2 million. In comparison the Egyptian operation cost £4.9 million and the Indian one £17.2 million. In 1987–8 the differential widened still further: the Latin American operations received a total of £10.13 million out of £245 million, of which Brazil again received £3.2 million. The Egyptian office allocation rose to £5.7 million and the Indian one to £18.6 million.[44]

The FCO and the British Council were the main sources of evidence for the FAC inquiry during its six months in session and it is obvious that they were separated by a very different concept of what cultural relations and cultural diplomacy are or should be. Indeed, these divergences and even confusions caused the members of the FAC some irritation. The difference in perspective is not surprising and would not even be a problem, were there some clear definition and policy statement which could allow the relationship between the two to be defined, reviewed and modified as circumstances require. Clearly, however, there has never been a serious attempt to define the nature and requirements of cultural diplomacy within the FCO itself, since this is effectively taken for granted as an inseparable part of the diplomatic effort as a whole. In contrast, the British Council tended to assert that cultural relations with the outside world were not only useful in improving Britain's standing and an insurance policy the nation could hardly do without, but also intrinsically valuable in their own right. Although this was not a point likely to be appreciated in government circles at this time, the FAC supported this view in its conclusions: 'Not only the political and commercial values of a nation but also its cultural values should be represented overseas and for their own sake' (p. xii). In general, the report represented a swingeing critique of FCO attitudes to cultural diplomacy and called for an adequate definition, a separate budget and substantially increased funds:

> The FCO – despite the recent policy statement in its memorandum 'Britain's Overseas Cultural Relations' – has failed to convince us that a figure of between 27 per cent and 33 per cent of FCO diplomatic funds should be considered the correct proportion to be spent on cultural diplomacy. We are left with the impression that the proportion owes more to historic practice than reasoned evaluation. (pp. x–xi)

It went on to say, 'By every criterion, including even its own, the government is devoting insufficient resources to cultural diplomacy' (p. xii).

The Report received surprisingly wide coverage in the national press and its recommendations (that we should think differently, do more and spend more) were almost unanimously welcomed. Three months later, in October 1987 the government reaffirmed its belief in cultural diplomacy but rejected the call for separate and increased funding, reiterating once again that public expenditure was not to rise as a proportion of Gross Domestic Product (GDP) and that within this there seemed no reason to increase the proportion allocated to cultural diplomacy. Its essential point was baldly stated, predictable and painfully familiar: 'We do not, however, share the Select Committee's assessment that there is any fundamental difference between the objectives of cultural diplomacy and those of the rest of our diplomacy. (Conclusion 1.) On the contrary, although the activities may be different, the objective is essentially the same: the vigorous promotion of British interests.'[45] Once again the British ostrich buries its head in the sand as the competition becomes fiercer. Since that cold douche the subject has more or less disappeared from the newspapers again, to resurface who knows when, although there was a crumb of comfort for Latin America towards the end of 1988 when the FCO made available to British Council offices in Mexico and Brazil extra resources for scholarships.

Conclusions

The problems outlined above are deep-rooted and have been with us for a very long time. Some observers still insist that the problems are largely imaginary and can be safely ignored. Against this view, however, what does seem surprising, given that since the 1920s we have been supplanted by the USA world-wide, that we lost a huge Empire after 1947, that since then we have been out-produced and out-marketed by those we supposedly vanquished in World War Two and that we are now a reluctant member of a large European community, is that in matters of overseas trade and cultural diplomacy one comes across responses which are almost identical to those of sixty years ago. Perhaps all nations forget, or fail to learn, but there seems to me to be a tenacity in our parochialism and insularity, our resistance to genuine interaction with foreign cultures, foreign languages and foreign people, which is startling in a country with Britain's kind of historical past, that of a 'world island'.[46]

It would seem that we need a major transformation of our attitude to culture, in both the anthropological and the artistic-literary senses of the word. (The same might be said of the United States, another pragmatic nation which may also be ill-equipped to cope with its apparent decline, but we in Britain appear to be blinded by the past and we do not have the USA's geographical and economic advantages.)

Only such a transformation of our own culture can in its turn transform our cultural receptivity to other cultures. With the prospect of a single European market in 1992, and in a world in any case characterised by increasing interdependence and intercommunication, Britain, which could still be so influential, seems likely to slip ever further behind, as Spain did three centuries ago. The idea that Britain, once more a small galleon in a large and dangerous world, should jettison the cultural knowledge, experience and know-how gathered in the days of Empire, seems desperately unrealistic. On the contrary, Britain needs to know more than ever what is going on in the wider world and is fortunate to have the cultural and diplomatic infrastructure which a weightier past bequeathed to it. The planet remains a vast and complex place, the future is unpredictable and we need to maintain close relationships with all nations and regions. There is great scope for expansion of our trading and cultural relations with Latin America in particular, if only because current levels are so depressingly low. Given the communications explosion, we may be sure that Latin America will not for much longer seem so far away.

The job is partly political and partly educational. Britain's usable global past and enriched multicultural present might seem to provide a remarkable opportunity to reverse decline and confront the challenges of the twenty-first century. There seems little sign that either the government or the education system, both inclined more to rhetoric than to real change, are fully aware of the opportunity and the probable consequences of failing, yet again, to take advantage of what will therefore prove to have been a mirage.

Needless to say, I believe that cultural diplomacy has a major role to play here: we should do more of it, state our commitment to it, sustain it and do it better by educating and training those involved for the job they are actually doing. There should be increased broadcasting by the BBC External Services and there should be British Council representation in every country in the world. (These institutions themselves presented no such immodest, or indeed 'unrealistic', demands to the FAC: the British Council pleaded only for another £5–10 million and the BBC for an extra 1½ per cent or £1.5 million.) This was implicitly the view taken by every section of the British press, when the FAC report on cultural diplomacy appeared. A *Times* leader on 3 July 1987 was typical: 'The standards set by the BBC External Services arguably do more good for the image of Britain abroad than many a diplomat in a local embassy. The same argument can be applied to the language teaching, the student exchanges and artistic performances organized under the auspices of the British Council.'[47]

It seems to me that we should have some mechanism for integrating our systems of education, information, trade and diplomacy, one which would retain the current semi-autonomy whilst concentrating, accumulating and maximising efforts, linking all relevant organisations[48] by both formal and informal connections, with appropriate checks and balances, within overall planned objectives, including a regularly reviewed statement on the role of cultural diplomacy. This would involve the FCO's renouncing the outdated attitude that it always and in every circumstance knows best where matters relating to 'abroad' are concerned. Meanwhile, current government policy seems to aim at an ever-increasing instrumentality, subordinating education to centrally established policy objectives, whereas the North American and French models of educational and governmental interpenetration would seem, each in its different ways, to point to a far more open and mutual relationship which does not involve shackling and frustrating some of the most creative minds in society.

We should have a different approach to the Civil Service, including the FCO. The old tradition of 'generalists' who are 'conversant' with all branches of government and the service itself is slowly disappearing and should be further telescoped. FCO (and British Council) staff should be more fully professionalised and become equally fully 'conversant' with foreign cultures and foreign languages. It goes without saying that educationalists for their part should learn more about business, government, administration and international relations. Readers may object that demands for a complete transformation of our social culture in general and our cultural institutions in particular are utopian – to which I would respond that these seem to me to be the logical corollaries to the 'enterprise culture' and the only possible route to survival in an age of – simultaneously – intensified competition and mechanisation on the one hand and increasing global awareness of the rights of others and the requirements of planetary survival on the other.

Really, then, Latin America, 'the land that England lost', is just one case study within an overall perspective and it is difficult to draw definitive conclusions relating specifically to that region. We need the kind of political and economic analysis which my fellow participants in the Study Group have made (see subsequent chapters) of the extent to which British and Latin American interests coincide or conflict and of the real state of the current relationship(s). We need to apprise ourselves of the policies and intentions of our EC partners, both individually and as a Community, and to make the most of our relationships with Spain and Portugal. More controversially, perhaps, we need to cease, at least, after half a century, to be quite so politically and economically deferential to the United States, not least in Latin America. We need a speedy resolution of the Falklands/Malvinas dispute, because no future US government is likely to give the kind of support which the Reagan administration gave in 1982. We need to understand Latin America's historic memory of Britain, and Britain's historic memory of Latin America, in order to know how to proceed in the present and in the future.

Many experts believe that Latin America's relationships with the United States and European countries are changing rapidly at present:

> The silent partner in Latin America's international relations during the last decade has been Western Europe. While the trade and financial ties between Europe and Latin America are not as strong as those between the United States and Latin America, there are a host of areas in which Europe has taken new and important initiatives. The role of Western Europe in the Triangle is still evolving. It is imprecise, but clearly of increasing interest to the states of the hemisphere. It is as much a cultural and historical role as it is a 'dollars and cents' role at this time. But its evolution will deeply affect both the ties between the United States and Latin America and the latter's role in international affairs in the coming decades.[49]

Currently, there seems to be a more generalised popular interest in the region than at any time in British history. The British (especially the younger generation) are at last in a frame of mind where Latin American culture is striking them as peculiarly attractive and I see no reason why this should diminish, given Latin America's predictable cultural effervescence in the next half-century. Relations with Latin America will become closer whether those now in power – in the widest sense – will it or not. The only question is whether progress will be facilitated, neglected or even impeded. The academic infrastructure is largely in place, but it is unused to acting in the real world, its staff are demoralised and even defeatist – the parallels with the British Council, the BBC and even the FCO are striking – and the system needs a new beginning, with some horizon for hope. I see little prospect of this unless British governments and the Foreign Office itself begin to see international relations and cultural diplomacy in a wholly different light. It is one thing to brush aside informed public opinion at home; it is quite another to close one's mind to the perceptions that observers from other cultures may have of our actions and intentions.

Notes

1 I should like to thank the following organisations for assistance with the factual information used in the preparation of this study: the Foreign and Commonwealth Office, the BBC Latin American Service, the British Council, the Central Bureau for Educational Visits and Exchanges, the Central Office of Information and the

Publishers Association. Given the nature of the subject, I chose not to solicit the opinions of individuals within these organisations, other than through the printed word, and the views expressed here are entirely my own.

2 The same was true a century ago. D. C. M. Platt, in *Business Imperialism 1840–1930: An Inquiry Based on British Experience in Latin America* (Oxford: Oxford University Press, 1978), concludes that British diplomacy was 'static' and 'largely negative' (see pp. 21–39); and Joseph Smith, in his *Illusions of Conflict: Anglo-American Diplomacy toward Latin America, 1865–1896* (Pittsburgh: Pittsburgh University Press, 1979), likewise confirms that British policy was 'a combination of indifference, ignorance and neglect, based on the reality that Latin America possessed no political or strategic importance for Britain' (p. 21).

3 The modern debate was initiated of course by Matthew Arnold, and has proceeded through the works of F. R. Leavis, T. S. Eliot, Richard Hoggart, Raymond Williams and Stuart Hall. Hoggart's case is particularly interesting, since the author of *The Uses of Literacy* went on to become a senior official with Unesco and subsequently, in 1986, chaired the committee which drew up the British Council's important Activity Review no. 5, *The British Council and the Arts*. Hoggart quotes Richard Auty to the effect that Britain is 'a deeply philistine country with, paradoxically, one of the great cultures of the world' (p. 5). Another seminal contribution to the debate had come on the occasion of the British Council's fiftieth anniversary lecture – at Chatham House – on 24 September 1984, when Sir Anthony Parsons, formerly British ambassador to the United Nations and of Falklands renown, made a stout and candid defence of the Council under the title 'Vultures and Philistines: British Attitudes to Culture and Cultural Diplomacy'. The lecture reviewed the scene from Dickens' Podsnap through World War Two Colonel Blimps to the present day.

4 S. Jenkins, 'Cultural diplomacy: Britain's Washington coup', *The Economist* 2 November 1985, p. 25. This brilliant piece of journalism – one of a number of important interventions by Jenkins – is a major point of departure for the whole discussion of cultural diplomacy in recent times.

5 Britain's diplomatic representation ('total diplomatic effort') in Latin America consumes 4 per cent of the FCO budget, while trade with Latin America (exports and imports) represents less than 2 per cent of the British totals.

6 Quoted in N. Bowen, *A History of Canning House* (London: Hispanic and Luso-Brazilian Council, 1979), p. 24.

7 One honourable exception is the excellent *Gran Bretaña y América Latina: vínculos de ayer y hoy*, a fifteen-programme radio series produced by Pablo Aguirre for the BBC Latin American Service which began in May 1988. For useful single-country studies, see J. P. King, 'The influence of British culture in Argentina', in A. Hennessy (ed.), *The Land that England Lost: Essays in British–Argentine Relations* (London: Lester Crook Academic, 1989), and 'Las relaciones anglo-argentinas despues del conflicto del Atlantico Sur', a paper presented by J. P. King to an international seminar at EURAL (Centro de Investigaciones Europeo-Latinoamericanas), Buenos Aires, April 1988.

8 Alberto Lleras, 'Otra vez nos descubren', *Visión* (29 October 1965), p. 21 (in English, this is 'Once again, we are discovered'). Lleras' explanation for the renewed interest was that the world was now at last 'complete', that the ex-colonial powers were looking to zones other than those they had administered and that Latin America was the 'most European' region of the developing world.

9 'British diplomacy in Latin America since the emancipation', *Inter-American Economic Affairs*, 21:3 (Winter 1967), p. 37.

10 See *Report of the British Economic Mission to Argentina, Brazil and Uruguay* (1930), FO371/14178 (London, Public Record Office).

11 H. O'Shaughnessy and J. Rada, 'Latin America and Europe: towards a new relationship', in *Britain and Latin America: An Annual Review of British–Latin American Relations* (London: Latin American Bureau, 1978), p. 1. Books on this topic have multiplied in the last decade. See, for example, *The European Challenge: Europe's New Role in Latin America* (London: Latin American Bureau, 1982), E. Durán, *European Interests in Latin America* (London: RIIA, 1985), and W. Grabendorff and R. Roett (eds.), *Latin America, Western Europe and the United States: Reevaluating the Atlantic Triangle* (New York: Praeger, 1985). W. Grabendorff of the Institute for European–Latin American Relations (IRELA, Madrid) and G. Ruiz Giménez (Asociación de Investigación y Especialización sobre Temas Iberoamericanos) edited a special issue of the magazine *Síntesis* (no. 4, 1988) on *América Latina y Europa Occidental* and Grabendorff convened a symposium on the same topic at the 46th International Congress of Americanists in Amsterdam, July 1988.

12 A rather bitter editorial in the last issue of the *Economist para América Latina* (11–24 February 1970) compared the journal to 'a ship that set sail on unknown seas' and sank 'just as the lookout had finally caught sight of land'.

13 R. Gravil, 'Anglo-U.S. trade rivalry in Argentina and the D'Abernon Mission of 1929', in D. Rock (ed.), *Argentina in the Twentieth Century* (London: Duckworth, 1975), pp. 41 and 45.

14 Peter Beck has studied the use of association football in cultural diplomacy in 'To play or not to play: that is the Anglo-Argentine question', *Contemporary Review*, 1423 (August 1984), pp. 70–4. See also his 'England v Germany 1938: football as propaganda', *History Today*, 32 (June 1982), pp. 29–35, for an illuminating historical parallel.

15 In recent years there have been significant exhibitions such as those of Brazilian modern art at the Barbican Gallery in 1984 and the highly successful Diego Rivera exhibition at the Hayward Gallery in 1987. A still more ambitious exhibition of Latin American art since Independence is planned for the Hayward in 1989. Major seasons of Latin American, Mexican and Argentine films were staged at the National Film Theatre in 1987–8 and more are planned for the coming years.

16 Published annually by Trade and Travel Publications Ltd, The Mendip Press, Bath, and edited since 1973 by John Brooks.

17 The Report, submitted to the University Grants Committee in 1986, was entitled 'A Review of the Requirements of Diplomacy and Commerce for Asian and African Languages and Area Studies'. Sir Peter was given £1,200 and no secretarial assistance. See *Times Higher Education Supplement*, 'Growing fears for our languishing languages', 18 July 1986, p. 11.

18 'Bosses told to learn lingo', *The News* (Portsmouth, 28 May 1988).

19 'Our man speaks wrong language', *The Guardian*, 3 June 1988 (report on FCO, *Overseas Development Administration Expenditure 1988–89*, Minutes of Evidence, House of Commons Foreign Affairs Committee).

20 John Harvey-Jones, *Making it Happen* (London: Collins, 1988).

21 'No reign in Spain', *The Guardian*, 27 January 1987, p. 13.

22 F. J. Poppleton, *An Investigation into the State of the Study of Latin America in Secondary Schools in the United Kingdom* (London: Institute of Latin American Studies and

Gerald Martin

Hispanic and Luso-Brazilian Council, 1972). See also J. Cross, 'The forgotten world', *Times Educational Supplement*, 22 July 1983, pp. 14–15.

23 University Grants Committee, *Report of the Committee on Latin American Studies* (London: HMSO, 1965).

24 See H. Blakemore, *Latin American Studies in British Universities: Progress and Prospects* (London: The Hispanic and Luso-Brazilian Council, 1971), R. A. Humphreys, *Latin American Studies in Great Britain: An Autobiographical Fragment* (London: Institute of Latin American Studies, 1978), and D. J. Cubitt, 'Issues in area studies: the case of Latin American Studies in Britain', *Journal of Area Studies*, 6 (Portsmouth, Autumn 1982), pp. 13–18, and 'The Latin American model for area studies programmes', *Vida Hispánica*, 32:2 (Autumn 1983), pp. 47–51. Also of interest is W. C. Atkinson, *British Contributions to Portuguese and Brazilian Studies* (London: The British Council, 1945; rev. ed. 1974).

25 See Humphreys, *Latin American Studies* p. 53; D. S. Zubatsky, *Doctoral Dissertations in History and the Social Sciences on Latin America and the Caribbean accepted by Universities in the United Kingdom, 1920–70* (London: Institute of Latin American Studies, 1973), and the booklets issued by the Institute of Latin American Studies since 1967: *Theses in Latin American Studies at British Universities in Progress and Completed*, *Latin American Studies in the Universities of the United Kingdom* and *Latin American Studies in the United Kingdom: Staff Research in Progress or Recently Completed in the Humanities and Social Sciences*.

26 In defence of his adventurous but much criticised Pelican Latin American Library (PLAL), Richard Gott wrote in 1973: 'It is the lack of balance in the origins of the authors in the PLAL that worries me, more than allegations of Leftist bias. I can find a hundred Frenchmen to write about Allende, or the military, or the Catholic Church, or the Tupamaros, or foreign investment, but I am hard pressed to find many Englishmen who can put pen to paper and produce a readable, scholarly book on a subject of importance' (*Latin America Review of Books* (London and Leeds, 1973), p. 218). Times have changed.

27 For information on Latin American Studies in other European countries up to 1978, see C. Mesa-Lago, *Latin American Studies in Europe* (New York: Tinker Foundation, n.d.), and P. Mason (ed.), *Latino-Americanistas en Europa* (Amsterdam: Centro de Estudios y Documentación Latinoamericanos, 1985); and for United States coverage, see the *Latin American Research Review* (1966–), the organ of the US Latin American Studies Association.

28 The British Council, *Statistics of Overseas Students in the United Kingdom, 1982–3* (London, 1984), pp. 8–11. See also the British Council annual reports, the annual Department of Education and Science publication, *Educational Statistics for the United Kingdom*, and the House of Commons Foreign Affairs Committee report *Cultural Diplomacy* (London: HMSO, 1987), quoted extensively below. Figures for overseas students need careful analysis, given frequent changes in the basis of calculation.

29 Statistics provided by CBEVE, June 1988.

30 *Report of the British Economic Mission to South America*, quoted by Frances Donaldson in *The British Council: The First Fifty Years* (London: Cape, 1984), pp. 17–19.

31 Jenkins, 'Cultural diplomacy', p. 28.

32 The only major work in English on this subject is J. M. Mitchell, *International Cultural Relations* (London: Allen & Unwin and The British Council, 1986). The British Council magazine, *Britain Abroad* (1987–), is also a useful source. See also J. Frankel,

International Relations in a Changing World (Oxford: Oxford University Press, 1979), esp. ch. 1, and S. Jenkins and A. Sloman, *With Respect, Ambassador: An Inquiry into the Foreign Office* (London: BBC, 1985). A new magazine for diplomats, *Foreign Service*, began publication in the Autumn of 1985.

33 Quoted by R. Mauthner, 'Cultural bagmen', *The Financial Times* (Supplement), 27 June 1987, p. I, and in House of Commons, Foreign Affairs Committee, *Cultural Diplomacy*, p. 2.

34 J. M. Mitchell, 'Britain's rules, OK?', *Times Higher Education Supplement*, 16 October 1987, p. 13.

35 'Vultures and Philistines' lecture (see n. 3 above).

36 S. Jenkins, 'The British Council – a case for treatment', *Times Literary Supplement*, 6–12 November 1987, pp. 1232–3. This article gave rise to a good deal of correspondence.

37 Jenkins, 'Cultural diplomacy', p. 26.

38 Donaldson, p. 18. See also Tessa Blackstone's review of Donaldson, 'A world of goodies and baddies', *Times Higher Education Supplement*, 25 January 1985, p. 17. Blackstone was one of the authors of the notorious Central Policy Review Staff (Berrill) Report of 1977, which recommended abolition of the Council.

39 Jenkins, 'Cultural diplomacy', p. 29.

40 See Mitchell, *International Cultural Relations*, p. 239; Jenkins, 'Cultural diplomacy', p. 26; and House of Commons, Foreign Affairs Committee, *Cultural Diplomacy*, pp. 14–18.

41 See House of Commons, Foreign Affairs Committee, *Cultural Diplomacy*, p. 58.

42 *The Times*, 1 July 1987. See also British Council, *Annual Report 1986–7*, p. 16.

43 F. Baveystock, 'The British Council battles on: more demands, but less money', *Foreign Service* (Spring 1987), p. 10.

44 British Council, annual reports for 1986–7 and 1987–8. In the latter there are only two one-line references to Latin American countries in a thirty-six-page booklet. R. Hoggart, in *The British Council and the Arts*, provides a number of examples of the inadequacy of the Council's arts policy towards Latin America and shows that arts spending on the region is negligible.

45 See Foreign and Commonwealth Office, *Cultural Diplomacy. Observations by the Government* (London: HMSO, October 1987), p. 3.

46 See A. Gamble, *Britain in Decline: Economic Policy, Political Strategy and the British State* (London: Macmillan, 1985), ch. 2. David Howell MP succinctly summarised the overall reasons for Britain's poor diplomatic performance as follows: 'One of the arguments we have heard in the past has been that our weakness in overseas marketing and world competition arises from our incurable insularity and lack of interest in everybody else's cultures, needs and tastes' (House of Commons, Foreign Affairs Committee, *Cultural Diplomacy*, p. 241).

47 'The cost of culture', *The Times*, 3 July 1987.

48 The main ones are the FCO, the ODA, the Central Office of Information, the Department of Trade and Industry, the Confederation of British Industries, the British Council, the BBC, CBEVE and the representatives of higher education.

49 R. Roett, in Grabendorff and Roett (eds.), *Latin America, Western Europe and the United States*, pp. 277–8.

3　British policy towards Latin America

Robert Graham

In the gradual scaling down of Britain's global role since 1945, few reasons have been found in Whitehall to pay anything other than sporadic attention to Latin America.[1] The generalised absence of pressing commercial, cultural, strategic and security considerations has fostered in turn both indifference and ignorance in official circles about the region. The record of successive governments, whether Conservative or Labour, has been consistent in the low priority accorded the region and in the low level of ignorance. Even such a seasoned British diplomat as Sir Michael Palliser, who visited the region on a three-week tour in 1976 after becoming Permanent Under-Secretary at the Foreign Office, regaled his audience at the Hispanic and Luso-Brazilian Council on his return with the discovery: 'Each country in the area is different from its neighbours.'

Relatively free of superpower rivalry, Latin America has been viewed by Britain primarily in commercial terms; yet the region has absorbed a declining percentage of Britain's exports and this in turn has tended to reduce the profile of its importance. In 1986 only 2 per cent of British exports went to Latin America and the Caribbean – roughly the same value as annual sales to Denmark. Direct access by air from Britain extends to only four cities outside the Caribbean: Bogotá, Caracas, Rio de Janeiro and São Paulo. The national carriers of France, Italy, the Netherlands, Spain, Switzerland and West Germany all possess more extensive direct links.

The low level of trade, however, is not the whole story, as Britain has other interests to defend. If commercial advantage, cultural penetration and political influence are the yardsticks of a nation's overall influence, then Britain arguably obtains a better return on the input of official resources than it rightly deserves.[2] Although it is impossible to measure, Britain perhaps obtains more for its limited input in Latin America than France or West Germany. Certainly the impression prevails within government and among Westminster politicians that Britain is somehow 'keeping its end up' in Latin America – and because Latin Americans themselves dislike the idea of Britain neglecting the region, they on occasions credit the UK with a greater presence than in fact is the case. On both sides therefore there is an element of wishful thinking which nevertheless plays a part in mutual perceptions, and permits the low priority accorded Latin America to exist generally without controversy and in relative silence.

The most eloquent measure of Latin America's limited importance in the overall conduct of post-war British foreign policy has been the derisorily infrequent presence of senior British officials in the region. Ministerial visits, though often far too tied up with protocol, act as important symbols of interest and commitment. On occasions such visits can even be catalysts for strengthening commercial, cultural and political ties. Nevertheless, in an age when air travel has broken the historic barriers of distance, no British Prime Minister has formally visited a single Latin American country. Mrs Thatcher briefly set foot in Mexico in 1981, but this was solely for the purpose of attending the Cancún Summit.

Only three British Foreign Secretaries have visited Latin America since 1945. The first such visit was by Sir Michael Stewart in 1966 (to Argentina, Chile and Peru). This burst of interest, which included a visit by the Queen to Chile and Brazil in 1968, was then followed by a gap of no less than fourteen years before Lord Carrington visited Brazil, Mexico and Venezuela in 1980. In the wake of the Falklands conflict and with the onset of the debt crisis, the region has merited greater attention with Sir Geoffrey Howe making three separate visits since 1984. (He went to Mexico in 1981, to Costa Rica in 1984, to Brazil in 1985 and to Colombia and Mexico in 1987.) Yet no other region has received such scant official attention, confirming that Latin America trails behind Africa, the Middle East and Asia in official priorities.

In a major debate on Latin American policy in 1972, held in the House of Lords, Lord Gore-Booth argued that it was very difficult for the British government to give Latin America the priority which many people wished to give it. There were,[3] he said, too many other things on the government's plate making the lack of priority 'purely a physical problem'. Clearly this practical argument on the allocation of government time is an important consideration, although it ignores any responsibility the government might have to help raise consciousness about Latin America. Here, the level of government attention devoted to the region has consistently lagged behind public interest. At least since the 1960s the extent of public interest in, and awareness of, Latin America has expanded significantly. Evidence of this interest is apparent in a number of ways:

1 the substantial growth since the early 1960s in the number of academic institutions and facilities specialising in Latin American studies;
2 the creation of numerous solidarity groups linked to countries and political movements in Latin America;
3 the spread of political ideas and contacts through such platforms as the Socialist International;
4 the higher profile and greater transparency of commercial and financial activity, especially as a result of the debt crisis;
5 the rise in quality media coverage plus the amount of television news, current affairs, film and nature/ecology programmes devoted to Latin American subjects;

6 the increase in the number of Latin American authors (particularly novelists) being published in English; and

7 the rise of environmental groups, which have paid particular attention to the ecological impact of the destruction of tropical rain forests in Latin America, the threat of pollution in Antarctica from commercial and scientific interests and the risks to coral reefs in the Caribbean from the growth of tourism and fishing.

As public interest in Latin America has broadened it has become much harder to place policy into a neat capsule. There are more actors and many more strands both to policy and to the type of links Britain enjoys with Latin America. The political constituency of Latin America within Britain has expanded so that one can talk of 'official' and 'unofficial' policies. Official policies refer to the combined actions of government; unofficial policies can embrace opposition campaigns over arms sales, pressure to exert sanctions because of human rights abuses and lobbies to ease credit restrictions. All these elements interact, altering, often imperceptibly, the texture of policy towards Latin America.

The traditional actor has been unquestionably the Foreign Office. The latter has presented and represented the broad Establishment view which incorporated the collective interests of the banks, business, government and the services. For years, no one really disputed the way the Foreign Office defined the commercial and strategic importance of Latin America and represented Britain's interests. This, after all, was its acknowledged role.

Under the Thatcher government, however, the Foreign Office has lost this pre-eminence, perhaps permanently. The change partly reflects the personality of Mrs Thatcher and the way in which she handled so much of the successful Falklands conflict, but it is also a natural evolution of the Whitehall bureaucracy accommodating European integration and a more complex interaction of ministries and interest groups. On key foreign issues in Cabinet, the Foreign Secretary in the Thatcher administration has not necessarily been even the *primus inter pares* with ministers. The Treasury, Ministry of Defence, Home Office and Department of Trade and Industry have been on occasions more influential; furthermore the all-controlling influence of the Prime Minister's Office can be found even in an area of limited priority like Latin America.

Is there a policy?

In the discussions of the various papers on Britain and Latin America considered by this Study Group, it has often been argued that there is no policy towards the region – and, for that matter, nor has there ever been one. Britain has merely, it is alleged, reacted to a series of historical circumstances. This view implies a total irresponsibility on the part of the Foreign Office whose job is both to assess Britain's role in Latin America and to draw up policy guidelines for action. One may be able to blame the internal power structure of the Foreign

Office for creating a situation where 'high fliers' avoid Latin America if they can
and where active promotion of ties with Latin America earns few if any rewards.
It is also possible to challenge the Foreign Office as to how, when faced with
budgetary cuts from the Treasury, it has reacted. However, the Foreign Office
cannot be accused of possessing no policy. Since the Second World War, the
Foreign Office has had a clear-cut and remarkably consistent policy. The fact
that this policy has been pursued with limited energy or even neglected is another
matter. The fault on this score must lie more with government, Parliament and
public-opinion formers, although the Foreign Office tends to be selected as the
natural scapegoat, as was the case over Britain's failure to anticipate correctly the
Argentine invasion of the Falklands in 1982.

In 1945 Victor Perowne, the head of the Foreign Office's South America
Department, wrote an internal paper called 'The Importance of Latin
America'.[4] As its title implied this was the first attempt to put the region in a
post-war context, laying down the broad parameters for policy. The paper
concluded that Britain should reassess traditional attitudes towards Latin
America. Perowne argued that this was necessary because the region was
showing a new awareness both of its own resources and of its voice in world
affairs. In language which today appears quaint rather than offensive, Perowne
declared: 'We can no longer afford to dismiss them merely as inconvenient and
rather ridiculous dagoes living at the world's end. We must recognise the need to
pay them more, and reasoned, attention if our interests are not to suffer ... ' The
broad thrust of his arguments for paying attention to Latin America hold good
today. They also continue to form the core of official policy towards the region
even though Perowne himself has long since been forgotten.

Perowne maintained that the region's importance was due to:

1 the availability of a large spread of raw materials, especially in the context
   of the war effort;
2 the extent of British investment (valued in 1945, for example, at £389m in
   Argentina and £237m in Brazil);
3 the potential of Latin America as an export market;
4 the significance of the region – from the Rio Grande to Cape Horn – for
   US strategic interests; and
5 the potential influence of the Latin American block of nations with a
   distinct identity in the emerging world order.

His recommendations included that Britain pay 'suitable personal attention to
worth-while nationals of the individual countries' and that their sensitivities be
recognised; that credit facilities be made available where possible to encourage
trade; that the government work to eliminate 'all bones of contention', especially
the claims of sovereignty affecting the Falklands, British Guiana (Guyana) and
British Honduras (Belize); that good use be made of cultural diplomacy through
the British Council. He also had the foresight to recommend in discreet
language that Britain's role should be a European one acting alongside – but not

necessarily in total accord with – the United States. (He talked of 'not conspiring' against the USA.)

Perowne's prescriptions were uncontroversial and not very original, but this was not so surprising. Britain's colonial presence was effectively limited to the small, easily managed Caribbean states. Questions of trade, investment and finance had been at the core of Britain's relationship with the region since the countries acquired independence from Spain and Portugal in the nineteenth century, and were likely to remain so.

Bones of contention

Perowne's argument that the region needed cultivating because of outstanding 'bones of contention' has proved depressingly prescient. Those disputes he specifically mentioned – Venezuela's claim to British Guiana (Guyana), Guatemala's claim to British Honduras (Belize) and the Argentine claim to the Falklands/Malvinas – are still unresolved. Britain has only managed to abrogate complete responsibility for one of these disputed claims (that between Venezuela and Guyana) as a result of Guyana's independence. Venezuela's claim itself is still on the table for roughly one-third of Guyana's territory (which is potentially resource-rich though virtually uninhabited).

Belize's independence in 1981, on the other hand, did not absolve Britain's responsibility for protecting this small weak state against the claims of Guatemala. The advent of a civilian government in Guatemala (in 1986) pledged to resolve disputes without resort to force has enabled Britain to resume diplomatic relations and has minimised the prospect of conflict. Although conflict with Guatemala is now improbable, the UK is obliged to retain 1,550 military personnel in Belize under a mutual-defence agreement. This, incidentally, is the largest acknowledged foreign military presence in a Central American country and Belize is the only sovereign state (except Brunei and Cyprus) where Britain retains a permanent presence outside the NATO sphere.

As for the Falklands, the fate of this colonial dependency is no closer to solution. The issue is discussed in depth elsewhere (see chapter 9), but here it is worth stressing that the 1982 Argentine invasion and the ensuing conflict complicated a negotiated solution to Argentina's claims of sovereignty. Military expenditure on new defensive facilities that include an all-weather air-base in the South Atlantic and the declaration of a 150-mile fishing zone round the Islands creates an extra dimension. To this must be added Britain's claims to large tracts of Antarctica (mostly disputed either by Argentina or Chile) (see chapter 10).

The three disputes involve deeply felt issues of national sovereignty and Latin American nations have a poor record among themselves of resolving territorial disputes. Few South American borders are entirely defined by mutual consent and recognised by treaty. The British Crown was requested by Argentina and Chile in 1967 to mediate over their disputed territorial claims in the Beagle

Channel, and the judgement in the Queen's name was finally given in 1977. It was not, however, accepted and the dispute was referred to the Vatican and eventually resolved in 1985. In this context, Britain seems to have operated more on the inertial principle of the late Generalissimo Franco who was reported to have had two trays on his desk – one for problems resolved by time and the other for problems to be resolved in time. The experience of the Falklands suggests that the generally low profile of Latin America in British official thinking allowed the consequences of failing to resolve the problem to be underestimated. Equally the dimensions of the problem were poorly grasped so that Britain's defence commitment to Belize even imperilled the availability of Harrier jump-jets during the Falklands conflict.

The Cold War

The timing of Perowne's formative review excluded the context of the Cold War and it is possible that he would have advocated a more direct political role, either alone or in conjunction with the USA, if he had been writing a few years later. Britain, however, lacking the hemispheric interests and commitments of the USA in Latin America, never felt – or perceived – a Soviet threat to the same degree. Cold War considerations applied only exceptionally in British government eyes to Latin America. Thus, while Britain supported global containment of Soviet expansionism, no anti-Communist policy was tailor-made for Latin America.

The British government had its anxieties about the leftwards lurch of British Guiana (Guyana) in the early fifties. The electoral success in 1953 of the People's Progressive Party (PPP) with its left-leaning platform occurred at the height of the McCarthyite era in the USA. As a result the British government removed Dr Cheddi Jagan and his colleagues after only six months in office. The constitution was suspended and the whole intervention justified by Britain on the grounds of preventing a Communist take-over.[5]

This action occurred ten years before Guyana gained independence from Britain and was primarily anti-Communist rather than directed against a Soviet threat. Britain only became directly concerned about Soviet expansionism in the wake of the 1959 Castro Revolution in Cuba. The presence of revolutionary Cuba posed a potential threat to the stability of the colonies in the Caribbean (many of which would soon join the Commonwealth). However, the traditional divide between British and Hispanic colonial cultures helped insulate the English-speaking Caribbean from Castro's revolutionary rhetoric and the Foreign Office wisely chose to accommodate rather than confront Cuba. Britain has retained 'correct' diplomatic ties with Cuba and at a crucial early stage even indulged in the public endorsement of trade via the sale of Leyland buses.[6] Unlike the United States, the weight of Britain's ties with the English-speaking Caribbean tended to make the British government focus on Castro's Cuba as a regional problem rather than a global Soviet one. Britain's principal concern was to steer the Caribbean colonies towards independence and/or federation.

Britain, along with other European allies, supported President Kennedy's 'Alliance for Progress'. The Alliance was dressed up with JFK's high-sounding idealism, but in practice the Europeans saw it as no more than the USA throwing its political, economic and military muscle into Latin America to check the advance of Marxist revolution. Again, because Britain focused its concerns about the Soviet Union and the spread of Communism primarily in a European context, it only briefly shared the United States' sense of a Communist threat, during the 1962 Cuban missile crisis. Furthermore, by the mid-seventies and with the decolonisation process in the Caribbean almost complete, the specific threat even to regional stability posed by Cuba loomed less large. Today such concerns are in a low key. This was evident during the run-up to the US invasion of Grenada in 1983, when Britain maintained a more open-minded attitude towards the revolutionary Bishop government and its ties with Havana/Moscow than the Reagan administration. The pragmatic British approach has been justified – if nothing else by the gradual mellowing of the Cuban Revolution and its fast-fading appeal as a model. The Soviets, now heavily involved in domestic change, seem more concerned to forge better ties with the bourgeois governments of the region. All this suggests that the ideological tone in policy has been a relatively short-term phenomenon whose significance is waning.

A new awareness

The Cuban Revolution excited an interest in Latin America unprecedented since the rise of Perón in Argentina. New forces were clearly at work, wholly different from the crypto-fascist national populism of Perón in Argentina. The threat of revolution on a continent where many governments were run by corrupt, unrepresentative elites obliged Western governments, including that of the UK, to come to terms with the Castro phenomenon. At the same time, the example of Fidel Castro defying Yankee imperialism and that of 'Che' Guevara, the guerrilla leader, exercised a powerful romantic appeal on British students and set a new tone to intellectual debate. The need to know more about Latin America was apparent.

The government responded in 1962 by establishing the Parry Commission to examine the state of Latin American studies in British universities. The report resulted in the creation in the next few years of five Latin American centres (see pp. 35–6 above) with the addition of a sixth at the new University of Essex in 1968. These have become the bulwark of the UK's academic research and teaching on the region, whose scale and quality compares favourably with those in other European countries (see chapter 2).

A less direct response to the Cuban Revolution and JFK's Alliance for Progress was a government-inspired export drive in Latin America. Trade promotion in the 1960s became a fashionable panacea for the ills of Britain's sagging domestic economy. An export drive was the principal rationale behind the first Foreign Minister's visit to the region in 1966, by Sir Michael Stewart.

The results, however, were at best mixed. For instance, between 1967 and 1970, the height of the export-promotion drive, exports increased 42 per cent from Britain to Latin America. Although this might seem impressive, Britain increased European trade during this period by 43 per cent when Europe's economies were growing more slowly than those in Latin America. The early trade drives were bedevilled by poor forward planning, insufficient knowledge of the markets, lack of follow-up and an underestimation of the sheer volume of problems in dealing with bureaucracies and local agents. The availability of credit, subsequently a major inhibiting factor, does not appear at this early stage to have been such a problem.

By 1972, the Foreign Office was beginning to advocate a balancing of the commercial drive with more emphasis on a political approach. The same year also marked Britain's most ambitious post-war project dealing with Anglo-Latin American relations. The government sponsored a large conference/seminar on Latin America at Lancaster House. The seminar, attended by leading figures from the region, marked the coming of age of Latin America in official British thinking.

This government-sponsored initiative, however, was not fully exploited and subsequently fell foul of the first oil shock in 1973. The follow-up to the conference concentrated diplomatic and commercial efforts on the four countries with the largest economies – Argentina, Brazil, Mexico and Venezuela. The results in purely commercial terms were not spectacular. Brazil by the mid-seventies was still twenty-ninth in importance in the world as a British export market. Overall the declining share of Latin America for Britain's exports was not arrested. In 1970 this was 3.5 per cent (against 7.1 per cent in 1950) and it was down to 1.6 per cent at the onset of the debt crisis, twelve years later. While this was happening, British aid to Latin America was being scaled down, as were the resources devoted to the British Council.

The Duncan Report

One major government policy review formally relegated Latin America to a peripheral role. This was the 1969 Duncan Report on diplomatic representation overseas.[7] The message of this report was that British diplomacy needed to operate on a more cost-effective and manpower-efficient basis. In this context Duncan confirmed existing prejudices about the low priority of Latin America which was condemned to being an 'outer area of concentration'. These conclusions were resisted within the Foreign Office not least because Duncan implied a down-grading of a service proud of its role and jealous of its privileges. The Duncan Report ended up by provoking more debate than action and its impact on Latin America was less than feared by those anxious to preserve British relations with the subcontinent.

In terms of the size of diplomatic missions, Latin America was not unduly pared down. Indeed, if one looks at the immediate post-war staffing levels, the

Table 3.1. *Official UK representation in Latin America, 1945, 1955, 1965 and 1985 (includes Defence Attachés, Honorary Consuls; excludes paid locally engaged staff)*

	1945	1955	1965	1985
Argentina	33	32	32	5
Bolivia	8	7	10	7
Brazil	45	41	40	39
Chile	26	24	29	16
Colombia	14	16	17	11
Costa Rica	6	6	5	4
Cuba	11	9	16	11
Dominican Republic	7	8	6	3
Ecuador	6	5	11	11
El Salvador	6	5	6	7
Guatemala	7	7	2	2
Haiti (all staff resident at Kingston, Jamaica)	6	5	3	8
Honduras	7	7	7	8
Mexico	30	28	26	38
Nicaragua	6	5	3	6
Panama	7	7	10	7
Paraguay	2	2	4	7
Peru	16	16	19	13
Uruguay	9	9	15	9
Venezuela	18	16	24	20

Source: Unpublished information made available by the Research Department, Foreign and Commonwealth Office.

slimming-down process has not been as great as might be imagined (see Table 3.1). The two largest countries, Brazil and Mexico, contain staffing either similar to or even higher than in the pre-Duncan years. In 1965 Brazil's staffing totalled 40 and twenty years later the figure was 39, while over the same period the staffing of the Mexican mission has risen from 26 to 38 persons. A more erratic pattern is detectable between 1965 and 1985 among the medium-sized and smaller countries with staffing dropping notably in Chile, Colombia, Cuba and Peru but increasing in El Salvador, Nicaragua and Paraguay.

Staffing levels have been sensitive to perceived needs. The most obvious example has been the up-grading of staffing in Central America during the Reagan administration to monitor the civil war in El Salvador and the evolution of the Sandinista Revolution in Nicaragua. Meanwhile, substantial cuts have occurred in Argentina because of the break in diplomatic relations caused by the Falklands war. The only real casualty in representation has had nothing to do with the Duncan Report. In 1986 the Treasury leant on the Foreign Office to prune its budget and the axe fell on the embassy in Santo Domingo, the capital of the Dominican Republic. The decision had an extremely negative impact, partly because the Dominican Republic's ambassador in London was the doyen of the diplomatic corps. More importantly, Latin American diplomats viewed the closure of an embassy in a Spanish-speaking state in the Caribbean as evidence of Britain's fundamental identity with the English-speaking world and an indirect comment on Britain's interest in the Latin world. The fall-out from this incident has been sufficient to insulate against future closures.

The Foreign Office conducted its first post-Duncan internal policy review of the region in 1972. Others followed in 1975, 1978 and then in 1982, post-Falklands. Running through these reviews is a common thread of agreement on the relative importance and potential of the region which can be summarised as follows:

(a) As a source of raw materials, the importance of Latin America has increased. The region produces fourteen of the twenty-two basic strategic materials, including bauxite, copper, tin, cobalt, titanium and oil.

(b) As a bloc, Latin America is more visible at the United Nations and in multilateral fora on trade and finance issues (such as the Group of 77 and the North–South dialogue). This has been reinforced by the debt crisis, as well as Latin America's desire to be more independent of the United States and to act outside the Organization of American States.

(c) The technological advances of countries like Argentina and Brazil require close monitoring, especially as they approach the threshold of nuclear power.

(d) As an export market, Latin America has shown, and continues to show, a distinct preference for Western civil and military goods.

(e) As a capital-hungry market, Latin America has provided major opportunities for British financial institutions and continues to do so.

The 'access to strategic materials' argument has tended to be repeated without any apparent detailed investigation. The fact that the region possesses these raw materials seems sufficient in itself. The policy-makers have rarely assessed the cost, availability and alternative sources of such strategic materials. Is there a case for saying the potential strategic significance of the region to Britain and Europe has been underestimated? For instance, it is worth recording that Latin America offers an interesting alternative (though not entirely compensatory) source of supply for some of the materials currently produced by South Africa. Turmoil in Southern Africa could provide an added dimension to Latin America's resource potential (see chapter 8).

The argument would have carried more weight if the level of British direct investment had been more substantial. Direct investment has provided the traditional umbilical cord of national interest in a country and produced powerful lobby groups. In the case of post-war Latin America, there has been no recognisable investment lobby outside the plantation interests (bananas and sugar) in the Caribbean. British investment was on a sharp downward curve in Latin America even before the Second World War. By 1945, investment in Latin

America had fallen to just 10 per cent of the total overseas. This downward trend was accelerated in 1948 when Perón nationalised the railways in Argentina, which had absorbed the largest single block of British capital in Latin America. Perón paid out the relatively handsome sum of £150 million in compensation, but his action at a moment of retrenchment in Britain tended to place a blue pencil over the region. Other developing regions appeared more attractive and British investors preferred to deal with English-speaking elites in countries where nationalist sentiment was less hostile to foreign investment.

The new actors

Since the early 1970s a far wider panoply of institutions and groups has taken part directly and indirectly in the policy-making process. The single most significant development has been the alignment of British policies with those of the European Community (EC) as the twelve nations move closer towards integration.

The EC has become an important actor in foreign policy. This phenomenon is discussed in detail elsewhere (see chapter 5), but it should be stressed that the move to align external positions on political and commercial matters does constrain national policy initiatives. So far the effect has been one of degree, illustrated in the Latin American context by two examples. If the Thatcher government had been left to its own devices, Britain's policy towards conflict in Central America would have almost certainly been more openly aligned with that of the USA. However, Britain has gone along with the Community view – the lowest common denominator between the British government's unwillingness to provoke the US administration and the greater sympathy shown towards Nicaragua by Greece, Italy, Portugal and Spain. Similarly, the Thatcher government's inclination on human rights issues has been to rely upon quiet diplomacy, especially with respect to Chile where a strategic alliance of sorts is necessary because of the Falklands. Nevertheless, the Thatcher government has accepted the EC's outspoken condemnation of General Pinochet's human rights record.

While the EC is usually an unseen actor, more visible has been the emergence of well-organised pressure groups to challenge official policies. These groups have derived their strength from being issue-oriented, often connected solely with a single issue. They have grown up on the back of the greater diversity of information available on Latin America and the greater ease of access to the region. Politicians, as a rule woefully ignorant of Latin America, often have their first contact with the region through these pressure groups. Furthermore, in an era of weak parliamentary opposition, these groups have assumed some of the opposition's traditional role.

The international human-rights organisation, Amnesty International, was the first in the field. Its approach was genuinely international and sought to be free of ideological connotations. The smaller pressure groups, associated with a particular cause or country, have been unashamedly ideological. The overthrow of the Allende government in Chile in 1973 provided the touchstone for these groups' activities with the formation of the first of the country-based solidarity committees. The Chile Solidarity Campaign was formed to draw attention to the human-rights abuses of the Pinochet regime and to pressure the British government into applying sanctions. Chile Solidarity grew up when a Labour government antagonistic to Pinochet was in power in Britain and this gave it a wider platform. Thus when it was revealed that a British doctor, Sheila Cassidy, had been tortured by the Chilean security services, the ensuing public outcry forced the Labour government to withdraw the British ambassador from Santiago and to cancel arms sales to Chile. It is hard to prove the precise force of Chile Solidarity, which consists mostly of student activists, leftist academics, Chilean exiles and prominent writers, artists and actors, but its role in consciousness-raising and in lobbying the media, Parliament and the government cannot be ignored.

In January 1980 the Thatcher government chose to restore full ambassadorial relations with Chile and six months later arms sales were resumed, overriding the objections of Chile Solidarity. Nevertheless, all subsequent government policy towards Chile has been carefully measured, aware of the sensitivities of Britain's being seen to be too closely identified with a military dictatorship. Arms sales have taken place, but assurances have always had to be given that the material is not going to be used in domestic repression and the Chilean army, with a bad human rights record, has been kept at a distance while ties with the more 'moderate' Chilean navy have been fostered.

Other leftist solidarity groups followed that of Chile, notably those opposing military oppression in Guatemala, supporting democracy in El Salvador and backing the Sandinista Revolution in Nicaragua. The ultimate rationale of these groups has often seemed more anti-US, anti-Reagan and anti-Thatcher than in favour of their particular cause. They have attacked, for instance, the Thatcher government for politically motivated minimalist aid to Nicaragua. (The UK in 1986, for example, gave far more aid to El Salvador and Honduras, both allied to the United States, than to Nicaragua, which received only £86,000.) The Prime Minister may not have altered aid policy towards Nicaragua, but the very existence of Nicaragua Solidarity has broadened the nature of the debate.

These groups absorb a sizeable chunk of Foreign Office time through their lobbying efforts – letters need answering, delegations have to be met and ministers briefed for parliamentary questions. Indeed, purely on the grounds of the amount of official time they absorb, these groups enjoy a significance out of all proportion to their size and grass-roots support. Often the extra-parliamentary groups interlink and can be composed of similar, if not sometimes the same, personalities. They also join forces with, or take advantage of, Amnesty, and share some common ground with the Catholic Institute for International Relations (which devotes especial attention to Catholic Latin

America). UK church groups do not play the same important role over policy towards Latin America as they do towards South Africa, but the more activist have taken note of the impact of church groups in the United States concerned with Latin American issues.

The traditional organisations promoting relations between Britain and Latin America, such as chambers of commerce and cultural/social groups (such as the Anglo-Argentine Society), continue to be clubbish, commercially oriented and weighted in favour of Establishment views. In other words, their worries and concerns tend to be already accounted for by the Foreign Office. The same applies to a forum like Canning House,[8] specifically devoted to Latin America.

The only new pressure group operating close to the corridors of power is the South Atlantic Council, a bi-partisan grouping of Members of Parliament, academics and businessmen, formed after the Falklands conflict to promote better relations with Argentina in particular and Latin America as a whole. The strength of the Council lies in its substantial backing from within Parliament, although it does not carry the weight of the less well-defined Falklands lobby. Council members have proved a useful conduit for contact with Argentina in the absence of diplomatic relations. The Council has also published booklets on such topics as fishing in the South Atlantic.

The environmental groups are in a different category, directing their energies toward ecological issues which are usually well removed from traditional diplomacy. Their activities have been so successful in highlighting the environmental problems of the region that Western governments have had to pay more attention to the plight of the tropical rain forests, the greenhouse effect, the development of Antarctica and the protection of endangered indigenous tribes and species of wild fauna and flora. These 'mankind' issues, raised by international groups like Survival and Greenpeace, have become part of public consciousness and public concern is demanding a more active response, which Western governments cannot wholly ignore.

These extra-official pressures are not limited to the political and ecological. The onset of the debt crisis in 1982 obliged the British government to establish closer relations with the commercial banks at risk from default by Latin American debtors. The banks themselves, through the Bank of England and the Treasury, managed to convince the government – if it needed convincing – that international financial orthodoxy had to be sustained. In other words the commercial banks ensured their interests remained paramount in government thinking, at the expense of a more sympathetic attitude towards the debtor countries. Significantly, the one British initiative during the debt crisis concerned Africa and specifically excluded Latin America.[9] This was on the grounds that Latin America was composed essentially of middle-income countries whose debt was mainly with commercial banks, while African debt on the other hand had been contracted essentially by governments too poor to repay and therefore relief was essential. Diplomacy has prevailed, however, even at the cost of disagreement with the United States, in recent relations with the

Inter-American Development Bank (IDB). Britain, who joined the IDB in 1976, supported the 'Latin' candidature of Enrique Iglesias to be the new President.

The dominance of a financial and economic approach to the debt crisis has spilled over into the question of export credits. The Foreign Office has been pressing for a more relaxed and 'political' policy regarding export credit guarantees, on a case-by-case basis. Such a policy is considered essential to improve Britain's commercial presence (and therefore its political profile) in larger markets like Brazil. However, the Treasury has steadfastly refused to bend the rules.

The counsels of the Foreign Office have generally been heeded over the diplomatically sensitive topic of arms sales. The principal instance of the Ministry of Defence overriding the Foreign Office has been on matters relating to the Falklands. The Foreign Office has also controlled the vital diplomatic input necessary as a result of the spread of the international narcotics trade. The drugs traffic in many Latin American and Caribbean countries has become the single most important focus of British concern and this is reflected both in the nature of British ministerial visits and in the character of British aid. Aid is increasingly being directed towards help in police training, legal advice, communications equipment and transport to combat the illicit drugs trade (see chapter 11). This applies to drug-producing countries, like Bolivia and Peru, as well as to drug-transit countries in the Caribbean. The Foreign Office at the international level co-ordinates the respective roles of HM Customs, the Police and the Home Office. The kind of rivalry evident in the USA between law-enforcement officers, the Drug Enforcement Agency and the State Department over dealing with internationally sensitive drug matters has so far been avoided.

Change in the air

The presence of these new actors provides a richer texture and a more challenging background to discussion and decisions concerning Latin America, whose effect should be incremental. Policy has also been given a new dimension as a result of both the debt crisis and the consequences of the Falklands conflict.

The aftermath of the Falklands conflict has obliged Britain to deploy unprecedented efforts to offset the negative impact of waging war with a Latin American country and holding onto the Falklands/Malvinas in defiance of UN resolutions. The damage-limitation exercise has been vigorously pursued. This has taken the form of a sharp up-grading in the number of ministerial visits to the region and an expanded programme of sponsored trips to the UK by prominent Latin Americans. The latter have always been part of policy, as was counselled by Perowne. However, the programme has traditionally been inhibited by budgetary constraints. A larger budget is now available and the feedback from visitors has been one of positive propaganda, encouraging the idea of greater British interest in their countries.

There is a negative side to the Falklands issue. Dealing with the Falklands aftermath and monitoring Argentina absorb a disproportionate amount of human and financial resources. This in turn distorts policy, making it top-heavy in favour of defending Britain's position on the Falklands. To put it another way, Britain still risks being branded as a colonial power when as far back as the early 1970s Sir Denis Greenhill, the then head of the Foreign Office, was urging that the problem of the colonial heritage in Latin America be resolved with despatch. Britain's colonial presence is uncontested in the case of the remaining Caribbean Dependencies, but it is challenged over the Falklands.

So long as the threat exists of further conflict with Argentina – no matter how remote – policies have to take account of such an eventuality. Renewed conflict could profoundly destabilise Britain's relations with Latin America and this prospect inevitably circumscribes the success of the British diplomatic effort in rebuilding fences. The Falklands diplomatic damage-repair exercise has patched up relations with Peru and Venezuela, two of the countries most strongly supporting Argentina. Yet sensitivities persist. Early in 1988 Mr Tim Eggar, Parliamentary Under-Secretary of State with responsibility for Latin America, was obliged to cancel at short notice a visit to Brazil and Uruguay as a result of strong feeling generated by Britain's decision to hold a rapid-reinforcement exercise in the Falklands known as Operation 'Fire-Focus' (see chapter 9).

Whether or not this cultivation of Latin America in the wake of the Falklands/Malvinas conflict helped sustain Britain's trading relations is hard to gauge. Certainly Britain's trade appears to have avoided long-term damage (see chapter 6), although this trade performance tends to reinforce the position of those in government who see no need to alter Falklands policy. The enforced post-Falklands activity hopefully looks like acquiring a momentum of its own, but it will require some political muscle to help it along and this in turn raises questions about how, with limited resources, the best results can be achieved. British policy will need to be adapted to the new realities if these questions are to be answered satisfactorily.

Notes

1 I am very grateful to John Penney and the staff of the Foreign and Commonwealth Office Research Department dealing with Latin America for giving me access to the material needed to write this chapter. Needless to say, they are not responsible for any of the views expressed here.

2 The region accounts for 4 per cent of total overseas British diplomatic representation (money and manpower).

3 The House of Lords showed rather more interest in Latin America than the House of Commons. The latter finally held a debate on Latin America on 28 July 1988. It was the first debate since 1950, started at 2.51 a.m. and provoked speeches from only six MPs.

4 The paper by Perowne was dated 17 March 1945. See Foreign Office memorandum AS 1599/176/51. Public Record Office, London.
5 See Raymond T. Smith, *British Guiana* (Oxford: Oxford University Press, 1962), pp. 168–83.
6 This was in the early 1960s, when the US attempt to forge a complete Western trade embargo against Cuba was at its height.
7 See *Report of the Review Committee on Overseas Representation*, Cmnd 4107, July 1969.
8 Canning House is the name given to the Hispanic and Luso-Brazilian Council, established in 1943 to foster links between Britain and the Spanish- and Portuguese-speaking world.
9 This is known as the 'Lawson initiative' and was launched in April 1987. See chapter 7.

4 The United States factor in British relations with Latin America

David Thomas

North American students of the subject habitually bemoan the lack of sustained attention devoted to Latin America by US administrations and Congress. The United States approach, they complain, tends to be episodic and reactive and United States policies to rest, in the words of one critic, 'on either alarmism or do-goodism'.[1] British Latin Americanists might wish that they had it so good.

For most of the period since 1945 British policy towards Latin America has been understated almost to the point of inaudibility; apart from brief flurries of crisis-management, generally related to problems of post-imperial disengagement, Latin American issues have tended to languish towards the bottom of any list of British ministers' priorities. This is not to say that Britain has had no consistent policy towards Latin America, but in the higher reaches, at least, of both Conservative and Labour governments it has habitually been the consistency of more or less benign neglect. Nor is this altogether surprising. The UK docs not have major strategic interests in Latin America and, in contrast with the United States, British governments do not perceive events in the region as capable of posing direct or indirect threats to national security (as opposed to their possible impact on the wider global balance of East–West power and influence). By comparison with the great themes which have preoccupied British policy-makers since 1945, relations with the countries of Latin America were bound to be at best a matter of secondary concern.

At the same time the United Kingdom's position as a nation dependent on international trade and as a permanent member of the UN Security Council, with a diminishing but still extensive range of international interests and commitments, has ensured the retention of the world-wide network of overseas representation, including an active diplomatic presence throughout Latin America. By and large the purposes of this diplomatic effort have been the traditional ones of fostering friendly bilateral relations with individual countries with the aim of promoting British commercial and, to a lesser extent, political interests; or, where necessary, defending those interests against actually or potentially damaging actions and activities of host governments or other foreign competitors. There is little evidence of any serious or sustained effort (except by a few specialists) to develop a regional strategy or even a distinctively British set of policies. This is a predictable consequence of Latin America's lowly place in

Britain's order of international priorities, reinforced by the perception of the region as a natural sphere of United States influence and responsibility. Historical memories of the British contribution to Latin American countries' struggles for independence from Spain and of the dominant role which British capital and entrepreneurial activity played in the subcontinent's economic development, especially in the Southern Cone, in the nineteenth century and up to the First World War provide useful (and often overworked) material for diplomatic speech-making, but have not served to inspire a more active political role in the second half of the twentieth century.

From 1945 up to the early 1980s the fundamental premise of British policy towards Latin America has been that commercial interests necessarily took priority over political objectives. The memorandum of 1945 by Mr J.V. Perowne, the then Head of the Latin American Department at the Foreign Office – quoted by Robert Graham in the previous chapter – identified Latin America's importance to the UK as a source of raw materials, as the seat of the last major block of overseas investment and as an 'indispensable' market for British exports. His principal policy recommendation was that the government should take appropriate measures to promote the revival of Britain's export trade with the region. This, *mutatis mutandis*, has remained the overriding concern of British policy ever since. In 1966, as part of its strategy of export-led growth, the Labour government launched a major export campaign in Latin America spearheaded by visits to Argentina, Chile and Peru by the Foreign Secretary, Michael Stewart. Between 1967 and 1970 British exports to Latin America increased by some 40 per cent in value (in dollar terms), on a par with the growth of British exports to Western Europe and Japan during the same period. There were doubts, however, about whether such a campaign could be sustained and from the early 1970s British trade policy became more selective, with the major export-promotion effort concentrated on the four most important markets of Brazil, Argentina, Mexico and Venezuela. This persistent emphasis on the primacy of British commercial and economic interests in Latin America represents an object-lesson in the triumph of hope over experience: notwithstanding occasional and exceptional upward blips in the graph, as in 1967–70, the overall trend of British trade with Latin America both as a percentage of British trade world-wide and in terms of market share has been steadily downwards (see chapter 6).

Britain's unavailing pursuit of economic interest has generally been unaffected by considerations of political relations between the US and the UK. The contentious trade-policy issues which habitually complicate and sometimes embitter politico-commercial relations between Britain and the United States – questions of extraterritoriality, for example, or civil aviation – have seldom had a direct impact on British trade with Latin America. Notwithstanding occasional disagreement between the two governments over such matters as the sale of sophisticated weapon systems to particular countries, commercial competition between Britain and the United States in Latin America has typically been apolitical. This may be explained in part by the unequal nature of the competition. Britain's share of total imports into Latin America (excluding the Caribbean) fell from 6.8 per cent in 1950 to 2.3 per cent in 1986. During the same period the United States' share rose from 29.7 per cent to 40.8 per cent (somewhat below its high point of 43.6 per cent in 1970). In the period between 1983 and 1985 US imports from Latin America accounted for around 40 per cent of all Latin American exports and nearly 20 per cent of all US imports. In 1986 1.5 per cent of the UK's imports came from Latin America.

Cuba is to some extent an exception to this rule. Britain did not follow the US example when President Eisenhower imposed a trade embargo on Cuba in October 1960 and successive British governments have ignored periodic suggestions by the United States that the UK should constrain its trade with Cuba, for example by limiting export credit insurance cover through the application of political rather than commercial criteria. In this case the traditional British dislike of trade sanctions has combined with hopes of commercial advantage to outweigh calculations of the political benefits which might accrue from following the US lead on an issue of much greater political sensitivity to the United States than to the United Kingdom. Over time Britain has institutionalised its commercial relations with Cuba to the extent required to do business with a Communist country and in recent years Cuba has consistently occupied fifth or sixth place in the table of Britain's export markets in Latin America.

Notwithstanding the priority accorded to commercial interests, British policy has also sought to promote a range of broad political objectives. One consistent theme has been the need to encourage or preserve a generally pro-Western orientation among the countries of Latin America, particularly as expressed in their votes at the United Nations and in other international organisations. In the 1950s and early 1960s this objective was pursued both in the broad context of the Cold War and from a narrower British desire to dissuade the Latin Americans from aligning themselves with the more radical anti-colonialist forces. In this context the satisfactory resolution of Britain's remaining colonial problems in Latin America tended to be perceived as a desirable aim as much as anything in order to avoid antagonising the Latin American group in the United Nations. By the early 1970s, with a number of Latin American countries taking leading roles in the Group of 77 and the campaign for a new international economic order, the main thrust of British efforts to influence Latin American governments became directed to persuading them that their best interests lay in economic co-operation rather than confrontation with the industrialised West. In a speech at Canning House in March 1976 Sir Michael Palliser, then Permanent Under-Secretary at the Foreign and Commonwealth Office, spoke of Her Majesty's government's determination to engage Latin American governments in 'an across-the-board, politico-economic dialogue', to be pursued bilaterally at the regional level (for example, between the European Community and Latin American regional organisations) and at the multilateral level in the Conference on International Economic Co-operation. For a time this theme of active North–South dialogue was the staple of British diplomatic activity towards the Latin American countries individually and collectively. But although this willingness to discuss Latin American concerns with every appearance of seriousness may have helped to lower the temperature of the debate in some cases, it cannot plausibly be claimed to have had a significant impact on the substance of Latin American thinking. A subsidiary, but perhaps more practical, objective of the dialogue was to encourage Latin Americans to channel their desire to diversify their economic and political dependence on the United States into a more substantial and mutually beneficial relationship with the European Community. With the election of the Conservative government in 1979 the emphasis in British policy reverted to trade promotion until events in the South Atlantic, the Caribbean and Central America added a new dimension to British perceptions of Latin America and to their place in the Anglo-US relationship.

The contrast between the United Kingdom's commercially inspired and politically pragmatic low-key policy towards Latin America and the highly ideological, security-conscious approach of the United States is striking. Of course the size and scope of US trade with and investment in Latin America mean that economic and commercial considerations are a significant factor in US policy-making; and in particular cases the protection of private US economic interests has been an important determinant of US action. Thus the United Fruit Company's response to the threat posed to it by President Arbenz' land-reform programme contributed to the process which culminated in the indirect US intervention in Guatemala in 1954 which brought Arbenz down; Fidel Castro's progressive nationalisations of US companies in Cuba in 1959 and 1960 played a large part in determining the US attitudes which led to the Bay of Pigs invasion in 1961; the role of ITT in the destabilisation of the Allende government in Chile has been well documented. More recently, domestic economic lobbies persuaded the US Congress to emasculate some crucial components of President Reagan's Caribbean Basin Initiative and concern for the position of some major US banks caused the United States to adopt what some observers considered to be an excessively flexible approach to Argentina's external debt problem in 1984–5. Nevertheless, these examples probably tell one more about the dynamics of the US political system and US perceptions of the Communist threat than about the aims and objectives of US relations with Latin America and it would be a mistake to identify economic interests, important though they clearly are, as the decisive element in US hemispheric policy.

The criticism that US policy towards Latin America has tended to be episodic and reactive undoubtedly has some force, but inconsistencies in US policy tend to reflect tensions and contradictions between a number of ideas which have characterised US attitudes towards Latin America over a long period. The Monroe doctrine (1823) symbolised the notion that the Americas constituted a distinctive group of nations from which the alien influence of the Old World should be excluded. This concept has gone hand in hand with the tendency of North Americans to universalise their own historical experience and to seek to project it onto the countries of Latin America. If certain truths were self-evident to the drafters of the Declaration of Independence it stood to reason that they should be self-evident to the inhabitants of Latin American countries too (or at any rate to their political elites), notwithstanding the very different political culture they had inherited. An idealistic concern for the liberties and well-being of its hemispheric neighbours has been a persistent feature of US thinking about Latin America, even if it has often appeared to be more rhetorical than real. At the same time this self-appointed role as the promoter of the democratic ideal has all too often justified a paternalistic or coercive exercise of US influence and power in ways which were given their classic expression by President Theodore Roosevelt; it has also engendered the assumption that the interests of the United States and Latin America must coincide and therefore that any Latin American deviation from this principle must imply hostility to US interests, thereby justifying the exercise of US strength to bring the offender to heel. When President Theodore Roosevelt sent US troops to Cuba in 1906 he complained: 'I am so angry with that infernal little Cuban republic ... All that we wanted from them was that they should behave themselves and be prosperous and happy so that we would not have to interfere. And now, lo and behold ... we have no alternative save to intervene.'[2] Some seventy years later Henry Kissinger is reported to have said about Allende's Chile: 'I don't see why we have to let a country go Marxist just because its people are irresponsible.'[3]

These two quotations illustrate rather well the persistence of the basic duality in US policy towards Latin America, the tension between what Stanley Hoffmann has called 'the instinct for the use of force and the drive for harmony'.[4] Dr Kissinger's remark also reflects the overriding concern of US Latin American policy in the post-war period. Notwithstanding narrower bilateral or regional issues which have come to the fore from time to time, the outstanding characteristic of US policy since 1945 has been that it views Latin America in the context of global East–West strategic and ideological competition. Individual countries and the region as a whole have generally been given high priority by US policy-makers only to the extent that events there have appeared to threaten a gain for the Soviet Union at the expense of US interests and national security. Major US policy initiatives have similarly been inspired in large part as defensive or pre-emptive moves against Communist penetration.

The application of this principle has varied from administration to administration, but the underlying pattern has been quite consistent. The Rio Treaty of 1947 and the Pact of Bogotá which established the Organization of American States (OAS) in 1948 were natural progressions from earlier US efforts to promote hemispheric security and pan-American democratic solidarity. Yet almost from the start they were perceived by Washington as vehicles by which the United States, as the leader of the free world, would consolidate the defence of the Americas against the threat of international Communism. In 1954 this aim was defined quite clearly when, in a gloss on the Monroe principle that European powers should not 'extend their system to any portion of the hemisphere', the United States secured the passage by the OAS of a resolution which declared that 'the domination of the political institutions of any American state by the international Communist movement ... would constitute a threat to the sovereignty and political independence of the American States'.

That resolution was part of the successful campaign mounted by the Eisenhower administration to rally Latin American governments behind Washington's perception of the Arbenz government in Guatemala as Communist-controlled. The threat of Communist subversion was similarly invoked as an *ex post facto* justification for the US military intervention in the Dominican Republic in 1965, after the Cuban Revolution and the failure to dislodge Castro had lowered the threshold of US tolerance to real or imagined Communist threats elsewhere in the hemisphere and especially in the Caribbean. Even in the era of *détente*, when the view of the Cold War as a global zero-sum game had given way to more sophisticated conventions, the early, relatively relaxed assessments by the State Department and the CIA of the implications of an election victory by Allende in Chile were soon overtaken by Dr Kissinger's geostrategic judgement that the establishment of a second Marxist state in Latin America would pose an intolerable threat to vital US interests and to the credibility of the United States world-wide. President Carter's concentration on human rights marked a change of emphasis, but Carter's brave assertion in 1977 that the United States was 'now free of that inordinate fear of Communism which once led us to embrace any dictator who joined us in that fear'[5] turned out to be premature. Even before the end of the Carter administration, events in the Caribbean and Central America had pushed national security back to the top of the agenda; and with President Reagan's election the wheel turned full circle with a reversion to the 1950s view of the nature of the international Communist threat to Latin America and the appropriate US response.

OAS resolutions and coercive actions were not of course the only weapons at the disposal of the United States. The instinct for the use of force was indeed accompanied by a drive for harmony. The latter part of the Eisenhower administration saw the beginnings of an effort to promote economic development and democratic institutions as a means of inoculating Latin America against the virus of Communist infection: the Inter-American Development Bank grew out of an initiative by President Eisenhower in 1959. President Kennedy's Alliance for Progress was a highly ambitious attempt to set in train a genuinely collaborative programme to promote political stability by linking economic aid with social and political reform. The aims were grandiose, the reforms were necessary and the rhetoric was impeccable. But the Alliance for Progress was inspired by the need to contain the popular impact of the Cuban Revolution and the threat from Havana to 'turn the Andes into the Sierra Maestra of Latin America'. The US commitment to reform was genuine, but the instinct to protect US security interests was even stronger and the greatly increased programme of military assistance and counter-insurgency training which accompanied the development-assistance package turned out to have the greater impact. President Reagan made no bones about the objectives of his Caribbean Basin Initiative. In his speech on 24 February 1982 announcing the Initiative he drew a stark contrast between the 'positive future' which awaited countries friendly to the United States who stood to benefit from his initiative and 'the dark future foreshadowed by the poverty and repression of Castro's Cuba, the tightening grip of the totalitarian left in Grenada and Nicaragua, and the expansion of Soviet-backed, Cuban-managed support for violent revolution in Central America'.

This is not the place to attempt a cost-benefit analysis of the post-war hemispheric policy of the United States, beyond noting that just as its objectives have sometimes been contradictory, so have its results been patchy. In particular, the US habit of viewing events in Latin America through the distorting prism of East–West geopolitics has reduced the capacity of successive US administrations to develop appropriate Latin American policies for Latin American problems. This is not to say that the East–West dimension is absent from Latin American politics or can be ignored – Cuba has seen to that. In the Cuban missile crisis of 1962 fundamental issues affecting the East–West strategic balance and US national security were at stake. The same could not plausibly be said of Guatemala in 1954, the Dominican Republic in 1965 or Grenada in 1983. Policies based on containment of Communism have caused the United States to act in ways which have stirred up anti-US feeling in Latin America and have contributed to the decline of the OAS and the Rio Treaty as effective instruments of hemispheric solidarity. They have also produced unlooked-for results which have run counter to proclaimed US objectives. After the ouster of Arbenz in 1954 there was not another genuinely free election in Guatemala until 1985. The military-assistance programmes which accompanied the Alliance for Progress did help democratic governments in Venezuela and Peru to control revolutionary insurgencies, but they also encouraged the suppression of popular movements elsewhere and contributed to the spread of military rule, not only by nationalists of the right. In Peru, the lessons drawn by the armed forces from their counter-insurgency experience led in 1968 to the seizure of power by an authoritarian left-wing military regime hostile to the United States. Under President Reagan the US administration's Manichaean East–West perspective of the situation in Central America had the effect of restricting the options which it was prepared to consider in order to counter the perceived threat from Nicaragua.

To what extent have the very different British and US approaches to Latin America interacted and to what effect? The great asymmetry of these interests in Latin America, together with the greater importance accorded to other regions and international issues on the US–UK agenda and the shared perception of Latin America as an area of United States hegemony, have meant that consultation between the two governments on Latin American affairs has mostly been conducted at a relatively low level. The United Kingdom has consistently supported the US aim of denying the Soviet Union new footholds in Latin America while generally taking a more relaxed view of the imminence of the threat or of the extent of Communist manipulation of radical and nationalist movements. For Britain, distance lent, if not enchantment, then a certain pragmatic complacency to its view of the global implications of episodes of local instability in Latin America. Yet if in some instances doubts were expressed about the appropriateness of US reactions to perceived threats of Communist infiltration, considerations of Western solidarity and the place of Latin America in Britain's balance of interests *vis-à-vis* the United States prevented these doubts from becoming serious causes of friction. Thus while British governments have generally been alert to Cuba's potential for undermining Western interests in the Caribbean and Africa, they have never appreciated – still less shared – the complex of historical, territorial, ideological and even moral reasons which have made the survival of a revolutionary Communist state ninety miles from Key West a standing affront to US pride. From the outset Britain refused to join in US efforts to ostracise the Castro regime and in the mid-1970s a Labour government which had courted unpopularity with its own supporters by its qualified support for US policy in Vietnam felt able to restore the balance a little by putting more substance into Anglo-Cuban relations. More typically, however, the British calculation has been that such marginal benefits as might be gained from seeking closer political relations with Cuba would be outweighed by the displeasure this would provoke in Washington.

Elsewhere in the Caribbean, where British and US spheres of interest overlapped, Anglo-US consultation and co-operation was generally closer, although with a certain ambivalence on both sides in so far as British colonial disengagement was involved. Britain was reluctant to allow the United States a say in the decolonisation process, but expected the United States to increase its economic and security support to the region. For the United States, atavistic anti-colonial sentiment was at odds with the fear that British withdrawal would leave behind a succession of non-viable independent mini-states vulnerable to Cuban and Soviet subversion. Where the two governments shared a perception of imminent Communist gains they were capable of close and decisive collaboration, as was demonstrated by the destabilisation of the Jagan government in British Guiana in 1963. The one attempt by the United States in 1968 to mediate in the Belize–Guatemala dispute was unsuccessful. Thereafter the United Kingdom tended to look to the United States to exercise a restraining influence on Guatemala, whereas the United States was more concerned about what it saw as Belize's susceptibility to Cuban subversion.

Britain's principal concern in the 1970s, that the United States should not enhance Guatemala's military capacity, was taken care of by the US Congress independently of British urging when in 1977 it imposed restrictions on the supply of lethal military assistance to Guatemala because of its record of human-rights violations. The decision to reinforce the British garrison in Belize in 1977 was a unilateral decision taken by the British government, but one which was welcomed by the United States and in time, and for different reasons, by all the interested regional actors – including even Guatemala and Cuba. Indeed, the value placed by the United States on the British military presence in Belize is one reason for its retention today.

In the 1980s critical issues related to Latin America have played a more prominent part in relations between Britain and the United States than at any time since 1945. The two countries have been dominated throughout this period by leaders whose 'special relationship' was the product of reciprocal political attraction: their close and mutually supportive relationship on international affairs reflected an intuitive congruence of outlook reinforced, on the British side, by Mrs Thatcher's calculation of British national advantage as lying with demonstrative solidarity with the United States wherever possible. But as events in the South Atlantic, Grenada and Central America have shown, this instinct for collaboration was not trouble-free when either country perceived its vital national interests to be at stake.

The South Atlantic (Falklands) conflict was unique in that the United States was called upon to play a central role over an issue which it had traditionally viewed as of peripheral significance, but where the support expected of it by its closest ally in a matter of the highest importance to the UK posed serious risks to its own regional interests. Notwithstanding the advocacy of a softer line towards Argentina by some of the neo-conservative Latin Americanists in the administration, it is evident that Secretary of State Haig saw clearly that Argentina should not be allowed to get away unscathed with an action which might be held to legitimise the settlement of territorial disputes by force; and both he and President Reagan were very conscious of the damage which failure to stand by Britain could do to the solidarity of the Atlantic alliance. At the same time they were concerned throughout at the possible consequences of overt support for the United Kingdom for the hemispheric position of the United States. The Reagan administration's efforts since 1981 to improve relations with Argentina had been successful to the point that Argentina was giving covert military support to the United States in Central America: thus, relations with Argentina and the prosecution of US policies in Central America both stood to suffer. The administration was worried that failure to support Argentina against military action by an extra-continental power would provoke hostility to the United States throughout Latin America and further undermine its position in the OAS; and it feared that the Soviet Union would exploit Argentine resentment in order to make new inroads into Latin America. There were even some fears that the United States might become directly involved in the hostilities. Small wonder, then, that a negotiated outcome to the Falklands crisis was always the administration's preferred solution, provided that British interests were adequately safeguarded; and that Mr Haig insisted that the credibility of his eventually unavailing efforts to mediate required that the United States should preserve a public posture of even-handedness. Even after the intransigence of the Argentine junta had brought the United States into open and effective support for the United Kingdom, and Britain had decisively won the battle for US public and congressional opinion, the administration remained deeply concerned about the consequences for its future hemispheric relations.

In Britain, where the government had at first overestimated the capacity of the United States to restrain Argentina (just as General Galtieri had been encouraged to miscalculate the administration's ability to dissuade Britain from a military response to the seizure of the Falklands and the likelihood of US neutrality thereafter), the administration's publicly even-handed stance – until the failure of Haig's mediation effort – was viewed with some impatience and even mistrust, reviving memories of Suez. Disagreements within the administration were a further cause for concern: notwithstanding Defense Secretary Weinberger's unequivocal solidarity with the British cause and Haig's private assurances, the activities of the 'Latino lobby' gave rise to some apprehension. In the end, the United States' diplomatic efforts were recognised to have had the important effects of filling a political vacuum while the task force was deployed and of exposing the intransigence of the Argentine junta. Furthermore, the value of the military support afforded by the United States was very great indeed. Yet, as Sir Nicholas Henderson concluded in his first-hand account of the Anglo-US diplomacy of the South Atlantic conflict, 'American support was not something that was inevitable: it could not have been taken for granted and could have been lost at any time had [Britain] shown complete intransigence in negotiation.'[6]

The repossession of the Islands was not the end of the affair. Although the worst US fears were not realised, in the short term the United States probably did incur greater resentment in Latin America from its support for Britain against a fellow American state than Britain did itself. One by-product of the conflict was to give a boost to assertive Latin American solidarity *vis-à-vis* the United States, but on a North–South, not an East–West, axis. The political consequences for both Britain and the United States were mitigated by the unlooked-for aftermath of the war in Argentina itself, but by the same token the restoration of democracy in Argentina created an essential opportunity for the United States to seek to rebuild the bilateral relationship, sometimes in ways unwelcome to the United Kingdom. The British government accepted with resignation the United States' support at the United Nations for Argentine calls for negotiations over the future of the Falkland Islands, but it remains morbidly sensitive to the possibility that the discredited Argentine armed forces might regain the capacity to pose a military threat to the Falklands in the future. If US efforts to help the Argentine government to integrate the armed forces as an institution into the democratic structure of Argentina were to involve the supply of modern weapon systems and other forms of assistance designed to enhance the professional capabilities of the Argentine military, this could still provoke friction between the British and US governments. For its part the US administration has shown no enthusiasm for reviving its efforts to mediate between Britain and Argentina, although it has acted as the channel for indirect contacts over fishing in disputed waters in the South Atlantic. So long as the British and Argentine positions over the Falklands remain irreconcilable, with Britain unwilling to discuss the sovereignty issue as the price for normalisation of bilateral relations and Argentina unwilling to improve relations in the absence of a British commitment to discuss the future of the Islands, the scope for mediation is in any case limited. However, if this continuing deadlock were to become the source of renewed political instability in Argentina, or were to be perceived in Washington as creating a significant impediment to the promotion of US interests in Argentina and elsewhere in Latin America, then again the Falklands could become a contentious issue between London and Washington – particularly with a new US administration which had not shared the experience of the South Atlantic conflict and was less attuned to British sensitivities.

Washington's failure to appreciate the raw nerve which would be touched by US armed intervention in a Commonwealth country owning the British Queen as its Head of State – even if it did have a revolutionary Marxist government – was one cause of the spat which soured the post-Falklands honeymoon. Britain and the United States had a well-established tradition of consultation on Caribbean affairs and Britain, like the United States, had become concerned at the increased scope for promoting instability in the Eastern Caribbean opened up to Cuba and, to a lesser extent, the Soviet Union by the seizure of power in Grenada by the New Jewel Movement. Yet the British government, which had maintained a correct if uneasy relationship with the Bishop regime, did not share the more extreme US perception of the threat to regional security represented by the Cuban presence and the construction by Cuban workers of Point Salines airport – with participation by a British contractor and (a detail generally overlooked) a US dredging company. The mini-crisis occasioned by the self-destruction of the New Jewel Movement and the murder of Maurice Bishop in October 1983 was the subject of intensive consultation between British and US officials; yet although the fortuitous presence in the area of a US task force originally destined for Lebanon indicated that armed intervention against a target of opportunity was one option under consideration by the United States, the belated communication to the British government of the decision to intervene came as a shock. (According to the former Speaker of the US House of Representatives, Tip O'Neill, the British government might have been even more embarrassingly wrong-footed if O'Neill had not reminded President Reagan to telephone Mrs Thatcher on the eve of the US intervention.[7]) Over and above the British government's objections of principle, forcibly expressed by Mrs Thatcher after the event, what really hurt was the realisation that not only had it not been taken fully into the administration's confidence, but it had to some extent been misled as to US intentions. It was a salutary reminder that when a superpower gets the bit between its teeth it will not necessarily stop to ask its closest allies if it is going in the right direction. In the White House Britain's failure to endorse the US intervention was seen as base ingratitude for the risks the United States had run in its support for the United Kingdom in the

Falklands conflict. The bitterness eased, however, and both sides sought thereafter to ensure that their consultation on Caribbean issues would be sufficiently close to preclude a repetition of the storm in the Grenadan teacup – in Britain's case, not least in order to recover some of the influence it had lost with most Eastern Caribbean leaders by its failure to back the US intervention.

Consultation offered less scope for the reconciliation of divergent viewpoints in the case of Central America, given the extreme asymmetry of British and US interests in the region and the strength of President Reagan's personal commitment. The United Kingdom has no significant national interests in Central America apart from its commitment to the defence of Belize and an important British objective is for Belize to remain insulated from the wider Central American imbroglio. For Britain, as for many European governments, the importance of the Central American crisis was to a large extent a function of the weight attached to it by the Reagan administration and hence of its sensitivity in the complex of transatlantic relationships.

The British government can understand and shares the US aim of preventing a revolutionary Marxist takeover in El Salvador; it has no ideological sympathy with the Sandinista government in Nicaragua; it appreciates the wider strategic implications for Western security if the Soviet Union were to establish a military foothold on the Central American mainland. It is not convinced, however, by the more apocalyptic vision of the nature and extent of the threat to US security posed by Nicaragua which has been voiced in Washington. Nor is it comfortable with some of the means chosen by the United States to counter this perceived threat, as can be inferred from the consistent British adherence to the European Community position, first formulated in 1983, to the effect that the problems of Central America cannot be resolved by armed force, but only by negotiation of a peaceful settlement. Britain supported the Contadora process and subsequently the Arias peace plan.[8] It has participated quite actively in the series of annual 'San José' meetings between foreign ministers of the European Community, Central American and Contadora Group countries, despite initial reservations (which have proved to have some foundation) about the practical as opposed to the symbolic utility of these meetings, and despite the displeasure clearly articulated by the US administration before and during the first meeting at San José, Costa Rica, in September 1984.

In addition to British fears that US methods are liable to be expensively counter-productive, even in terms of the objectives proclaimed by Washington, the British government has clearly been apprehensive about the implications of the US assault by proxy on Nicaragua for the rule of international law. Regardless of the merits of President Reagan's categorisation of the Contras as freedom-fighters deserving of support in their just struggle against a totalitarian regime which had betrayed its original democratic promises, the provision of financial and material assistance to a rebel force seeking the violent overthrow of a recognised government (and one with which the United States still maintains diplomatic relations) is seen as contrary to established norms of international law

– as the International Court of Justice (ICJ) has confirmed. That the United States recognised this convention in the past is demonstrated by the efforts made to establish plausible deniability of direct US involvement in the overthrow of established governments in Guatemala and Chile (and the abortive expedition against Castro at the Bay of Pigs) or by resort to the legal fig-leaf of saving US lives to justify military interventions in the Dominican Republic and even Grenada. The British fear has been that the US administration's overt sponsorship of the Contras could not only lose the United States the high moral ground in relation to the Soviet Union, but also establish a precedent having dangerous repercussions on international stability elsewhere.

Notwithstanding such doubts about US behaviour in Central America, the British government's public position reflected Mrs Thatcher's sympathy, both instinctive and calculated, with the broad objectives of President Reagan's policy and her sense that Britain's interests are best served by being demonstrably helpful to the United States administration where possible. Thus Britain was one of the relatively few countries to send official observers to the elections in El Salvador in 1982 and 1984 and official government statements were generally supportive of President Duarte – but Britain did vote in favour of UN resolutions condemning human rights abuses in El Salvador in 1985 and 1986. By contrast, Britain did not send official observers to the Nicaraguan elections in 1984 and the government's public statements are critical of the Sandinistas; the UK abstained when Nicaragua obtained the UN General Assembly's overwhelming endorsement of the ICJ ruling on the illegality of US actions against Nicaragua. However, this predisposition to be helpful has its limits: despite some allegations to the contrary, there is no evidence that the British government has ever sanctioned the supply of British military equipment to the Contras, either directly or indirectly, and it would be very surprising if it had. British reservations about US policy have seldom been articulated openly. Given President Reagan's sensitivity on the issue and the domestic controversy in the United States over funding of the Contras, this was seen by the British government as a classic case for quiet diplomacy. It is also worth noting that Sir Geoffrey Howe's repeated appeals to 'all sides' in Central America to exercise restraint mean exactly what they say.

The Central American crisis is in many ways a paradigm of the impact of the Anglo-US relationship on British policy towards Latin America: the disparity between the British and United States interests at stake means that Britain's capacity to influence US policies and actions is strictly limited; and the low priority generally accorded to Latin America in the British scheme of things means that Britain's policy options are limited by calculations of their likely impact on other and weightier British interests in relation to the United States.

This pattern is unlikely to change significantly in the foreseeable future, regardless of the advent of a new US administration and perhaps sharper tensions in the permanent dialectic between administration and Congress. The present British government will expect an easier relationship with a Republican administration headed by President Bush than it might have formed with a Dukakis White House (although it would have been predisposed to seek the closest possible working relations with either). The extent to which both the content and the conduct of much of British foreign policy have come to reflect the Prime Minister's own perceptions and prejudices implies that the personal relationship between Prime Minister and President will continue to be one important factor in determining, within the broader Anglo-US framework, the British response to US attitudes and initiatives in contentious areas of policy affecting Latin America. Mr Bush will not automatically inherit the political and emotional rapport which characterised Ronald Reagan's partnership with Margaret Thatcher; nor is he likely to benefit to the same extent from her deep sense of gratitude for the support given to Britain by the United States in the South Atlantic conflict.

The South Atlantic is indeed the one area in which the normal calculations of reciprocal British and US interests do not apply; and the enduring deadlock between Britain and Argentina over the Falkland Islands is the most obvious potential source of future transatlantic discord. One possible irritant – US military co-operation with an Argentine government seeking to consolidate the country's democratic structures – has already been mentioned. On the other hand, if political developments in Argentina were to be such as to generate serious new tensions with the United Kingdom, this in turn could cause friction between Britain and the United States. The issues would almost certainly not be as clear-cut as in 1982 and London and Washington could well arrive at very different appreciations of the nature of the threat to their respective national interests and of the appropriate means of meeting it. In such circumstances the British government could find itself seeking a degree of support from the United States which the administration and Congress were not prepared to give; or the United States could feel obliged to promote an outcome which was perceived in London as paying insufficient regard to legitimate British concerns. Either way, if the British government were to feel that its closest ally had let it down the ensuing bitterness could have a disproportionately damaging effect on Anglo-US relations.

No other Latin American problem is so sensitive for the British government. Relations with Argentina aside, the nature of the interaction of British and US policies towards Latin America is likely to remain largely conditioned on the British side by a desire for collaboration in the pursuit of common or complementary objectives or, failing that, the calculations of wider Anglo-US and Western interests. Thus the new US administration will probably adopt a more measured, less Manichaean approach to Central America; but if, for example, the United States were to intensify its efforts to bring about the forcible removal of the Sandinista regime, the British government could be expected to react by directing its efforts primarily toward limiting the ensuing strains in the Atlantic alliance rather than by parading its reservations about US actions. Other regional issues could give rise to occasionally quite sharp differences between

David Thomas

Britain and the United States or face the United Kingdom with awkward choices between US and European Community positions. The instinctive approach of the present British government will be to seek to avoid or defuse such situations by consulting closely with the United States and influencing US assessments and policy decisions to the extent this is possible; but except in the rare instances where important British national interests are seen to be at stake, strictly Latin American considerations will take second place to the preservation of the transatlantic relationship.

Notes

1 Representative Bill Richardson, 'Hispanic American concerns', *Foreign Policy* (Fall 1985), p. 34.
2 Quoted by Thomas A. Bailey, *A Diplomatic History of the American People* (New York: Appleton-Century-Crofts, 1964), p. 500.
3 Quoted by Roger Morris, *Uncertain Greatness* (New York: Harper & Row, 1977), p. 241.
4 Stanley Hoffmann, *Gulliver's Troubles or the Setting of American Foreign Policy* (New York: McGraw-Hill, 1968), p. 177.
5 Speech at Notre Dame University, May 1977.
6 Sir Nicholas Henderson, 'America and the Falklands: case study in the behaviour of an ally', *The Economist*, 12 November 1983, p. 42.
7 Tip O'Neill, *Man of the House* (London: The Bodley Head, 1987), p. 366.
8 The Contadora Group, composed of Colombia, Mexico, Panama and Venezuela, was set up in 1983 to seek a peaceful solution to the Central American impasse. It provided the inspiration for the Arias peace plan, launched by President Arias of Costa Rica in 1987. The Contadora Group was broadened by the inclusion of a Support Group (Argentina, Brazil, Peru and Uruguay) in 1986 and changed its name to the Group of Eight in 1987.

5 Britain, Latin America and the European Community
Laurence Whitehead

David Thomas (in the previous chapter) has discussed how Anglo-US relations affect British policy toward Latin America. This chapter is concerned with how British participation in the European Community (EC) affects our relations with Latin America. Both the strength of our ties with the United States and traditional British reserve about Europe have impeded close harmonisation of policy between London and Brussels. The still unresolved conflict between Britain and Argentina over the sovereignty of the Falkland/Malvinas Islands sharpens that divide. So the first question to consider is whether Britain has, or can have, an autonomous policy toward Latin America, separate from those of both the United States and Europe.

Certainly the British government has a policy of its own on the Antarctic; we have substantial post-colonial interests in the Caribbean and residual colonial commitments both there and in the South Atlantic; we have a policy on drug-trafficking, a standpoint on the Third World debt issue, a set of general policies on trade, investment and commodity markets, all of which impinge on Latin America without being specifically tailored to the concerns of that region. Britain also has a tremendous historical presence in the region. Between the early nineteenth and early twentieth centuries we were the most significant external power in South America and one of the major sources of both political and economic influence in Mexico, the Caribbean and Central America as well. Yet since the bond defaults of the early 1930s and the liquidation of most of the assets in the 1940s, our direct political and economic stake has gone into such an eclipse that we have difficulty nowadays even in recalling the nature of our former presence. Thus, in July 1988, the House of Commons held its first general debate on the affairs of Latin America since May 1950. This took place between three and four in the morning of the final session before the holiday recess and only six Members of Parliament participated.

Despite this, even in the 1980s Britain retains a surprising degree of respect and influence in certain crucial areas. Although the teaching of Spanish and Portuguese is on the decline in our educational curriculum and few British businessmen have any familiarity with either the languages or the culture of Latin America, London remains a major centre of information-gathering and analysis concerning Latin American affairs; as a financial centre it still ranks second only to New York as far as the region is concerned; and a surprisingly high proportion of senior political and business figures in Latin America visit this country frequently, in some cases taking refuge here and in others acquiring their higher education from us. There is also a network of English-speaking settlers in many parts of Latin America, with a corresponding array of schools, theatres, English-language newspapers and so on. Yet we have no real Latin American policy and have not had one for at least forty years.

Of course we have always had a policy towards the United States (and perhaps even towards Canada). At least since 1941 the Anglo-US relationship has acquired fundamental importance in British foreign affairs, pushing relations with Latin America to the margins of British concerns. Since the late 1960s we have also developed an increasingly elaborate and entangling set of relationships with continental Europe (a development that British statesmen had traditionally sought to avoid during the many centuries in which we could use our naval resources to counterbalance pressures from the mainland). Thus, there is slowly emerging a Britain-in-Europe which could eventually transform our relations not only with peripheral areas of the outside world, such at Latin America, but even our relations with the United States. Indeed, the process of transformation may be faster than we realise, both because of the speed with which US dominance in the Western alliance is receding and because of the accelerating pace of economic integration in Europe. Yet political and psychological adaptations often seem to lag well behind these relentless 'material' processes. Certainly discussions of Britain's role in Latin America often reflect our puzzlement and nostalgia for the lost past rather than a correct appraisal of the manner in which we are likely to exercise a role in world affairs in the future.

The approach adopted in this chapter is to work backwards from a summary assessment of Latin America's changing international position to a discussion of the implications of this change for European–Latin American relations, followed by a consideration of the place that the slowly emerging Britain-in-Europe might occupy in this new configuration. This approach may fail to track down the Snark of an independent British policy toward Latin America, but it could also help us understand why the beast is chimerical.

Latin America's external relations

We refer to the subcontinent as 'Latin' America for a good reason. It has especially long-standing and intimate ties, not so much with Europe as a whole as with the Catholic romance-language countries of South-West Europe. Links with Denmark, Greece or Finland are not especially intimate, but cultural affinities with Spain and Portugal as well as France and Italy are extremely strong. In addition to the language, the religion and the family ties, consider the historical origins of such characteristic regional institutions as the *latifundio*, the *plaza pública* and the republican constitution – not to mention legal tradition. Similarly, in the political realm, the Latin American countries are all in a rather direct sense 'children of the French Revolution' with corresponding conceptions of popular sovereignty, individual rights, the Napoleonic role of the nation-state and the left–right ideological spectrum. Thus, when the Christian Democratic and Socialist Internationals expand their activities in Latin America they encounter numerous apparently familiar landmarks, as does Europe's jacobin left. Finally, in the economic realm, Latin America developed with an over-whelmingly outward orientation (coastal and indeed centrifugal) which lasted from the Conquest until about 1930. During that period of more than four centuries, the economic orientation was not so much outward as Europeward, first to the Iberian peninsula, then to Britain and to a lesser extent to France, Germany and Italy. It was only because the Europeans destroyed their own presence through internecine conflict that Latin America fell so completely under US influence during the middle half of the twentieth century. As this unrivalled US supremacy has gradually declined (both globally and regionally) since the 1950s, so Latin America's historical orientation towards Europe has begun to revive.

There is a marked contrast here between Latin America and other areas of the so-called 'Third World'. The retreat of Western influence in the Middle East has uncovered quite different historical orientations that remained subter-ranean during the brief interlude of Christian ascendancy. The decolonisation of Asia and Africa also gave rise to the expression of a wide range of local traditions that were at least partly a repudiation of European models. It is only in Latin America that contemporary trends towards decolonisation (or in this case resistance to Great Power hegemonies) actually involve reaching out to the new Europe being constructed after two great wars.

A few specific examples may help to illustrate this distinctiveness. The most unlikely Latin American leaders retain strong family ties in Europe. Former President Stroessner of Paraguay came from Hof, in Bavaria, not far from the Bolivian General Banzer's parental home. The former Brazilian President Geisel's family came from the Protestant north. Fidel Castro's father was born in Galicia, the former Mexican President Luis Echeverría's family is Basque and ex-President Miguel de la Madrid's name speaks for itself. The Peruvian novelist Mario Vargas Llosa sends his sons to London University, the French are embarrassed by the Salvadorean right-wing leader Roberto d'Aubuisson and Italian Freemasons move effortlessly from conspiracies in Argentina and Uruguay to Rome and back.

The last time any Latin American government attempted what might be called a 'Burmese' or 'Albanian' strategy of turning away from the outside world was in Paraguay before 1870. Recently Latin America has witnessed some striking examples of what are sometimes labelled 'de-linking' development strategies, but what they actually involve is 're-linking' external ties away from the United States and towards Europe. For example, Cuba entered Comecon in 1972 (perhaps the most extreme example of outward-oriented economic development in the entire history of independent Latin America). Currently

Sandinista Nicaragua goes to enormous lengths to cultivate strong ties with both Eastern and Western Europe. The link between Oxford in Britain and León in Nicaragua is, for example, but one of about forty vigorous campaigns to twin Nicaraguan urban settlements with sympathetic counterparts in Western Europe. In isolation each of these examples might be trivial, but taken together they have a cumulative effect. Institutions like the Catholic Church and the Christian Democratic and Socialist Internationals provide a bridge between Latin America and Europe (although it is weak between Latin America and Britain). These generalisations apply most strongly to South America and Southern Europe. (Portugal is very influenced by Brazil, of course, but the reverse is less true.)

One consequence of all this that is particularly striking to Europeans who engage in Latin American studies or analysis is the extraordinary ease of access that it grants to a wide range of Latin American elites. Westerners who study the Soviet Union generally find themselves shut out, regarded with suspicion and confined to the most marginal location in the social hierarchy. Similar difficulties apparently limit access and perhaps sour judgements not only about Khomeini's Iran but also about various African, Asian and Middle Eastern governments. Latin American societies may well be exceptional in their hospitality and openness to European visitors. Partly this may stem from the wish to attract foreign investment or financial assistance or even immigration; partly (as in the case of vulnerable democracies such as Costa Rica or Chile before 1973) a search for external approval to shore up a faltering internal regime; in some cases it may also reflect upper-class disrespect for the darker-skinned majorities over whom they generally rule; in such circles there often remains a strong element of cultural deference towards Europe. Thus the 'outward orientation' of the pre-1930 period was social and cultural as well as economic. Even when the economic aspect (which is what most registered with the Europeans) went into decline, the social and cultural legacy remained powerfully entrenched.

Over the past generation, of course, Latin America has achieved a degree of cultural emancipation and originality that has greatly raised its prestige in the outside world. There has been a growth of Latin cultural influence within the USA and this aspect of Latin American development has also made a considerable impression in much of Europe (although Britain counts as only 'half-in-Europe' from this standpoint). In the 1990s Japan might well emerge as a major source of *economic* influence in Latin America, rivalling the United States and overshadowing Europe. Yet in *cultural* terms the affinity with Europe will remain unsurpassed, whereas in that respect Japan still remains very remote.

In order to characterise accurately Latin America's external relations, it is necessary to take the argument one step further and to say something about the region's characteristic insecurity over its international identity. This is a difficult subject to discuss convincingly and the issue is by no means unique to Latin America (remember Acheson's dictum about Britain's search for a role), but it underlies a large range of more specific episodes that are hard to understand unless the problem of regional identity is grasped. Argentine attitudes to the Falklands/Malvinas issue, for example, are rooted in a deep insecurity over the country's international status. Chilean feelings about the Pinochet regime are strongly connected with the challenge to national esteem that arises from this government's pariah status. Obviously such current accusations as that the government of Panama has been taken over by drug-traffickers and that the political structure of Colombia, Mexico and other countries has been penetrated to a very high level by the same criminal interests, powerfully reinforce this sense of insecurity, as does the clash of values arising from the perpetually unresolved debt problem. Much of the 'dependency' literature (an attitude rather than a theory) can best be attributed to similar worries over regional identity.

However, in contrast to the 'dependency' perspective of the 1960s there is now growing acceptance among Latin Americans (and among Latin American-ists) that the most decisive factors determining the prospects for development within the region are domestic rather than international. This attitude informs much of the shift towards democracy that has taken place over the past decade; it has also been taken on board in much of the Latin American response to the debt crisis and, indeed, in such regional 'self-help' endeavours as the Cartagena Group, the Contadora Group and the Esquipulas peace agreement.[1]

In fact, rather than a concerted effort by external interests to shape Latin American affairs from outside, what the past decade has witnessed (apart from such special cases as Nicaragua and the problem of drug-trafficking) has been more of a tendency toward neglect and lack of interest. In the absence of a continent-wide threat of 'more Cubas', the inclination has often been to leave the Latin Americans to face the consequences of their own economic and political mistakes. To some extent this shift in the locus of responsibility may have been salutary, but there is a danger that it may now be overdone. Although domestic factors are – and should be – the most decisive influences shaping regional events, there remains an important international interest in the evolution of Latin American affairs. The region can provide a positive example and a source of good influence to the outside world if, for example, it succeeds in peacefully resolving the Central American crisis, in establishing stable democra-cies or in restoring economic growth. It can also exert a harmful influence, which would not long remain confined to the domestic realm, if for example it generated a series of criminal governments engaged in drug-trafficking and the export of violence or if its internal social and political conflicts become so unmanageable that they stirred up international rivalries.

European–Latin American relations

The new post-war Europe is of course composed of nations that have, in the past generation, undergone the most profound re-examination of their tradi-tions, assumptions and place in the world: defeat and occupation; loss of Empire; loss of Great Power status; the redefinition of alliances and antagonisms; the dismantling of Iberian autocracies; the gradual construction of a liberal-democratic multinational community. All this has occurred in Western Europe while Latin America has been struggling with still largely unresolved internal debates about the region's identity and commitments. Thus, Latin American attention is drawn to Europe not only by the strength of past cultural ties, or even by the sheer weight of the new Europe's economic presence, but also by the thought that our regional experience may offer some lessons of special relevance to Latin America's predicament and by the expectation that the adherents of at least some of the emerging political and social currents in Europe will be particularly well placed to understand and sympathise with Latin American dilemmas. In particular Spain and Italy seem well suited to play this role, although other minor European countries (Holland, Ireland, Scandinavia) also seem to respond strongly to this appeal. Of all the West European countries, the United Kingdom would seem the least likely to empathise with this point of view – even before the Falklands issue erupted to provide a focus of dissension.

The new role played by democratic Spain has received considerable recognition. In March 1988, to take a recent example, Felipe González was enlisted as the 'good faith' intermediary who might induce General Noriega to leave Panama and settle in Spain (with his ill-gotten gains). This is only the most recent in a long series of political initiatives, some dating back before González to the preceding Suárez government. The Partido Socialista Obrero Español (PSOE) has played a major role in channelling the attention and resources of the Socialist International into Latin America and Madrid now hosts the Institute for European–Latin American Relations (IRELA), established in 1984 by the European Community to strengthen relations between the two regions. Spain has also been active in supporting the Central American peace process and has pioneered certain bilateral agreements, notably an economic co-operation agreement signed with Argentina in 1987. An underlying aim has been to bolster civilian and democratic institutions, which are seen as under threat in Latin America just as they were until recently in Spain. Yet there are some important limitations on Spain's role, particularly if economic or financial assistance is involved. Since January 1986, Spain has been a full member of the EC and many Latin Americans have entertained the hope that Madrid would prove able to act from within to modify those aspects of Community practice that discriminate against the subcontinent. However, these expectations are likely to prove somewhat misplaced, in part because the Community was already firmly established before Spain entered, in part because Spanish energies will for at least some years be largely absorbed with the challenge of internal adaptation to the requirements of Community membership and finally also because Spanish public opinion may not be so strongly committed to the Latin American cause (or so agreed on how to promote it) as official rhetoric tries to suggest.

To act effectively on Latin America's behalf within Europe, Spain would also need to ally with other like-minded Community governments. Portugal has proved a weak reed in this respect. In the early eighties France, under a Socialist administration, offered some encouragement and may do so again following Mitterrand's re-election to the Presidency in May 1988. Latin American governments generally regard Michel Camdessus (formerly of the Bank of France and the Paris Club) as a constructive influence, as Managing Director of the International Monetary Fund (IMF), open to reasonable arguments from the debtors. In the last few years Italy has come closest to sharing a common perspective with Spain and, indeed, the recent Italian–Argentine deal is larger in scale and similar in inspiration to the González–Alfonsín agreement.[2] Rome and Madrid seem to share a fairly common view of the debt problem, of the problems of Central America and of the importance of assisting democratic consolidation. However, the Italian interest is much more focused on Latin America's Southern Cone (there are over 800,000 Italian passport-holders living in Argentina alone) and Italy has also taken a rather stronger line than Spain in edging the European Community away from Britain's 'Fortress Falklands' policy. Although Italy and Spain have recently shown some convergence on Latin American issues, this is not a fundamental bond uniting the two countries and in future the pattern could easily shift with variation in the fortunes of particular parties and politicians.

If these four romance countries have the strongest cultural ties with Latin America, it is West Germany which carries the greatest economic weight.[3] The German Foundations have also exercised a disproportionate influence. For example, in 1983 the Ebert Foundation published a document issued by the German Association for Research on Latin America (ADLAF), which also received support from the Adenauer and Thyssen Foundations. ADLAF pointed to a contrast between the official government policy of emphasising West Germany's obligations to Asia and Africa (that is, the same Third World obligations as the ex-colonial European powers) and the activities of West German non-governmental organisations (industry, political parties, churches and trade unions) which had for a number of years been focused on Latin America. It argued that 'the credibility of the Federal Republic as a democratic nation is linked, domestically and internationally, to its will and ability to demonstrate its responsibility in international politics', and therefore called for the provision of more resources for Latin America.[4] The following year the Naumann Foundation sponsored an international initiative aimed at the promotion of peace and democracy in Central America.[5] However, since the early 1980s the West German outlook has become by and large more introverted and the authorities in Bonn have tended to back away from unilateral initiatives in Latin America – particularly if they might offend the USA. The emphasis of German policy has therefore shifted to multilateral action through the European Community, as illustrated by the February 1988 meeting in Hamburg of Foreign Ministers from the twelve European states with representatives of twelve Latin American countries – the Central American countries plus the Contadora Group, Mexico, Venezuela, Colombia, but not Panama and the Contadora Support Group (Argentina, Brazil, Peru, Uruguay).

Before I consider the role of the Community there is one other point raised by the ADLAF report that deserves a mention here. It stated that

> understanding the cultural identity of Latin America is complicated by the fact that not only the Latin Americans themselves, but also their German partners interpret the 'Latin American reality' in different ways. This becomes particularly obvious in terms which seem to have identical meanings (e.g. society, individual, order, time, etc.). In reality, the same terms are associated with different ideas.

These differences of interpretation arise, of course, not only between Latin America and Europe, but also *within* both regions.[6] The report went on to list a series of respects in which Latin American self-images are under challenge and in flux (for example, ambivalence about the region's European heritage, about its place in North–South rather than East–West polarities and about the conflict between its aspiration to unity and the realities of its disunity). These were all perceptive observations which require the attention of all Europeans concerned with Latin America.

Latin America's ambivalence about the region's 'European heritage' will be particularly apparent in 1992, the 500th anniversary of Christopher Columbus' so-called 'discoveries'. The current struggle to define what Latin America 'really means' by democracy is another striking illustration of the same point. Yet Europeans need not be discouraged or turned off by these problems of interpretation. On the contrary, Latin American attempts to answer such questions can be enlightening and enriching for those whose own intellectual traditions or social circumstances may leave less scope for such forms of self-questioning.

Turning now to the past activities and likely future influence of the European Community, since this largely concerns current economic trends I have reproduced a selection of tables drawn from IRELA's 1987 statistical compendium. The broad picture is that Latin American trade with the twelve countries of the EC (EC–12) remains marginal and undynamic from the European point of view. Before the debt crisis began in 1982 Latin America purchased about 6 per cent of EC merchandise exports, but by 1985 (see Table 5.1) this had fallen to 4.1 per cent. (Japanese exports were similarly affected, whereas the USA saw a smaller proportionate fall in its share.) During the 1970s Latin America's share of imports into the EC–12 fell to about 5½ per cent of the total, a consequence both of the growing importance of trade among developed countries and of the increased price of oil imports from the Middle East (see Table 5.2). By 1985, however, this had recovered to 7.5 per cent – the same share as in 1970.

One counter-current was the rise in European arms exports to Latin America in the late seventies and early eighties (mainly from France, but also from Britain, Spain and other countries). Information on the arms trade is patchy and difficult to assess, but it seems clear that Latin American interest in such acquisitions has declined in the 1980s with the establishment of many civilian governments and the adoption of austerity measures in response to the debt crisis. Moreover

Table 5.1. *Latin America's share of exports from developed countries*

	1965 %	1970 %	1975 %	1980 %	1985 %
From EC–12	6.4	6.7	6.6	5.8	4.1
From USA	13.7	13.0	14.2	15.9	13.1
From Japan	4.8	5.1	8.1	6.3	4.1

Source: Economic Relations between the European Community and Latin America: A Statistical Profile, IRELA Working Paper no. 10 (Madrid, 1987), Table 5. (All the Tables in the rest of this chapter are based on Tables in this publication.)

Table 5.2. *Latin America's share of imports into developed countries*

	1965 %	1970 %	1975 %	1980 %	1985 %
To EC–12	8.7	7.5	5.5	5.5	7.5
To USA	17.3	12.0	12.2	12.0	12.6
To Japan	8.4	7.1	4.3	3.9	4.7

Source: IRELA Working Paper no. 10, Table 4.

competition from non-European sources (Israel, Brazil's domestic industry, and others) has become intense. Indeed, the most recent reports suggest that Latin American arms manufacturers could soon become more substantial rivals to the Europeans in such markets as the Middle East. (Argentina has entered into a joint-production agreement with Egypt, for example.) Even so Britain is negotiating its largest single military sale to Latin America since the Falklands, of eighty-four Scorpion tanks to Venezuela.

In general, any future upsurge in European merchandise exports to Latin America would require among other things an easing of the foreign exchange constraint arising from the debt crisis. Viewed from the other side, Latin Americans frequently complain that many of their exports are penalised by European integration. Temperate agricultural products and sugar have been directly and severely penalised by the Common Agricultural Policy, which not only displaces Latin American supplies from the EC market, but also disrupts trade in third markets. (For example, the EC has imposed a quota on the import of apples from Chile that has led to a complaint before GATT. The Chilean government argues that Europe is violating a 1986 promise to impose a 'stand-still' on new protectionist measures. Washington supports Chile on this, at least in part from fear that, otherwise, surplus Chilean apples will further depress the US market.) Other raw-material exports may suffer indirectly from the exclusion of Brazil and the Spanish-speaking republics from the benefits of the Lomé Convention, which are confined to the recently decolonised states of Africa, the Caribbean and the Pacific.[7]

Table 5.3. *Net direct investment in Latin America*

	1971–3	1983–5
Percentage from EC–7 countries[a]	18.5	35.4
Percentage from all other countries	81.5	64.6
Value of EC–7[a] investment ($m)	6,175	13,020

[a] Belgium, Denmark, France, Italy, the Netherlands, the United Kingdom and West Germany. These seven countries are all members of the Development Assistance Committee of the Organisation for Economic Cooperation and Development (OECD) which provides information on direct investment on a comparable basis for each country.
Source: IRELA Working Paper no. 10, Table 17.

Table 5.4. *Latin America's share of net direct investment in all Less Developed Countries (LDCs)*

	1971–3	1983–5
Percentage of investment from EC–7 countries[a]	21.8	36.2
Percentage of investment from OECD countries	50.3	45.8

[a] See note a, Table 5.3, above.
Source: IRELA Working Paper no. 10, Table 18.

The European Commission replies to Latin American complaints by pointing to the large trade imbalances which now exist (Latin America has had to compress its imports and boost its exports in order to generate the trade surplus required for debt servicing) and to the fact that the sub-continent receives proportionately more benefits under the Generalised System of Preferences (GSP) than any other region of the Third World. With the exception of agriculture the European Community is, it is said, far more liberal in its trading practices than the export pessimists seem to realise. In fact Europe is indeed a major market for many Latin American exporters, easier to penetrate than Japan, less likely to succumb to added protectionism than the USA and with strong currencies that make exports from a region with heavily undervalued exchange rates very lucrative. Over the next few years Latin American non-traditional exports are likely to experience an increasing penetration of the European market, even if traditional primary commodity exports continue to languish.

Turning to the capital account (see Tables 5.3 and 5.4) we can see striking evidence of the retreat of the USA as a source of external finance for Latin America and the relative expansion of the European (and to a lesser extent the Japanese) presence. Of course this shift in shares takes place in the context of an overall collapse in the availability of external capital in the 1980s, whether in the form of direct foreign investment, portfolio investment, commercial bank

Table 5.5. *Sources of Latin American external bank debt, end 1985*

	Outstanding Latin American debt ($bn)	Latin American debt as % of all sovereign lending
Originating in:		
United Kingdom	30.0	19.3
France	17.0	8.7
Germany	14.8	6.6
Switzerland	7.9	6.7
Spain	5.5	26.5
Italy	3.3	N/A
Netherlands	2.2	6.3
Belgium	1.6	N/A
Eight European total	82.4	–
USA	90.5	25.9
Canada	16.6	N/A
Japan	29.7	N/A
World	253.2	–

Source: IRELA Working Paper no. 10, Table 33.

lending, export credit guarantees or unrequited transfers. Nevertheless there is substantial evidence of a longer-term shift within the 'developed' countries with Western Europe in general and the EC in particular playing a gradually larger role. Indeed one striking finding (see Table 5.5) is that by the end of 1985 Europe's share of Latin American external debt taken as a whole was about as large as that of the USA. On the subject of external aid, however, the European contribution remains very modest in absolute terms, although – at least in the case of South America – it compares favourably with other regions. Here a contrast should be made between Central and South America. In general, aid to South America from all sources remains exiguous, but the European share has risen as the USA has turned away from the region (no longer 'threatened by Cuban expansionism') and the Europeans began to respond to the establishment of fragile civilian regimes. In Central America the USA has judged that its national security is at stake and has therefore provided far more aid than the Europeans. Yet if we consider not just the magnitude of the aid, but the purposes for which it is allocated, the European contribution has been widely viewed as more in keeping with the interests and aspirations of the recipient population. In particular it has concentrated on political and economic reconstruction, rather than on financial low-intensity war, and it has not discriminated between Central American governments.

The West German Foreign Minister, Hans-Dietrich Genscher, claimed a leading role in establishing an EC–Central American dialogue in 1983, as a response to the creation of the Contadora Group. The February 1988 summit at

Table 5.6. *Sources of official development assistance (net disbursements)*

	1970 %	1975 %	1980 %	1985 %
To South America from				
EC–7 countries [a]	19.2	41.9	67.4	40.8
USA	83.6	44.2	6.4	31.2
Japan	−3.9[b]	10.0	19.9	19.6
Total value ($m) (includes other OECD countries)	400.7	411.4	438.4	694.7
To Central America (including Panama) from				
EC–7 countries [a]	5.3	20.1	30.6	11.9
USA	94.5	75.2	61.0	79.3
Japan	0.2	1.7	6.1	2.3
Total value ($m) (includes other OECD countries)	82.5	122.3	288.4	927.1

a See note *a* to Table 5.3.
b Repayments of old loans exceeded new ones.
Source: IRELA Working Paper no. 10, Tables 26 and 27.

Hamburg was the fifth meeting in the series and was prompted by the 'Esquipulas II' peace agreement among the Central American countries in August 1987. At Hamburg the Central Americans put forward a three-year recovery plan that envisaged $1.5 billion in external financial assistance from a variety of sources (the EC, the Scandinavian countries, North America and the United Nations). In response, the European Commission pointed out that in 1988 EC aid to Central America would be worth 82m ECUs and that, if the aid programmes of individual EC members were included, the total would be 180m ECUs. The EC pledged to 'substantially' increase its aid, but without specifying a figure (it is worth recalling that in 1988 the total EC budget involved the expenditure of about 43 billion ECUs). However, Commission spokesmen took care to stress that the Community is forbidden by treaty to provide balance of payments support and also to discourage any expectation of changes in commercial policy that would affect the interests either of EC farmers or of ACP member states. Although willing to play an important co-ordinating role, the Community does not intend to displace the sovereign right (and duty) of member states to conduct their own national aid and development policies.

To conclude this discussion of EC policy, Esperanza Durán's judgement of three years ago still seems to hold up:

the Community has adopted less ambiguous positions on such issues as Central America, Chile, the Andean Pact and SELA [Sistema Económico Latinoamericano] than its often vacillating member countries ... its approach to Latin America as a whole has tended to tilt more openly against US policy than has been possible for its individual members ... This is one of the advantages that could be gained from a collective approach to the region.[8]

Whether the current British government would consider it an advantage is a matter to be considered below. It is interesting that the EC Commission praised the Esquipulas peace plan for bringing all sides together, contrary to the approach of 'certain other countries' that 'divide in order to conquer'. Yet the EC is also quite cautious about the Latin American causes it is willing to endorse and quite parsimonious with the resources it is willing to allocate to this aspect of policy.

Before considering the implications of all this for British policy it is as well to mention that not all collective European initiatives concerning Latin America are channelled through the European Commission. The European Parliament also plays a significant role, dating back to the Inter-Parliamentary Conferences that began in 1970. With direct election to the European Parliament from 1979 onwards, with the admission of Spain and Portugal in 1986 and with the increasing importance of parliamentary institutions in Latin America, these ties have become more substantial. The most direct evidence of how this form of European influence is making itself felt in Latin America is the plan to hold direct elections to a Central American parliament. The European Parliament is willing to furnish technical aid for this exercise and possibly to oversee procedures.

Another interesting illustration of the growth of these parliamentary ties was the Conference on Central America held at Oxford in April 1988. This brought together representatives from most of the major political parties from seventeen European countries, Canada and Central America. They worked out a series of recommendations to assist the peace process and the reconstitution of Central America which is a subject being discussed in all the European national parliaments.

This illustrates one final aspect of collective European influence. The Scandinavian countries (outside the EC) have also taken an active interest in some aspects of Latin American affairs (the Norwegian and Swedish Foreign Ministers sponsored the Oxford Conference). The smaller European countries have often been more generous than the EC with their aid and more willing to defend controversial points of view. Switzerland and Austria also have a presence on some matters. Another forum for co-ordinating West European views (mainly with regard to the defence of democracy) is the Council of Europe. Canada also has a substantial interest in Latin America and its viewpoint is often fairly close to the European position.

Britain half-in-Europe and Latin America

Britain is closer to the standpoint of the USA than to most of the European positions sketched out above. A checklist of the major issues concerning Europe and Latin America in the 1980s is sufficient to dramatise this difference –

Central America, debt relief and redemocratisation. Presumably we support Latin American efforts to establish civilian democracies, but not to the extent of achieving a compromise settlement with President Alfonsín concerning our differences over the Falklands. Presumably as a medium-sized power we prefer the rule of law (and the verdict of the International Court of Justice) to the rule of force. Yet as Mrs Thatcher told *The Financial Times* (23 November 1987), 'We have troops in one form or another – some as military advisers and trainers – in thirty countries in the world and of course in the Falklands, and that means we are still a global power and we do our bit.' The presence of the troops in Belize, she went on, demonstrated to the USA how Britain understands what the United States feels 'about some of the threats from Central America ... It keeps a stable democracy there right on the American front.'

Presumably, we have an interest in the stability of the international financial system and, as Stephany Griffith-Jones argues in chapter 7, in Latin America's recovery from the debt crisis. But for us, in contrast to most of Europe, the financial dimension is so much greater than the trade dimension that any debt relief we granted would largely serve to boost the exports of our competitors. Perhaps for that pragmatic reason, or perhaps out of a commitment to the principles of sound finance, the Governor of the Bank of England has warned British banks not to make 'excessive' provisions for Latin American debt (that is, provisions on the scale that West German and Swiss bankers regard as prudent) and the Chancellor of the Exchequer backed former US Treasury Secretary Baker in resisting any comprehensive scheme for debt relief, although Establishment Europeans in France, Italy and Spain and even the Managing Director of IMF, Michel Camdessus, increasingly seem to recognise the urgency of adopting a new approach, as do the Japanese.

It should be apparent that these differences in emphasis on current policy issues reflect a deeper difference in historical experience and psychological outlook, distinguishing the United Kingdom from most of the countries of continental Europe (and particularly from the 'romance' four). The political, religious and cultural ties of Latin America are with Southern Europe, whereas those of Britain are with North America. The same applies to the question of empathy. In recent memory Southern Europeans have experienced conquest, the external imposition of political and economic models, relative powerlessness and profound uncertainty about national values and identity. The British have experienced little of this. It is hardly surprising, then, if we now find ourselves somewhat out of sympathy with European initiatives and at a loss to identify a new basis for our Latin American policy.

For the time being a stance of close identification with Washington, wariness of European initiatives and determination to, if necessary, 'go it alone' in the Falklands may serve as a substitute for working out a more balanced and forward-looking policy. Yet in the longer run we could be confronted with the inconvenient consequences of this posture. Despite all the assertiveness of the Reagan years, it seems probable that US preponderance in the western hemisphere will continue to decline (the trade and budget deficits certainly point that way); furthermore, even before the end of the Reagan years, it was increasingly accepted in the United States that the US approach to Latin America was in need of considerable revision. Whether or not British policy anticipates the resulting changes, the United States is likely to become less Thatcherite in the 1990s. For example, some major new debt initiative is likely to emerge from Washington in the first years of the Bush administration and if so, whatever the British Chancellor of the Exchequer and the Governor of the Bank of England have said beforehand, they are likely in the event to fall in behind it. Likewise, reliance on force to promote 'democracy' in Central America will probably give way to some more flexible and constructive stance.

As such changes take place in Washington, the British position could well become more isolated and backward-looking. Nowhere is this prospect more in evidence than in relation to 'Fortress Falklands'. A future US administration that needed to mend its fences with the major countries of South America would surely seek to distance itself from British rigidity over this issue. Recent straws in the wind include the resumption of US sales of 'spare parts' for the Argentine military and the election of Dante Caputo, the former Foreign Minister of Argentina, as 1988/9 President of the UN General Assembly. Indeed, we seem well on the way to surrendering the international support that so strengthened our moral position in 1982 in the wake of Argentine aggression under General Galtieri.

In the longer run, therefore, Britain's broad alternatives will be to tag along behind whatever new Latin American policies may emerge in Washington (and for some time these could be quite incoherent and unstable) or to adopt a nostalgic stance toward the outside world or to come to terms with the policies slowly emerging from Europe. Both the logic of our position in Latin America and the continuing Community pressure on us to participate more fully and wholeheartedly in common European initiatives point in the direction of the third alternative. Neither of the other approaches has the potential for innovation or constructive leadership offered by a more unified and coherent Western Europe. However, we are at present still only 'half-in', and that Europe is still only half-built. Much will therefore depend upon the direction taken by the Community during the next phase of policy harmonisation and upon the way the British government chooses to apply its influence.

Policy toward Latin America is, of course, a very minor and incidental aspect of the general debate about Britain's place in a prospectively more unified Europe. Nevertheless it illustrates in microcosm many of the broader cross-currents. If Britain exerts her influence to make the Community more open on questions of international trade, and more determined to eliminate the absurdities of the Common Agricultural Policy, that will produce a more economically outward-looking Europe which would, among other things, be much to the benefit of Latin America (although Anglo-Latin American trade might not initially change much as a result). On the other hand, if British economic influence is devoted mostly to blocking European inclinations to accept a write-down of Latin American debt, the effects would be very much the reverse. In the short run, and from a narrow financial perspective, this stance might seem to be in the British interest, but on a longer view a healthy international trading system requires removal of the Third World debt 'overhang' and this may only be possible through the kind of co-operative international economic leadership for which the EC is well suited.

Britain's stance on Latin American political issues has also been somewhat affected by our status 'half-in-Europe'. On Central America, for example, the existence of a relatively firm European counterweight to the Reagan administration's perspective produced a mild degree of differentiation between London and Washington that might not otherwise have occurred. Britain avoided involvement in some of the most questionable excesses exposed by the Irangate scandal (for example, Colonel North's records indicate that both in 1984 and in the spring of 1986 he failed to secure the British government's approval for his plan to re-export British Blowpipe missiles to the Nicaraguan Contras via Pinochet's Chile). London even indirectly extended considerable aid to Nicaragua (by contributing to EC aid initiatives targeted at the five Central American republics without discrimination). On the subject of the Falklands, by contrast, European perceptions of the political progress achieved by Argentina since 1982 make no impression on London. Rome and Madrid may have signed ambitious commercial agreements with Buenos Aires, but trade restrictions continue in force against British exports to Argentina because we still refuse to discuss any modification to the present costly and irrational status quo. Eventually, if Britain were to become a more wholehearted participant in a more united Europe, the Europeans could help us disengage gracefully from this backward-looking 'Fortress Falklands' posture. On our own, or only 'half-in-Europe', we are more likely to remain stiff-necked. Apart from our exclusion from the Argentine market, and the garrison costs which have already largely been incurred, it has been argued that continuation of the present policy seems surprisingly costless. It is indeed difficult to point to other major direct costs of the policy so far, but we risk becoming increasingly isolated on this issue as opinion in Europe and the Americas continues shifting gradually towards Argentina. For a medium-sized European state acting in isolation, the indirect costs of complacency could abruptly become rather substantial (for example, if the Argentine political climate changes again after the May 1989 elections).

It is not just Britain, of course, that can be unduly inward-looking. Between now and 1992 there is a distinct prospect that the European Community may be so absorbed with its internal processes of economic integration and policy harmonisation as to neglect its embryonic external relations. This risk is of particular concern to those Latin Americans who fear that another five years of economic and political deterioration like those since 1982 would take regional problems beyond a point of no return. There is indeed a lack of synchronism between Europe's slow methodical construction and Latin America's intensifying socio-economic crisis. Over the next decade a more effective Europe could well emerge, capable of exerting an economic and political influence in the world comparable to that of the USA and Japan. This prospect does not seem to depend very much on whether the British choose to participate very actively or to fall in from behind. When it materialises, the consequences for Latin America will be of considerable importance. Yet it takes a long time, longer perhaps than the Latin Americans can afford to wait. If we so choose, the British could help to speed up the process and to accentuate the Community's internationalism. If we prefer to remain only half-in-Europe, still nostalgic for our few remnants of Empire or for the fading certainties of the United States' early post-war leadership, we can surely delay and obstruct – though not prevent – the eventual outcome. Our policy (or lack of policy) towards Latin America will be essentially a by-product of this broader choice.

Notes

1 The Cartagena Group was formed by the main Latin American countries in 1984 to explore regional approaches to the debt crisis. Both the Contadora Group and the Esquipulas accords involve Latin American countries in a search for peace in Central America.

2 In 1986 the Italian government's outlay on foreign aid rose 58 per cent in value, reflecting the priorities of parties such as the Socialists and the Radicals, who were gaining increasing influence within the government. In 1987 a unified Directorate General for Co-operation was created within the Foreign Ministry, and Italy now budgets to spend 0.4 per cent of GDP on aid (compared to only 0.28 per cent currently spent by Britain). About 40 per cent of Italian aid goes to multilateral organisations like the UN agencies and the World Bank, which have generally been underfunded by both Britain and the USA. Minister Antonio Badini recently described Italian aid policy as follows: 'We want to intervene in areas where human dignity is suffering, but also in areas where aid can help democracy where it is fragile, or to further pacification in areas of conflict.' By these criteria, Argentina and Peru were among the ten nations selected for priority assistance in September 1987. Two months later Presidents Alfonsín and Cossiga signed a bilateral treaty under which the Italian government is to act as guarantor for up to $5 billion in investments in Argentina between 1988 and 1992 and Argentina is to assure the free repatriation of capital and profits to Italy. A bilateral agency was set up to supervise the investment process, with the stipulation that the treaty would only be valid under democratic regimes in both countries. The following month Alfonsín negotiated a similar bilateral treaty with Spain, this time for up to $3 billion over four years, with the same stipulation about democracy.

3 For example, the Federal Republic is the largest single source of credits and public guarantees to Argentina, surpassing even the USA. When Economics Minister Bangemann visited Buenos Aires in 1988, however, he rebuffed the suggestion that West Germany might follow the examples set by Italy and Spain, saying that such bilateral preferential arrangements with non-Community countries were contrary to the spirit of EC solidarity and the norms of the General Agreement on Tariffs and Trade (GATT).

4 Dieter W. Benecke, Michael Domitra, Wolf Grabendorff and Manfred Mols, *The Relations Between the Federal Republic of Germany and Latin America's Present Situation and Recommendations* (Bonn: ADLAF & Friedrich Ebert Stiftung, 1984), p. 6.

5 One result of this was the publication of *The Central American Impasse*, edited by Giuseppe di Palma and Laurence Whitehead (London: Croom Helm, in association with the Friedrich Naumann Foundation, 1986).

6 See also Wolf Grabendorff, 'De las dificultades en el trato de lo ajeno: estereotipos y prejuicios en las relaciones entre América Latina y la República Federal de Alemania', *Zeitschrift für Kulturaustrauch* (Stuttgart), March 1980.

7 For example, West Indian bananas benefit compared to Central American supplies. When President Arias appealed in 1987 to the EC to extend Lomé benefits to Central America, it was pointed out that this would leave Ecuador as the one major banana exporter penalised by the Community. But to admit Ecuador would awaken demands from Bolivia, and so on. In the 1970s Commissioner Soames hinted at a compromise by which Latin America would remain outside Lomé, but be eligible for STABEX support if export earnings fell. At the time nothing came of this idea, which in any case illustrates the illogicalities of EC trade policy in this area.

8 See Esperanza Durán, *European Interests in Latin America*, Chatham House Paper 28 (London: Royal Institute of International Affairs, 1985), p. 78. It was not easy for the EC to hold steady with a policy on Central America so out of line with that of the Reagan administration, but Britain and Germany were persuaded to go along with the majority European view. Commissioner Claude Cheysson's role in this should not be underestimated.

Part II
Economic relations

6 Trade, aid and investment since 1950

David Atkinson

Historically the United Kingdom had very strong commercial links with Latin America, as a major source of finance for investment and as a leading trade partner, but this episode of British history came to a close well before the scope of this study begins. Indeed, the main trend of post-war commercial relations has been to erode further linkages between the two areas, consigning Latin America to the periphery of UK economic interests. This chapter examines the main trends in British–Latin American commercial relations, the reasons for the limited and declining importance of these relations and possible future developments. For analytical purposes, trade, investment and aid will be dealt with separately, but it should be remembered that in practice they are very closely interwoven.

Trade

Exports

As a destination for UK exports Latin America has declined steadily in relative terms since 1950. In 1986 the Latin American market accounted for only 1.4 per cent of UK exports, down from 7.1 per cent in 1950 and 4.5 per cent in 1960 (see Table 6.1). Indeed, throughout this period Latin America has been one of the least important regional markets for UK goods. To put the position in perspective, the total value of UK exports to Latin America in 1987 was £1.19 billion, slightly less than the £1.22 billion of exports to Norway and only marginally more than the £1.09 billion of exports to India.

The decline in the relative importance of Latin America as a market for UK goods has been more or less matched by a decline in the importance of the UK as a source of goods for Latin America. The share of the UK in the total imports of Latin America declined from 6.8 per cent in 1950 to 2.3 per cent in 1986 (see Table 6.2). The region's diminished importance has been exacerbated by the disruption to UK–Argentina trade since the Falklands/Malvinas war in 1982. Yet even excluding Argentina the trend was still firmly downwards. Allowing for the loss of exports to Argentina, the share of exports to Latin America in total UK trade would probably only have been about 1.7 per cent and 1.6 per cent in 1982 and 1986 respectively.

Table 6.1. *UK trade by major region*

	Exports (% share)					
	1950	1960	1970	1980	1982	1986
Europe	30.7	32.9	46.7	58.5	54.7	57.9
EC	11.1	15.3	29.2	46.7	44.2	47.7
North America	11.0	15.3	15.3	11.2	15.0	16.5
Asia	28.4	22.1	13.7	8.7	9.5	9.2
Middle East	5.7	5.0	5.1	8.4	9.9	7.2
Africa	13.2	12.8	9.9	7.7	6.8	3.7
Eastern Europe	1.7	3.7	3.7	1.8	1.3	1.9
Latin America	7.1	4.5	3.5	2.2	1.6	1.4
Caribbean	1.8	3.1	1.6	0.9	0.7	0.6
Others	0.3	0.6	0.6	0.5	0.5	1.5

	Imports (% share)					
	1950	1960	1970	1980	1982	1986
Europe	27.6	31.9	41.9	57.0	59.7	66.3
EC	12.8	14.5	26.9	43.7	46.8	51.8
North America	15.0	20.7	20.5	15.0	14.3	11.7
Asia	23.6	17.4	11.6	9.9	11.0	12.1
Middle East	5.7	7.3	5.8	9.0	5.9	2.1
Africa	11.5	9.6	11.0	4.3	3.8	3.0
Eastern Europe	3.3	3.8	4.2	1.6	1.9	1.6
Latin America	7.8	6.7	3.7	2.1	2.1	1.5
Caribbean	4.8	2.3	1.1	0.6	0.6	0.4
Others	0.8	0.3	0.2	0.5	0.8	1.3

Source: International Monetary Fund, *Direction of Trade Statistics* (Washington, DC), various editions.

Table 6.2. *Latin American imports: market share of main trading partners (%)*

	1950	1960	1970	1980	1982	1986
UK	6.8	5.0	5.0	2.6	2.0	2.3
US	29.7	36.7	43.6	37.9	37.7	40.8
Japan	N/A	2.9	6.8	8.4	10.3	11.7
France	N/A	2.8	3.4	3.7	3.6	4.8
Germany	N/A	8.0	9.6	6.5	5.5	7.1
Above five countries as percentage of total Latin American imports	N/A	55.4	68.4	59.0	59.1	66.8

Source: International Monetary Fund, *Direction of Trade Statistics* (Washington, DC), various editions.

Table 6.3. *UK trade with the main Latin American economies*

	% share of UK exports to Latin America					
	1950	1960	1970	1980	1982	1986
Argentina	25.0	25.5	15.7	16.4	4.3	1.0
Brazil	27.8	11.7	21.7	20.6	17.5	28.0
Chile	3.7	8.2	7.3	5.3	6.3	6.4
Colombia	3.9	5.6	4.6	4.0	5.6	5.5
Mexico	2.8	12.5	12.2	17.8	18.2	15.4
Peru	6.0	5.0	3.6	4.4	4.4	4.6
Venezuela	8.6	16.9	12.0	12.5	16.4	16.2

	% share of UK imports from Latin America					
	1950	1960	1970	1980	1982	1986
Argentina	47.1	32.3	19.5	10.8	5.2	2.2
Brazil	20.0	9.6	18.8	27.9	37.9	41.7
Chile	2.6	11.2	19.4	11.9	9.5	9.7
Colombia	0.0	2.9	2.6	3.2	2.9	7.2
Mexico	2.1	1.9	1.9	10.5	8.1	8.7
Peru	6.3	5.8	4.6	7.3	7.9	6.2
Venezuela	7.0	23.6	15.2	11.0	12.0	7.1

Source: International Monetary Fund, *Direction of Trade Statistics* (Washington, DC), various editions.

Table 6.4. *UK trade with main Latin American economies by selected product category (1986): shares of total exports (%) and imports (%)*

				Exports			
	Argentina	Brazil	Chile	Colombia	Mexico	Peru	Venezuela
Primary products	21.9	14.3	11.6	6.9	5.2	6.5	20.7
Beverages & tobacco	20.9	4.5	9.0	4.0	2.3	3.6	15.1
Crude materials	0.0	1.6	1.1	1.4	0.1	0.4	1.6
Manufactures	70.4	79.5	86.5	91.8	94.5	92.9	77.6
Chemicals	35.5	22.1	22.8	22.7	14.2	29.4	16.3
Manufactured goods	10.2	7.2	14.4	10.9	6.2	6.5	7.5
Transport & machinery	17.1	44.6	43.2	51.2	69.7	50.2	45.5
Other (n.i.e.)	7.7	6.2	2.0	1.3	0.4	0.6	1.7

				Imports			
	Argentina	Brazil	Chile	Colombia	Mexico	Peru	Venezuela
Primary products	93.0	61.7	43.9	92.8	76.9	23.3	96.9
Food	68.3	33.6	20.5	78.5	7.1	3.3	2.4
Crude materials	17.0	20.4	21.2	12.8	11.8	19.0	18.5
Fuel	0.0	0.1	0.0	1.4	57.4	0.0	76.0
Manufactures	6.7	38.1	51.4	7.2	22.6	76.7	3.0
Other (n.i.e.)	0.3	0.2	4.7	0.1	0.5	0.1	0.1

Note: n.i.e. not included elsewhere.
Source: Department of Trade and Industry, *UK Overseas Trade Statistics* (London: HMSO, 1987).

The importance of Argentina had in any case been declining rapidly even before 1982. Throughout the period Brazil has been the largest market for UK exports, accounting for 28 per cent of the total in 1986 (see Table 6.3). Venezuela and Mexico accounted for 16.2 per cent and 15.4 per cent in the same year. Together, these three markets accounted for almost 60 per cent of the total in 1986, a proportion even higher than in 1970, despite the fact that the major shift in emphasis away from Argentina towards Mexico and Venezuela had already occurred before then.

In terms of products, UK exports are heavily concentrated on manufactures (see Table 6.4). In 1986 transport and machinery alone accounted for 50 per cent of total exports. Examination of the major categories of exports from the UK to the six largest Latin American economies (excluding Argentina)[1] reveals trends that are indicative of the development of both Latin American markets and UK exports. Power-generating equipment was the most important UK export to all six countries in 1970; in 1986 it was still the most important in two countries and among the top five in the others. Chemicals also appear among the top five imports from the UK of all six countries in both 1970 and 1986, as do industrial and special machines. Metal-working equipment, however, among the top five imports of all six countries in 1970, figured in none by 1986. Similarly iron and steel, among the top five imports of Brazil and Colombia in 1970, had disappeared by 1986. On the other hand, by 1986 telecommunications equipment had emerged among the top five in Brazil and Mexico.

The underlying reasons for the lack of interest shown by UK exporters in the Latin American market can be grouped under three headings: general factors, not specific to Latin America; the image projected by Latin America; and outright neglect.

Among the general factors, which are not specific to Latin America, the prime reason has been the reorientation of the UK towards the European Community (EC), which was already occurring well before the UK's accession to the Community in 1972. During the period 1950–86 the share of UK exports accounted for by the EC rose from 11.1 per cent to 48.1 per cent, a reflection of the demise of Britain as a colonial power and the realisation that as a small manufacturing economy its future had to lie in integration with the rest of Europe. The reduced emphasis on the colonies, however, had an even more profound impact on trade with Africa and Asia than on relations with Latin America.

In no small part a key factor behind the diminished share of the UK in Latin American imports has been the decline in the British share of the world market because of the UK's lack of international competitiveness. This overall position may also have meant that UK exporters spent more time and energy defending their market share in traditional markets than in pushing forward into new areas.

A further problem has arisen out of institutional/organisational arrangements for encouraging exports from the UK. There is a perception among many observers that the various governmental agencies supporting UK exporters – the Department of Trade and Industry (DTI), Export Credits Guarantee Department (ECGD), Foreign and Commonwealth Office (FCO), Overseas Development Administration (ODA) and Latin American Trade Advisory Group (LATAG), along with various Chambers of Commerce and private-sector institutions that could provide project and trade financing – are not as well co-ordinated and do not act in concert to the same extent as occurs in some closely competitive countries, such as France or Japan. Thus, 'UK Inc.' appears to be somewhat at a disadvantage when compared with 'Japan Inc.' or 'France Inc.' Moreover, while this problem is not unique to Latin America, it may in fact have a more adverse impact on exports to Latin America than to other developing areas because of the generally low level of interest shown by successive UK governments towards Latin America.

UK exporters have no doubt also been influenced by developments in Latin America itself. Image problems date back at least as far as the external-debt problems of the inter-war years, when British investors as a major source of foreign finance suffered badly. This can only have added to the inherent unattractiveness of Latin America in the immediate post-war period. Recent developments with regard to the external debt of Latin America have reinforced these negative perceptions (see chapter 7).

Inward-looking policies in Latin America were a further negative factor. Such policies produced a relatively slow rate of growth of imports and a low level of trade relative to Gross Domestic Product (GDP) in many countries. As a result, economies such as Brazil and Mexico, respectively the eighth- and ninth-largest non-Communist economies measured by nominal GDP, have levels of imports in dollar terms lower than those of Hong Kong, Taiwan, Singapore or even Saudi Arabia.[2] Furthermore, while Brazil's GDP is over twice the size of that of South Korea, the total value of its export and import trade in 1985 was only 65 per cent that of the latter. These factors have combined to produce a serious image problem for the region which has provided little incentive for UK exporters to turn away from tried and trusted markets towards Latin America. The problem can only be remedied, however, by the actions of government and key business sectors in the various countries that make up Latin America.

There would also appear to have been an element of neglect of Latin America by UK business. A study by LATAG and the DTI looked at industrial sectors where the UK was perceived to have a comparative advantage in world trade and examined the relative performance of UK exports to Latin America in those sectors. The results showed that the market share of the UK in these areas – chemicals, machinery for special industries, electrical power and switch gear, other electrical machinery and scientific instruments – was well below what could have been expected from the measure of comparative advantage, to the tune of £900 million of lost exports per year. This loss, it should be remembered, is equivalent to 80 per cent of all UK exports to Latin America in 1987.

On a more simplistic level, Latin America accounts for only 1.5 per cent of UK exports, but 3.2 per cent of world imports. In contrast, Africa accounts for only 2.9 per cent of world imports but 3.7 per cent of UK exports, while Asia accounts for 10.1 per cent of world imports and 9.2 per cent of UK exports, which suggests some imbalance in the focus of UK exporters. The fact that the key markets in Asia and Africa – India, Hong Kong, Singapore, South Africa and Nigeria – are all former British colonies points to a key reason for the neglect of Latin America: the absence of colonial ties and a common language.

External debt may well continue to cast a long shadow over the future growth and relative importance of Latin America as an export market. The debt burden, in the absence of new initiatives, will constrain investment and import growth and prolong the image problem of the countries concerned. Moreover, as well as constraining the growth of demand for UK exports, the level of external debt means that credit availability will remain relatively scarce both from the private sector and through the ECGD, although cash-based export opportunities undoubtedly exist and countertrade (a sophisticated form of barter) plays an increasingly important role. Here UK government policy could play an important part in enhancing commercial ties by expanding available cover from the ECGD, by lending more itself directly and by demonstrating greater flexibility in its approach to middle-income countries that are experiencing debt-servicing difficulties.

Against this background it is hard to foresee how Latin America will be anything other than on the periphery of UK export activity, at least in the shorter term. Yet despite these daunting problems there have been some encouraging developments, which are all too often obscured by the 'high profile' blackspots, but nevertheless are important because of the potential opportunities that they open up.

First, growth of demand in almost all of the Latin American economies has now resumed and is accepted as the highest policy priority by almost everyone. One way or another this is likely to involve a reduction in the net resource transfer from Latin American debtor countries to creditor countries. If this were to be achieved by 'confrontational' means using, for example, unilateral measures to achieve debt reduction, the short- to medium-term effect on trade would most probably be highly disruptive. Yet this is not a very likely scenario. Much more likely is an 'accommodating' approach that will facilitate an expanding market, albeit at a relatively modest and possibly uneven pace. The net result will be that the market will continue to grow, in many respects more healthily than it did in the 1970s, with import demand focused on productive goods for investment in contrast to the more indiscriminate boom of the earlier years. Indeed, latest figures show that exports from the UK to some Latin American countries have already been expanding quite rapidly for some time. For example, exports of manufactured goods to Brazil have increased at a real annual rate of 10 per cent since 1982, one of the fastest-growing UK markets anywhere. Exports to Chile have shown a similar trend and, of the smaller markets, Uruguay, Costa Rica, Guatemala and Honduras have all shown significant growth rates, although in the case of Guatemala this was from virtually a zero base.[3]

Secondly, economic policies in Latin America have in the main been refocused since 1983, with much greater emphasis on trade. In many cases, for example, Mexico, adjustment policies have also been explicitly linked to the reduction of tariff barriers. Thirdly from an organisational point of view, there have been signs that assistance to exporters has been improved somewhat. Of particular note is the effort of LATAG. LATAG has selectively targeted specific sectors from which to promote UK exports to Latin America based on the comparative-advantage study mentioned earlier. Initially export promotion also focused on specific countries, although both targeted countries and industrial sectors are now being expanded. The results of this approach have been generally good with a marked increase in growth of exports in the targeted sectors. Nonetheless, the message that there is business to be done in Latin America needs to be reinforced as export potential from the UK expands. Finally, many of the UK's traditional markets in Africa are also badly afflicted by external-debt problems and in most cases are less well placed to recover in the future than is Latin America. At the same time British industry is 'leaner and fitter' and a great deal more competitive internationally than for some time. As a peripheral market, Latin America may stand to gain from both these developments.

Imports

Imports from Latin America to the UK, like exports from the UK to Latin America, have been declining steadily in relative importance. By 1986 Latin America's share of total UK imports had falllen to 1.5 per cent compared with 7.8 per cent in 1950 (see Table 6.1). Again, similar to export trends, Latin America as a whole was the least important regional supplier of goods to the UK market in 1986 (except for the Caribbean). Imports into the UK from Finland alone, for example, exceeded those from all of Latin America. Even imports of Eastern European goods accounted for the same share of overall imports as did those from Latin America.

Yet Brazil, by far the largest individual exporter to the UK from Latin America, in 1986 ranked twenty-second as a supplier of goods to the British market and was the third largest source (after South Africa and Hong Kong) of UK imports outside the OECD area. Imports from Brazil, however, accounted for 41.7 per cent of all imports into the UK from Latin America in 1986 (see Table 6.3). Moreover, the value of imports from Brazil was four times larger than those from any other Latin American country. Chile and Mexico were the next largest suppliers, having roughly equal shares of the market.

David Atkinson

Since 1950 there have been a number of noteworthy shifts in the relative importance of individual countries, a reflection both of specific political and economic trends in Latin America and the changing import requirements of the UK:

Argentina, from being the largest supplier in 1950, had declined dramatically in importance even before the Falklands/Malvinas war. Chile also declined in importance significantly;

Peru and Venezuela retained their relative importance through the period;[4] and

Colombia and Mexico, on the other hand, not only increased their share of Latin American exports to the UK market, but were the only two Latin American economies to increase their respective shares of the total UK market during 1950–86.

Although there has been a modest swing towards manufactures, UK imports from Latin America remain heavily biased towards primary products which accounted for 65 per cent of the total exports of the largest seven economies in 1986 compared with 76 per cent in 1970. For goods from Argentina, Colombia and Venezuela, however, the proportion of primary products is still over 90 per cent and for Mexico 77 per cent (see Table 6.4). Indeed, Mexico and Chile have become more reliant on primary products for exports to the UK (crude oil and copper, respectively). The shift towards manufacturing has, in fact, been concentrated largely on Brazil and Peru. Manufactures accounted for 38.1 per cent of imports from Brazil in 1986 compared with only 7.7 per cent in 1970 and 76.7 per cent of imports from Peru in 1986 compared with 23.1 per cent in 1970.

There have, however, been some significant changes in the top five exports of the major seven Latin American economies to the UK since 1970. For example, Mexico now exports petroleum, textiles and iron and steel, reflecting its development in this period. For Brazil, telecommunications equipment ranked fifth, an indication of the growing sophistication of Brazilian industry. Textiles no longer rank among the top five exports of Chile, reflecting the difficulties experienced by manufacturing industry in that country in the 1970s and early 1980s and the new policy emphasis on encouragement of sectors with a comparative advantage in world trade (agriculture and minerals). Colombia also demonstrated its emergence as a manufacturer of basic goods.

The decline in importance of Latin America as a source of UK imports can be traced to over-reliance on primary-goods exports and the parallel failure to develop competitive manufacturing industries during a period when the UK has been reducing its need for primary-goods imports in relative terms. To see the lack of competitiveness of Latin American exports, we need look no further than the inroads into UK market trade by manufactured imports from the Far East. Moreover, it is surely no coincidence that Brazil, the largest exporter from Latin

America to the UK, also has experienced the most rapid increase in manufactured exports.

Though much of the decline can be attributed to the development strategies of Latin America and the subsequent deterioration in the terms of trade for commodity producers, their difficulties in UK markets have not been helped by discriminatory tariffs levied by the EC and by other restraints on trade such as the Multi-Fibre Arrangement (MFA) in the textiles sector. The colonial legacy also means that sixty-five former colonies of the EC have preferential rates of access not enjoyed by Latin American countries through the Lomé Convention. The EC's Common Agricultural Policy with its strong price-support structure has also discriminated against Latin American producers; grain and sugar producers have been particularly hard-hit.

Yet, while discriminatory trade policies are undesirable and should be eliminated, they are also something of a double-edged sword in that they can provide an artificial stimulus to the development of alternative or more sophisticated products. For many Far Eastern economies, for example, there is little to suggest that restraints on trade have made real growth unacceptably low. Indeed, it is precisely to more sophisticated products that many middle-income Latin American economies must turn if they are to overcome the seemingly interminable long-run deterioration in the terms of trade facing primary-commodity producers. Thus, as a real or potential problem, the existence of discriminatory trade policies should not be exaggerated. With appropriate policies, it seems probable that markets in the UK could be found. Trade barriers, while objectionable, are not insurmountable and, in any event, are likely to be a fact of life for some time to come. Thus, they should not become an excuse for inadequate development policies.

According to most medium-term forecasts[5] the UK looks set to remain a relatively buoyant market for imported goods, although the expansion will continue to favour producers of manufactured goods rather than producers of primary goods. Nevertheless, where Latin America is an efficient producer of primary goods and is not discriminated against, there should be potential to improve market share. Yet this will probably not be enough to arrest the decline in the relative importance of Latin America or elevate it to anything other than peripheral status unless the region can continue to reorient its development strategy to encompass a major expansion of manufactured exports.

Trade policy issues are likely to continue to inhibit the growth of certain exports to the UK. To a large extent these are questions to be resolved within the EC framework. Nonetheless, in some areas the UK government does have considerable latitude, for example in relation to agreements covering textiles, clothing and shoes. Indicators of market penetration suggest that on this score the UK may be more 'closed' than, for example, Germany or France. Conversely, the same indicators show that the UK is more 'open' to imports of non-ferrous metals, metal products and other manufactured goods.

Finally, Brazil as the largest trade partner in Latin America is also building up a sizeable bilateral trade surplus with the UK ($378 million in 1986). At some point in the future this could strain relations between the two countries if the imbalance is not reversed.

The arms trade

Military supplies and technology were an expanding area of business for the UK, and indeed for Europe, from the mid-1970s up to the early 1980s as Latin America shifted away from the United States as its main supplier. From the latter half of the 1970s into the early 1980s sales from the UK even exceeded those of the USA ($750 million compared with $650 million from 1980 to 1982). The UK's sales, however, were greatly overshadowed by those of France which sold $1,900 million of military equipment in the same period, a substantial increase on the mid-1970s. While it is not possible to be precise, one estimate has suggested that 15–30 per cent of the UK's arms sales in this period were to Latin America. Since 1982, among identified transactions, air-to-ship missiles were sold by British Aerospace to Brazil, patrol boats were purchased by Mexico and trainer/counterinsurgency aircraft have been sold to Ecuador. The Conservative government has also tended to encourage arms sales more openly.

Future developments will depend to a great degree on political relationships and the complexion of governments both in the UK and in Latin America. With the return of civilian governments in most of Latin America and the budgetary constraints under which most governments find themselves, it seems unlikely that military spending will expand very rapidly. Moreover, this is a highly competitive market and Britain will also face increasing competition from Latin American arms producers, particularly Brazil and Argentina.[6]

Services

There is no reliable data available on trade in services between the UK and Latin America. What is clear, however, is that this is a not insignificant, and growing, market. In 1985, excluding payments of interest and travel, Latin America (including the Caribbean) paid out almost $17 billion, the equivalent of 27 per cent of the value of total imports, for services from abroad. Expenditure on travel abroad by Latin American residents amounted to another $3.7 billion (in 1980 it had been a massive $10 billion) while expenditure on travel in Latin America had earned those countries about $9 billion.[7]

A relatively high proportion of the supply of services in auditing, advertising, banking and insurance, data processing and hotel management in Latin America is provided by multinational firms. Given that the UK is generally competitive in most of these sectors there would appear to be considerable scope for future development. The UK, however, does not play a significant role in the travel/tourism sector either as a destination for Latin American visitors or as a

Table 6.5. *UK outward direct investment (excluding oil companies, banks and insurance companies): book value of assets 1962–81*

	(% shares and £ million) 1962		1974		1981	
Western Europe	13.4	(455.4)	27.4	(2866.6)	23.2	(6611.8)
North America	23.1	(785.3)	21.8	(2271.6)	34.6	(9883.9)
Other developed countries	27.1	(922.9)	30.1	(3138.2)	20.4	(5823.7)
Africa	12.1	(413.6)	7.0	(730.9)	6.7	(1911.1)
Middle East	0.4	(14.2)	0.6	(63.8)	0.8	(236.4)
Asia	15.5	(529.2)	8.3	(868.4)	8.3	(2380.3)
Latin America & Caribbean:	8.2	(277.4)	4.6	(476.5)	6.0	(1711.3)
Argentina	1.5	(49.3)	0.7	(70.7)	0.3	(95.2)
Brazil	1.1	(37.2)	1.9	(193.1)	1.5	(421.1)
Chile	0.1	(4.2)	0.1	(12.6)	0.3	(94.4)
Colombia	N/A		Neg.	(5.0)	0.1	(26.8)
Mexico	0.8	(28.0)	0.5	(51.3)	1.0	(277.9)
Peru	N/A		Neg.	(3.8)	Neg.	(6.7)
Uruguay	N/A		Neg.	(1.3)	Neg.	(5.2)
Venezuela	0.3	(10.2)	0.1	(12.8)	0.1	(32.5)

Note: Neg. = negligible.
Source: Business Monitor MA4, *Census of Overseas Assets* (London: HMSO, 1981).

source of tourists to Latin America.[8] This must surely be a neglected sector of potential business between the two areas, although its development is hampered by the relative absence of direct air links.

Trade in services is now a major area of international commercial relations and will probably grow even more rapidly in the future. Services are also forming an increasingly large part of international trade negotiations (for example in the Uruguay Round of the General Agreement on Tariffs and Trade (GATT) negotiations) as the developed countries, the USA in particular, push to have services included within the GATT framework. It is likely, therefore, that trade in services between Britain and Latin America will increase in the 1990s, since this is an area where Britain has long enjoyed a comparative advantage.

Investment

Direct investment

In the nineteenth century, the UK was the pre-eminent source of foreign investment in Latin America, although it had been overtaken by the USA by the turn of the century. Nevertheless, even in 1930 35 per cent of the stock of British direct investment overseas was still located in South and Central America, compared with 21 per cent in Asia, 16 per cent in Canada, Australia and South Africa combined, 7 per cent in Europe and 2 per cent in the United States.[9]

By the early 1960s, however, all this had changed. In 1962 the stock of UK investment in the five major Latin American countries – Argentina, Brazil, Chile, Mexico and Venezuela – totalled £128 million and accounted for only 3.8 per cent of total UK investment abroad. Even including the rest of Latin America and the Caribbean, the share only increased to 8.2 per cent (see Table 6.5). During the period 1962–5 the proportion of investment in these five countries increased slightly, but then fell steadily to just over 3 per cent in the early 1970s. The period through 1978 saw something of a revival as the share rose again to almost 5 per cent, but was followed by a reversal through to 1981 as the proportion returned to the levels of the early 1960s.

For comparison, by 1981 over 28 per cent of UK overseas investment was located in the United States, approximately 23 per cent in Europe, 26 per cent in Canada, Australia and South Africa combined, 8 per cent in Asia and 7 per cent in Africa. Moreover, the countries of the Caribbean accounted for almost as much of total UK investment as Latin America.

Yet despite the relative insignificance of the region as a whole, Brazil, which accounted for 44 per cent of all UK investment in 1981 in the eight Latin American countries in Table 6.5, is among the most important host countries for UK investment outside of the OECD area, a reflection of Brazil's status as the largest country in terms of GDP and manufacturing value-added outside the OECD and its position as Britain's largest trade partner in Latin America. Thus, Brazil accounts for as much of total UK investment overseas as Singapore, India, New Zealand and Kenya, although it accounts for less than Zimbabwe, South Africa (at least until 1981), Nigeria and Malaysia.

Although investment in Brazil accounts for such a large share of all UK investment in Latin America, it has declined from a peak of 69 per cent in 1978. This decline in share was due to an increase in the proportion of UK investment located in Mexico. After a period which had seen investment in Mexico fall as a proportion of the total from 22 per cent in 1962 to 11 per cent in 1978, investment surged in the next three years to 29 per cent of the total. Throughout the period 1962–81 (that is, pre-dating the Falklands war) the proportion of UK investment located in Argentina declined sharply. Whereas in 1962 Argentina had accounted for 39 per cent of UK investment in the eight countries, the most important destination for UK investment, by 1981 this proportion had dropped to only 10 per cent. Investment in Venezuela also declined, both in relative terms and indeed in terms of the real value of the assets. Investment in Chile has shown large swings since 1962. There was a big increase in the period 1965–8, but the Allende years saw a large fall not only in proportional terms, but also in nominal terms as the book value of assets fell from £15.4 million in 1968 to £12.6 million in 1974. During the period 1978–81, however, Chile recovered some of its lost importance as its share of UK investments in the eight countries rose again to 9.8 per cent.

As might be expected, the flows of investment to Latin America from the UK show a similar pattern to the value of the outstanding assets, but provide a little more information as the available data are more recent (see Table 6.6). During

Table 6.6. *UK net outward direct investment flows*

	1970	1975	1977	1980 (£ million)	1983	1984[b]
Latin America (largest six countries)[a]	10.6	79.2	155.1	167.9	140.5	368.2
Total UK	546.2	1094.2	1884.8	3390.7	3312.5	5819.4
			% share			
Latin America (largest six countries)[a]	1.9	7.2	8.2	5.0	4.2	6.3

[a] Argentina, Brazil, Chile, Colombia, Mexico and Venezuela.
[b] Includes investment by oil companies.
Source: Business Monitor M4, *Overseas Transactions* (London: HMSO), various issues.

the years 1970–7 the proportion of investment flows going to Latin America steadily increased, with flows to the largest six economies peaking at 8.2 per cent in 1977. Indeed, direct investment flows to all developing-country areas in this period was increasing as a proportion of the total, mainly shifting away from Canada, Australia and South Africa. It should be noted, however, that in 1977 Nigeria alone accounted for as large a share of investment flows as the six largest Latin American economies alone. After 1977 the share of investment flows declined again so that in 1983 the proportion accounted for by the six Latin American countries was only 4.2 per cent. Investment flows to Africa, however, were now accounting for only 2.3 per cent of the total and net flows to the Middle East were negative.

In 1984 data included for the first time investment by oil companies. With this new element, investment flows to the six Latin American countries rose to 6.3 per cent of the total. For comparison, in 1984 flows to Western Europe, Africa and the Middle East were negative, although flows to the Caribbean and Central America and the rest of Latin America accounted for a surprisingly large 18.9 per cent of the total.[10]

It should perhaps be no surprise that UK investment in Latin America has been relatively insignificant in the context of overall UK investment in the post-war period, as there is a strong correlation between trade flows and foreign direct investment. It has been estimated, for example, that 34 per cent of world trade is accounted for by intra-company flows. Colonial ties, the reorientation of the UK towards the EC and the history of Latin America itself have all played significant roles in determining the location of direct investment abroad and the relative insignificance of Latin America.

In the inter-war period the closure of various markets, as tariff barriers rose during the depression years, encouraged Imperial Preference and with it a swing towards the Commonwealth. In the case of Latin America there was also the problem associated with the debt defaults of that period which affected a great deal of UK investment. In the immediate post-war years the UK continued to develop its investment links with the Commonwealth – in particular Australia, Canada and South Africa (at that time still a member). One estimate suggests that during the years 1946–60 approximately 80 per cent of recorded UK direct investment overseas went to these three countries. This was a reflection of their rapid expansion, strong links with Britain and the fact that for much of the time this period was one of post-war reconstruction with formal trade and exchange controls in Europe and elsewhere. As we have seen earlier (see Table 6.1), the major countries of Europe accounted for only 11.1 per cent of UK exports in 1950, compared with Asia's 28.4 per cent and Africa's 13.2 per cent.

As the EC developed, however, and as it became clear that the UK would eventually become a member, British foreign investment began to concentrate on the EC. This trend continued for much of the 1960s through to the second half of the 1970s. Since the late 1970s the USA has displaced the EC as the focus of UK direct investment overseas. There has been a tremendous upsurge in investment which took the share of North American (mainly the United States) in UK investment from 21.8 per cent in 1974 to 34.6 per cent in 1981. Furthermore, in 1983 and 1984 the US was still accounting for a massive 52.8 per cent and 59.7 per cent respectively of UK investment flows. It is beyond the scope of this paper to attempt to explain the apparent lemming-like rush into the USA, although it is probably related to factors which are relevant to the neglect of Latin America. First, cultural and linguistic similarities; secondly, stability, both politically and with regard to investment policy; and thirdly, the boom in the US economy.

Cultural and linguistic differences between the UK and Latin America are fairly obvious. Nevertheless, culturally Latin America would appear to have a good deal more in common with the UK than either Africa or Asia, even though the colonial links are missing. Stability of governments and policies have not been Latin America's strong points. Although investment in Latin America in the nineteenth and early part of the twentieth centuries bore little relation to the types of post-war investment, the experience of debt defaults in the inter-war period coloured perceptions of Latin America in the immediate post-war period. This was reinforced by subsequent experiences in certain countries, where specific sectors were nationalised, for example, oil in Venezuela and copper in Chile. Moreover, from the late 1960s until very recently there has been a strong strain of anti-foreign-investment sentiment running through economic policy, especially pronounced in the rhetoric of various governments on the subject. In practice many countries have tempered their rhetoric with a heavy dose of pragmatism, although while there was a readily available alternative source of foreign savings, such as untied commercial bank finance for general balance of payments financing purposes, there was hardly much incentive for governments to encourage actively foreign direct investment in their countries. It should be recalled, however, that the development model of the 1950s and early 1960s adopted in most parts of Latin America was fairly receptive towards foreign capital. This was an opportunity not seized upon by the UK as it was preoccupied with the baggage of colonialism, fundamental industrial complacency and its own economic problems and perhaps put off by the experience of the inter-war period.

Economic performance cannot be ignored in any investment decision and this has been evident in the flows of UK investment to Latin America. Thus, for example, in the 1970s, as certain Latin American countries such as Brazil, Mexico and Chile looked to be at last fulfilling their potential, the proportion of UK direct investment located in these countries rose substantially. Yet it cannot be denied that the performance of Brazil and Mexico has lagged behind that of Hong Kong and Singapore, so that – especially given historical and colonial ties – it is hardly surprising that UK companies have preferred to invest in those two countries. Conversely, the dismal economic performance of Argentina was mirrored in its decline in relative importance as a destination for UK investment abroad.

The relative attractiveness of Latin America in the future will be closely tied to the problem of external debt. It might be reasonable to ask why anyone would want to invest a dollar in Latin America when the secondary market price of a 15- to 20-year loan asset is only worth 50 cents or less. This may be an overly simplistic view of investment, but it nevertheless illustrates the difficulties that Latin America will experience in attracting foreign investment. By and large, foreign investment follows economic performance – not vice versa.

Yet there are positive developments which will make Latin America relatively more attractive than in the past. First, the last few years have seen a pronounced shift in attitudes towards foreign investment, largely out of necessity as other sources of foreign savings have dried up. The Andean Pact countries, for example, have drastically revised their foreign investment code to ease previously highly restrictive conditions. Secondly, economic policies have also shifted, again out of necessity, and generally tend to favour exports more than hitherto, which along with lower real wages is making Latin America more attractive as a manufacturing base from which to export. Thirdly, investment in the immediate future will be encouraged by debt–equity conversion programmes, such as that successfully operated by Chile.

Portfolio investment[11]

Data do not exist to provide any reasonably accurate gauge of this aspect of economic relations between the UK and Latin America, but crude estimates suggest that Latin America has not been an attractive destination. Nevertheless the removal of exchange control in the UK in 1979 and the subsequent outflow of capital provided a ready supply of funds for this type of investment. Moreover, as a result of the debt crisis and the diminution of bank lending, Latin American countries have been forced to think more seriously about attracting such funds. Multilateral agencies have also focused more attention on this aspect of

Table 6.7. *UK aid flows to Latin America*

	1979	(£000) 1983	1986
Argentina	5	0	0
Bolivia	888	1,199	1,953
Brazil	888	5,574	880
Chile	2,131	442	373
Colombia	1,242	635	1,018
Costa Rica	623	1,836	11,538
Dominican Republic	77	176	42
Ecuador	1,897	176	836
El Salvador	448	783	239
Guatemala	14	0	10
Haiti	5	19	331
Honduras	230	6,670	1,258
Mexico	1,186	2,827	803
Nicaragua	246	64	86
Panama	63	43	70
Paraguay	267	1,281	221
Peru	882	4,427	1,214
Uruguay	35	16	13
Venezuela	0	3	10
Belize	7,172	2,885	3,179
Falklands	915	9,053	10,252
Total	19,214	38,109	34,326

Source: Overseas Development Administration, *British Aid Statistics,* 1976–80, 1981–5, 1982–6.

investment in developing countries. For example, a Mexico Fund and, more recently, a Brazil Fund have been established.

The debt problem has stimulated a search for innovative ways of dealing with the existing debt overhang. One such avenue is the establishment of a fund for portfolio investment utilising a debt conversion scheme. A major UK bank, Midland, was the first to establish a fund of this kind. Doubtless more will follow. As capital markets have become ever more global, the attraction of a 'high-yield' fund based on portfolio investment in developing countries is likely to increase, notwithstanding recent setbacks in the wake of the collapse of stock markets in the OECD economies in October 1987. As Latin America returns to sustained growth, the region should begin to provide an acceptable risk–reward trade-off and hence grow as a destination for such funds.

Aid

UK official bilateral aid to Latin America is insignificant, particularly if aid for the Falkland Islands and Belize is excluded; in 1986 it was valued at £21 million, less than 3 per cent of total aid (see Table 6.7). Moreover, of this total

£11.5 million went to Costa Rica alone. Bolivia, Honduras, Peru and Colombia were the main recipients of aid (other than Costa Rica) in 1986. Since 1983 aid has been cut, in some cases substantially.

The reasons for the low level of aid to Latin America are not hard to find. First, there is the policy of 'aid to the poorest', instigated by the Labour government (1974–9). As almost all the Latin American countries are classified as 'middle-income' countries and have a relatively high average level of GDP, these countries do not qualify under such a policy. Secondly, as the incumbent Conservative Minister for Overseas Development, Chris Patten, noted in a speech at Chatham House in 1987, there are four criteria which determine the allocation of aid: political, commercial, humanitarian and developmental. Thus, the UK gives two-thirds of bilateral aid to Commonwealth countries, largely for political reasons. However, with regard to commercial criteria the Minister said: 'If a project or programme is sound, and if British goods are reasonably competitive, then I do not believe that tying [aid] should of itself be regarded as objectionable.' Latin America has been included in tied aid funds in recent years, even though it is not a priority area in general government perceptions.

Given these criteria, particularly the commercial and political objectives, it should, however, be no surprise that Latin America ranks so low in UK aid priorities. The speech referred to above, for example, did not once mention Latin America, while it dwelt at length on Africa. Moreover, despite the conclusion of the House of Commons Foreign Affairs Committee in 1987 that aid should reflect the degree of poverty within a country as well as its real income per head, which might increase the amount given to Latin American countries, political and commercial realities are likely to dictate that Latin America remains insignificant with regard to UK aid flows.

Conclusions

The facts are hard to deny – Latin America has declined in importance to the UK and vice versa as far as trade and investment is concerned. And, as aid is closely linked to these two elements of commercial relations, a similar trend emerges in this area as well. Much of this decline can be ascribed to the UK's own economic decline and the reorientation of the economy toward the European Community. In that respect there is little that could have or should have been done specifically to reverse the trend. This is not the whole story, however. There has also been significant neglect of Latin America by UK businessmen, a situation exacerbated by the serious 'image' problems for which the Latin American countries are largely responsible themselves. The issue then is how to reverse the twin problems of neglect and a negative image, although realistically it has to be recognised that in the short term at least Latin America, constrained by external debt problems, will remain on the periphery of UK commercial relations.

David Atkinson

Although there are tentative signs that these two problems are being tackled, albeit slowly and probably on an insufficient scale, greater efforts should be made to overcome what appears to be an inherent prejudice against and ignorance of Latin America in the consciousness of British businessmen. There is no natural Hispanic base in the UK, unlike in the US, but there is a fund of goodwill towards the UK that still exists in Latin America which could and should be exploited. A focused, co-ordinated effort by government agencies and support of UK exporters, along with educational assistance in all its forms, and a more flexible stance by the UK government on the external debt problem would contribute to ensuring that potential in Latin America is fully exploited. Ultimately, however, it is hard to escape the conclusion that the consolidation of a fast-growing and dynamic market in Latin America accompanied by a more receptive attitude to foreign investment and trade, on the one hand, and a 'leaner and fitter' British industry hungry for markets on the other, are prerequisites for a major stimulus to UK–Latin American economic relations. (This theme will be returned to in chapter 12, below.)

Notes

1 The six are Brazil, Chile, Colombia, Mexico, Peru and Venezuela.
2 See World Bank, *World Development Report 1987* (Washington, DC, 1987), Table 10, pp. 220–1.
3 Trade between Britain and Guatemala was one of the casualties of the absence of consular and diplomatic relations between the two countries. Diplomatic relations were finally restored, after an interval of nearly twenty-five years, in 1987.
4 Venezuela saw its share rise sharply in the 1950s following increased UK purchases of oil. By 1986, however, the share was down to the same level as in 1950.
5 See, for example, International Monetary Fund, *World Economic Outlook* (Washington, DC, April 1988).
6 Britain did, however, win a number of very valuable military contracts with developing countries outside Latin America in 1988 and is also negotiating a huge contract with Venezuela (see chapter 5).
7 See Inter-American Development Bank, *Economic and Social Progress in Latin America* (Washington, DC, 1987), p. 453, Table 45.
8 There has been some growth, however. For example, the number of British visitors to Brazil increased from 21,294 in 1980 to 34,552 in 1982.
9 See Peter Uwe Schliemann, *The Strategy of British and German Direct Investment in Brazil* (London: Gower Press, 1981).
10 The main reason for this high share, however, was the negative flows recorded for several other regions.
11 Portfolio investment is defined as stock-market-type investments and excludes commercial bank loans.

7 Financial relations between Britain and Latin America

Stephany Griffith-Jones

The key issues to be addressed in this chapter are:

(1) Why did British banks become so heavily exposed in Latin America in the 1970s and early 1980s, when other British links (such as trade and direct investment) with the subcontinent were relatively weak and declining during that period?

(2) What initiatives could (or should) be taken in the United Kingdom (by government, banks, exporters) to:

(a) relieve the burden of debt on developing countries' economies?

(b) strengthen the stability of British and British-based banks?

(c) change the asymmetrical nature of British links to Latin America, so that the importance of trade and other links is enhanced relative to that of the currently dominant financial links?

The evolution of UK financial links with Latin America

As is well known, international private banks played a major role in funding the very large deficits that Latin American and other Less Developed Countries (LDCs) experienced after the early 1970s. Within this very rapid expansion British-based banks played a major role, as London was, and still is, the major international financial centre in the world and also the main centre for the so-called Euro-dollar market, through which most of the loans to LDCs and to Latin America were carried out. The importance of London as an international financial centre has its origins in the leading role played by Britain in the world economy and in international trade up to the beginning of the twentieth century. As Britain lost pre-eminence in world production and trade, it still maintained – through the City of London – a very big role in financial markets, as well as other trade-related service markets (such as commodities trading and insurance underwriting). Specifically, in the case of the rapid growth of the Euro-markets, the relaxed regulation of overseas lending (either of British or particularly of foreign banks), combined with far tighter US regulations of international lending by US banks, played a major role in the establishment of London as the main world centre of the then rapidly growing Euro-dollar market.[1] Largely due to the

Table 7.1. *Banks in the UK and Bank for International Settlements (BIS) area: external claims on Less Developed Countries (LDCs) and Eastern Europe[a] (US$millions, end of year)*

	Average annual rates of change (%)						Net loans from UK as % of BIS total		Outstanding UK claims 1983[c]	
	1976–9		1979–83		1983–6		1976–9	1979–83	US$(bn)	% of BIS total
	BIS[b]	UK[c]	BIS	UK	BIS[d]	UK[e]				
Eastern Europe and Yugoslavia	26.6		−2.1	−2.4	10.2	12.9		26.9	13.5	23.2
Latin America and Caribbean	24.8		13.0	12.7	1.4	0.2		16.8	34.8	17.1
Middle East[f]	28.8		10.3	11.9	−0.3	−7.1		49.2	20.4	43.1
Africa	57.5		5.4	18.7	6.7	3.5		57.2	7.7	21.9
Asia	24.6		12.9	17.4	7.9	1.7		24.0	11.1	19.4
Sub-total	27.8		9.1	10.2	3.9	1.4		24.1	87.5	21.8
Total lending	26.6	25.1	12.1	14.0	15.2	11.7	23.4	28.8	456.3	26.0
Functional groups										
Oil exporters	47.5		7.9	10.0	1.2	−8.5		37.0	26.4	30.4
Non-oil LDCs	22.6		13.2	16.0	3.7	3.2		21.3	47.6	18.6
10 heavily indebted LDCs[g]	30.8	39.3	13.6	11.6	1.5	1.9	23.0	16.7	42.3	18.8
SE Asian NICs[h]	26.0	28.3	17.2	21.4	3.5	1.0	16.0	20.1	6.4	17.5

 These series show the evolution of the external net financial assets of commercial banks in the UK and in the BIS area. The figures are not consolidated, excluding claims of branches and subsidiaries of banks with head offices in the UK and in the BIS reporting area, but including the latter's claims on their outside area branches and subsidiaries. Regional groups have been standardised to suit the geographic and functional groupings in the table.

[b] The 1976 data cover the Group of Ten countries (Belgium/Luxembourg, Canada, France, Italy, Japan, the Netherlands, Sweden, the UK, the USA and West Germany), Switzerland and some offshore branches of US banks. In 1978 this coverage was extended to banks in Austria, Denmark and Ireland. The rates of growth in the Table, therefore, reflect both the relative changes in claims by banks in the old sample and the increased coverage in 1979.

[c] Includes claims in foreign currencies with details only for a few countries and no regional aggregates.

[d] Also includes claims by banks in Finland, Norway, Spain and six offshore centres.

[e] Covers claims in all currencies.

[f] Includes Bahrain until 1985. Since then Bahrain is included among the offshore centres reporting to the BIS.

[g] Argentina, Brazil, Chile, Colombia, Mexico, Peru, the Philippines, Venezuela and Yugoslavia. BIS data for Nigeria do not include claims by US banks.

[h] Indonesia, Malaysia, South Korea and Thailand (Newly Industrialising Countries).

Sources: Bank for International Settlements (BIS), International Banking Developments (quarterly series); Bank of England Quarterly Bulletin, series 14.1 (various issues).

rapid growth of Euro-market lending opportunities in London, the number of foreign banks based in London grew by 50 per cent (to over 400) between 1975 and 1985.

As has been widely discussed, an important and growing proportion of Euro-currency lending was channelled during the 1970s and early 1980s to developing countries, of which a very large share went to Latin American countries. Banks based *in the UK* (both British and others) played a major role in this lending. As can be seen in Table 7.1, the share of UK-based lending in total bank lending (as covered by Bank of International Settlements (BIS) statistics) to developing countries and Eastern Europe reached 21.8 per cent in 1983; this was only slightly lower than the share (26.0 per cent) of UK-based lending in total international lending. As regards regional distribution, it is worth noting that the proportion of UK-based lending to Latin America was relatively low, reaching 17.1 per cent in 1983, as much lending to Latin America was handled from the United States. Since 1983, relatively little has changed in terms of market shares, with outstanding claims on these countries growing mostly in response to involuntary lending in rescheduling packages.

Although exposure of British-based banks has a certain significance for the UK economy and for the role of British institutions such as the Bank of England in regulating and supervising UK-based financial institutions, the key variable in understanding British–Latin American financial relations relates to lending by British-owned banks. These banks' lending to Latin American countries was very high during the seventies. By 1980, British-owned banks had outstanding claims on Latin America of around US$20 billion. Somewhat surprisingly, given the increasing doubts about Latin America's continued debt-servicing capacity, British banks increased their exposure to Latin America further in the early eighties: in 1983 British-owned banks' exposure, at around $30 billion, was 50 per cent larger than that in 1980. This rapid growth of British banks' lending to Latin America was significantly faster than the growth of US lending to Latin America in that period. US banks, which in the early seventies had initiated lending to developing countries and, in particular, to Latin America were beginning to feel over-exposed and were slowing down their growth in lending. The British banks, which had become involved somewhat later, still seemed keen to expand their lending and their share of the market. By late 1985, UK banks were disputing with Japan the role of second-largest creditor to Latin America (with both having exposures of over $30 billion), compared with US banks' exposure to the subcontinent of around $90 billion.

As can be seen clearly in Table 7.2, the UK banks' share of lending to Latin America in their total international lending at the end of 1985 (at about 20 per cent) was far higher than that of any other European country, except for Spain. Spain's high level of lending to Latin America can be more easily explained, given far stronger trade, political and cultural links between Spain and Latin America. British banks' share of lending to Latin America is, however, far higher than that of Swiss, Dutch and German banks (at around 7 per cent) or the

Table 7.2. *Geographical distribution of European commercial bank credits, end of 1985 (percentage)*

Debtors:	Western industrial countries	Eastern Europe	LDCs	Latin America[a]	Latin American share of LDC total
Creditors:					
West Germany	65.5	6.7	27.8	6.5	23.4
France	63.1	4.7	32.2	8.7	27.0
Netherlands	84.1	1.9	14.0	6.3	45.2
Spain	54.4	1.9	43.3	26.5	61.3
Switzerland	79.2	1.9	18.9	6.7	35.4
United Kingdom	49.5	5.6	45.0	19.3	42.9
USA	38.4	0.8	60.8	25.9	42.7

a Does not include Dutch and British Antilles, Bahamas, Barbados and Bermuda.
Source: Institute for European–Latin American Relations (IRELA), *Western Europe and the Latin America Foreign Debt* (Madrid, June 1987), calculated on the basis of Central Banks' figures.

French banks (at just below 9 per cent). The British share is only slightly lower than that of the US banks; although US banks also became heavily over-exposed in Latin America, the expansion of their lending into that subcontinent is far more closely related – than in the British case – to very important links in trade and direct foreign investment; furthermore, US political interests in the region also contributed to encourage private lending by US banks, particularly at a time when US aid flows were declining and the belief in external funding for LDCs via private international flows was becoming increasingly fashionable in Washington.

British banks' involvement in lending to Latin America clearly did not reflect growing trade links. Indeed, the share of British exports to Latin America was falling in the seventies and early eighties; by 1980 it had declined to around 2.2 per cent of total British exports and by 1986 it had reached an all-time low of 1.4 per cent of British exports. By the mid-1980s, also, the share of total UK aid going to Latin America had fallen to below 3 per cent. These two figures are in sharp contrast to the fact that about 20 per cent of British banks' total international exposure by 1985 was in Latin America.

The fact that it is the financial relationship that is so dominant in British–Latin American links (and that all other links are both in relative and absolute terms so weak) implies that British perceptions of Latin America – in government circles, in the press and to a certain extent in public opinion – tend to be dominated by purely financial considerations. Furthermore, discussion of the debt problem tends perhaps to focus excessively on the purely financial dimension without taking sufficient account of trade and political considerations (for example, the negative effects of the debt crisis on British exports is only rarely noted in Britain – in marked contrast to the debate in the USA). I shall return to this issue below.

The question of why British banks lent so much to Latin America can be explained at two different levels. First, it needs to be pointed out that British-owned banks – partly because of their historical tradition and partly because they are part of the highly internationally minded City of London – tend to think of themselves as global financial institutions and seem rather detached from their British roots. For this reason, British banks seem to study more closely and follow, the initiatives being taken on the other side of the Atlantic by their US counterparts, who led the rush into Latin American lending, and appear unconcerned by the weakness of other British links with Latin America. The importance of the City as the major world centre from which international lending was being carried out, by banks of all nationalities, clearly contributed to their enthusiasm.

Secondly, it should be pointed out that the high exposure of British banks in Latin America is to an important extent explained by the particularly heavy involvement of two of the four British clearing banks (Lloyds and Midland). As can be seen in Table 7.3, the level of exposure of these two British banks in Latin America was almost double the exposure of the other British banks; further-more, both for Lloyds and Midland, the ratio of Latin American loans to equity was as high as the average for the thirteen most heavily exposed US banks. Lloyds and Midland have also played a consistently key role not only in participating in lending to Latin America, but also in leading it via their large participation in the local management of syndicated loans.[2]

To a certain extent, Lloyds and Midland had specific reasons for their great expansion of lending to Latin America. This is perhaps clearest in the case of Lloyds, a bank traditionally involved in international lending and having a powerful international division; furthermore, Lloyds has – via its own links and through the acquisition of the Bank of London and South America (BOLSA) – an important network of branches and offices in Latin America. Thus, Lloyds has branches in Brazil, Argentina, Ecuador, Uruguay, Paraguay and Guatemala, and representative offices in Mexico, Colombia and Venezuela. It also owns minor institutions in Honduras, Panama, Colombia and Brazil.[3] Normally, in the seventies, the existence of a branch or a representative office in a country tended to increase the incentive of international banks to lend to that country via the Euro-market; Lloyds was certainly no exception to that trend. In the case of Midland, there is also a clear reason – though an unfortunate one from the bank's point of view – for its very high Latin American exposure. The reason is that in 1980 Midland was extremely keen to extend its international operations; as its then General Manager, Malcolm Wilcox, clearly said,[4] his ambition was for Midland 'to be and be seen to be a major international bank'. Midland was particularly keen to acquire a US bank, which would provide it with a large US-dollar deposit base, as well as enlarge its international network. As is well known, Midland purchased Crocker, with extremely problematic consequences given that bank's bad portfolio. When Midland later sold Crocker, it had to retain its high Latin American exposure. Without Crocker's claims on Latin

Table 7.3. *Exposure to Latin America of some major international banks, 1982.*

	Loans (US$ million)	Loans/Equity[a] (%)
Canadian banks		
Royal Bank of Canada	3,510	149.1
CIBC	2,155	109.6
Bank of Montreal	3,450	178.4
Bank of Nova Scotia	2,610	189.5
Toronto-Dominion	1,740	121.7
Total[b]	13,465	148.6
US banks		
Citicorp	10,450	188.8
Bankamerica	7,590	144.7
Chase Manhattan	6,500	176.0
Morgan Guaranty	4,370	143.0
Manufacturers Hanover	6,720	228.3
Chemical New York	4,240	187.4
Continental Illinois	2,290	109.5
Bankers Trust	2,670	163.0
First National Chicago	2,310	136.4
Security Pacific	1,380	77.2
Wells Fargo	1,510	117.0
Crocker	2,250	169.0
First Interstate	1,470	70.9
Total[b]	53,750	155.1
Japanese banks		
Dai-Ichi Kangyo	2,086	82.5
Fuji	1,580	55.8
Sumitomo	2,255	82.4
Mitsubishi	1,759	75.7
Sanwa	1,896	79.5
Mitsui	1,200	73.3
Tokai	1,495	92.3
Taiyo Kobe	944	67.6
Daiwa	510	50.8
Kyowa	498	52.7
Saitama	522	65.6
Hokkaido	574	86.6
Bank of Tokyo	2,974	211.4
Industrial Bank Japan	1,509	70.8
Long-Term Credit Bank	1,475	90.0
Nippon Credit Bank	973	91.7
Total[b]	22,250	82.1
British banks		
Barclays	3,500	68.5
Lloyds	5,800	165.7
Midland	5,200	150.0
NatWest	2,900	65.2
Total[b]	17,400	105.3

a Includes general provision.
b Weighted average.
Source: S. Griffith-Jones, M. Marcel and G. Palma, *Third World Debt and British Banks* (Fabian Society Working Paper, London, May 1987).

America, estimated to reach around $2.8 billion, Midland's exposure would not have been higher than that of Barclays or NatWest. What is, however, particularly surprising in this context is that Midland both increased its lending to Latin America and allowed Crocker to continue doing so in 1980 and 1981.

Both Barclays and NatWest, on the other hand, had other priorities than lending to LDCs, although they did lead several syndications for these countries. In the case of Barclays, it is the most involved in domestic retail banking among the London Clearers, showing by far the lowest share of international assets in its portfolio. (The shares of international assets in total assets for each UK clearing bank in the early 1980s were: Barclays, 32 per cent; Lloyds, 60 per cent; Midland, 62 per cent and NatWest, 52 per cent.) Moreover, in the international market its interests concentrated in geographical areas away from Latin America, such as Africa and especially South Africa. Finally, NatWest became more specialised in merchant banking and concentrated its cross-border operations in the USA and other OECD countries. This bank was probably more reluctant to risk lending to LDCs due to its past troubles during the UK secondary banking crisis of the early 1970s.

The management of the debt crisis

The main features of debt crisis management since 1982 have been amply discussed elsewhere.[5] As is well known, all international banks lending to problem debtor countries grouped themselves in steering committees, which represented all banks in negotiations on rescheduling/new money with debtor nations. On the whole, banks have acted in unison (which is clearly different from the experience of the 1930s, when creditors formed several – often rival – groupings). This unity has been a source of bargaining strength for the banks *vis-à-vis* the debtors, but has implied that banks of different nationalities and sizes have had to adopt common positions, even though their objectives and national regulations on supervision and taxation matters are significantly different. US banks have played a leading role, because they were often the largest creditors to problem debtors and because US banking rules are on the whole the most stringent. In recent years, the view has been expressed by some bankers – particularly European ones – that perhaps banks of different countries could have separate negotiations with debtors. This has not so far occurred, except for very special cases such as that of Peru. The banks on the whole continue to act in unison, possibly with growing tensions amongst them as the debt crisis has continued and in some respects deepened.

Because British banks were so heavily exposed in Latin America and in the Third World, they have played a fairly important role in the steering committees for Latin American countries (see Table 7.4). However, British banks have very rarely had a leading role on these committees, except in very small countries (for example, Honduras).

Table 7.4. *British banks' participation in steering or advisory bank committees of indebted developing countries*

	Barclays	Lloyds	Midland	NatWest	Others
Argentina		X			
Brazil		X^c			
Chile			X		
Colombia	X		X		
Costa Rica		X			
Cuba			X		
Ecuador		X^a	X^d		
Honduras		X^a			
Mexico		X			
Panama		X			
Peru			X^c	X	
Venezuela		X^b			
Ivory Coast			X		
Malawi			X	X	X
Morocco	X				
Nigeria	X^a				X^e
Zaire					X
Zambia	X				X
Philippines	X				
TOTAL	5	8	7	2	4

Note: X indicates participation.
a Chairman; *b* Co-Chairman; *c* Deputy; *d* originally Crocker Bank; *e* Co-ordinator.
Source: D. Lomax, *The Developing Country Debt Crisis* (London: Macmillan, 1986).

The Bank of England has played a more active role in debt-crisis management than the commercial banks; together with the US Federal Reserve, in the early stages of the debt crisis, it encouraged 'involuntary' new lending by British banks and helped organise bridging loans via the Bank for International Settlements. However, particularly in relation to Latin American debt, the 'blueprint' for debt-crisis management has basically been defined by negotiations between the US government and the Latin American debtor governments. For example, the key Mexican packages – in 1982, 1984 and 1986 and above all the innovative 1988 package for debt-repurchase – were basically first negotiated in Washington and New York.

Not only are bilateral agreements with Latin American debtors negotiated in the USA, but so also are broader initiatives whether public or private. For example, the Baker Plan – not particularly effective, but representing a new approach – was launched by the US government largely in response to the unwillingness of Latin American debtor governments to continue servicing their debts. As regards the essential step of making meaningful loan-loss provision for Third World debt, this initiative was in fact first taken by continental European banks (especially Swiss, West German and Dutch ones). Then, in May 1987, Citicorp – followed by the major US banks – drastically increased their provisions. Only then did British banks act, raising their provisions to levels similar to those of the US banks.

An All-Party Parliamentary Group Report[6] produced in early 1987 summarised the UK response to the debt crisis very clearly: 'Apart from according generous aid-debt relief to the poorest countries, the Government has not launched any innovations. Treasury caution has determined the agenda at the expense of our interest in developing countries. The Government *have preferred a reactive response, closely attuned to the US position*' (my italics). An IRELA document (see source note for Table 7.2, p. 125) puts a similar conclusion in stronger language: 'given the similarity in bank exposure and vulnerability, as well as in economic policy, the US Administration's major ally in its global strategy is the British government'; the IRELA report supports this analysis with the fact that the British government – together with the Japanese and Canadian – supported the US proposal to amend the voting rules of the Inter-American Development Bank in favour of greater conditionality, a proposal which met with much Latin American resistance; this attitude contrasted with that of the West German and other European governments, which proposed a compromise formula.

The British government, however, has played an innovative role in relation to debt to low-income countries (and particularly African ones). First, it took the lead in granting RTA (retrospective terms adjustment) in the late seventies and early eighties to the poorest countries; furthermore, together with West Germany, the UK has made the largest transformation of past loans into grants. Similarly, the UK government (through the so-called Lawson initiative) launched, in April 1987, an important proposal to assist the poorest and most indebted African countries, an initiative which included a reduction in interest rates to be paid to governments. This proposal was adopted by Western leaders at the Toronto Summit in June 1988.

On African debt the UK government is innovative and takes the initiative, while on Latin American debt the UK government is conservative and tends to respond reactively to initiatives by other actors, mainly US ones. The possibility of more coherent European initiatives – in which the British could play a large role – has not been pursued with sufficient vigour. If European countries were able and willing to co-ordinate positions and take initiatives, they could easily do so, given their weight in international financial institutions.

In this context, it seems relevant to mention that European Community (EC) countries have 28.6 per cent of the vote in the IMF (with Britain having the largest share – 6.63 per cent – which is second only to the US share of 19.14 per cent). The fairly passive role played by the UK government – on matters such as new initiatives on debt for middle-income countries and on issues such as conditionality – does not seem to correspond to the potential influence it could have, based both on its voting share and on its widely respected expertise in these matters.

So far, we have highlighted British attitudes to and perceived interests in the debt crisis. Very briefly, it seems worth noting that the debt crisis – and the accompanying deterioration of the international economic environment – has had a very marked negative effect on Latin America's growth and development, with particularly negative effects on income levels of poor and vulnerable people and on levels of investment.[7] To the extent that the British government (and/or public opinion) has an interest in development and political stability in the region, then alternative management of the debt problem could provide a possibly valuable contribution towards it. Concern with Latin American development and the sustainability of democracy in the region carry far greater weight in US analysis and initiatives (such as the Bradley Plan) than in British documents and proposals. With a few distinguished exceptions (such as the All-Party Parliamentary Report quoted above), British documents tend to treat Latin American debt too much as a purely financial problem, thus ignoring the development and political dimensions. To a certain extent, this may reflect the fact that links between the UK and Latin America are so heavily biased towards the financial.

The link between the debt crisis, foreign exchange shortages and the level of UK exports to Latin America is also a theme which hardly receives attention in British analysis of the problem (again there is a sharp contrast here with the USA, where a number of detailed studies on the link for the US economy have been prepared in Congress, government departments, and elsewhere and the issue is clearly brought out in most discussions of the debt crisis). In fact, though weaker, the link between lower British exports (and fewer British jobs) and the decline of Latin American imports (related to the debt crisis) is an important one. It has been estimated[8] that around 200,000 jobs may have been lost in the UK as a result of sharply reduced imports from heavily indebted countries (British exports to Latin America and Africa between 1980 and 1986 *fell* by 32.6 per cent and 51.2 per cent respectively). Particularly badly hit were British manufacturing exports, as debtor countries cut back most on investment.

Furthermore, it has been estimated[9] that a significant proportion of any debt relief offered to Latin America by UK banks, as part of a general strategy by the region's creditors to lower debt-service payments, could return to the UK in the form of higher exports. For example, a 1 per cent reduction in interest rates could provide $2,000 million in debt relief with the UK contribution equal to $195 million; if all the reduction in debt-service payments were spent on additional imports, UK exporters could enjoy an increase in sales to Latin America of around $50 million at current market shares, equivalent to over a quarter of the debt relief granted. Should such debt relief be linked to measures for encouraging British exports to Latin America so as to increase market share, the impact of any debt relief could be further magnified.

Possible British initiatives in the new stage of the debt crisis

Since early 1987, it would seem that a new stage has been entered in debt crisis management. As a result of greater assertiveness of debtors in limiting debt servicing and of the deterioration in the international environment which makes such debt servicing more difficult, in mid-1987 major US, British and other banks made substantial provisions against their developing-country loans. These provisions have been interpreted by developing-country governments – and by many observers – as a recognition that Third World countries will not in fact be able and willing in future to service their debt at 100 per cent and that the banks are recognising that in due course they will have to make concessions.

The need for debt relief by Latin American countries is still strongly resisted by many of the major creditor banks. Understandably, opposition is particularly strong amongst banks where Latin American assets are a high proportion of total assets and capital and which have relatively lower provisions against those loans. (As I have noted above, two of the major British banks are in this category.) Opposition to debt relief – or less drastic options, such as interest capitalisation – is far weaker from bankers, whose institutions are relatively less exposed in Latin America (either because they lent less and/or because they have sold off part of their exposure on the secondary market) and have made greater provisions against potential losses. It is thus perhaps not completely surprising that amongst the most radical proposals for debt or interest relief are those made by the Chairman of American Express and by the Managing Director of Deutsche Bank, both major financial institutions which are less vulnerable to such measures.

Opposition to debt relief for middle-income Latin American debtors by industrial governments is also being eroded, although it has by no means been eliminated. The Japanese government made a proposal in favour of debt reduction for middle-income debtors at a meeting of the Group of Seven (USA, UK, France, Italy, West Germany, Canada and Japan). This was the same meeting, in Toronto in June 1988, in which the G–7 had responded favourably to the 'Lawson initiative' on African debt. At the time, several members of the G–7, notably the USA, made it clear that they were not yet ready to adopt such a radical proposal for middle-income debtors in Latin America, but the Bush administration has shown itself much more sympathetic than its predecessor to innovations in managing the debt crisis. At the time of writing, no new initiative has yet been taken by the Bush government, but a thorough review of debt options has been launched and a new initiative is confidently expected early in the life of the new administration.

Undoubtedly, the need for more radical solutions will depend significantly on the evolution of the international economy, in particular on key variables such as commodity prices, international interest rates and new capital flows to Latin American economies. An important element in any equitable scheme for debt or interest relief would be to make it contingent on fluctuations in those key variables.

Some fairly small steps have clearly been taken which accept that Latin America's (and other LDCs') debt cannot be serviced in foreign exchange at 100 per cent of its value. This is shown by the growing number of debt–equity swaps, exit bonds (as in the Argentine case), debt–barter operations (such as the Peruvian government has negotiated with Midland Bank and with the Soviet Union) and debt–development swaps (such as Bolivia has done with environmental groups and such as UNICEF is trying to promote for low-income countries to enhance expenditure on vulnerable groups, particularly children).

Furthermore, in December 1987 the Mexican government announced a scheme whereby Mexico would buy – at discount – an important part of its debt. The scheme seemed to have received US government blessing, as US Treasury funds were part of the deal. Though of limited success, this initiative marks an important and operational step towards recognising that the value of the debt is below its face value and that therefore debt-servicing should reflect this. It was basically a Mexican–US initiative with inputs from the US banks, Morgan Guaranty (who advised on the scheme) and the US government, elaborating an idea already presented by the Mexican authorities in mid-1986.[10]

It should, however, be pointed out that British bankers have been contributing creatively to the debate on how to modify the present debt management strategy into a far more workable one. Especially important contributions have been made by David Suratgar, Director of Morgan Grenfell, Hervé de Carmoy, Chief Executive International at Midland UK and David Lomax, Group Economic Advisor of the National Westminster Bank.[11] The Lomax proposal is particularly interesting on two accounts: it is very similar to the procedure suggested by the Mexican government and it accepts that commercial banks will have to make important concessions.

The time is clearly ripe for new initiatives; in fact, new initiatives – à la Mexico – are clearly being taken. It seems important that the British government and British banks act in a way that accelerates the implementation of new initiatives and uses the opportunity to broaden links between the UK and Latin America.

In this context, an idea presented some time ago by a senior British banker, Peter Leslie,[12] could provide an interesting base for a British initiative. Leslie has suggested that parts of the bankers' medium-term LDC debt, which are 'immobilised' due to rescheduling or non-repayment, could be mobilised on the basis that the proceeds were used to create fresh lending. In the scheme there was a link with export credit, whereby the corresponding export credit agency or Central Bank would extend facilities to a bank for it to 'discount' a certain amount of a country's debt, provided that the bank then used the additional cash to make a new export credit to the same country. If the new loan was guaranteed by the government agency, it would make sense in the current circumstances for the 'old debt' to be bought at a discount by the export credit agency from the bank and for the agency to charge proportionally lower interest rates to the developing country for that 'old loan'. The new loan would be used – as normally export credit guarantee loans are – for the purchase of British goods and services. Such a scheme would have the virtue for the Latin American country of lowering the value and the debt-servicing of the 'old debt', while generating new credit to fund imports. (We are assuming that this credit would be additional and that the goods and services imported would be essential for development.) It would have the advantage for Britain of encouraging exports to a region where they have been depressed. Though obviously involving costs and problems, such a scheme (or some variation on it) could link a solution to the existing debt overhang to the broadening of British links to Latin America from purely financial ones into trade ones, and could free some additional resources within Latin America for increased involvement. More broadly, a British initiative (either unilaterally or jointly with other creditors), which both accepted the almost inevitable need for some concessionality or forgiveness for Latin American debt and promoted British trade interests, would encourage both in the UK and in Latin America the broadening of economic links (for example via direct foreign investment and aid), as well as improved political relations.

It is important to combine any initiative for debt relief explicitly with broader initiatives on the trade front (such as are discussed in chapter 6, pp. 111–12, above). There is clearly a large potential for enhancing the prospects for British exports in Latin America and financial measures (such as partial debt relief and/or increased trade finance) must be seen as only part of a broad package of measures.

On the financial side, British expertise and influence in international financial matters need to be applied to the search for alternative solutions in debt crisis management, which defend both the interests of creditor banks and governments as well as those of debtor economies. It is not just the potential for trade for Britain which should be considered, but also the role which Britain – and the EC – should play in encouraging sustained and democratic economic development in Latin America.

In the long term, lessons need finally to be learnt on unregulated lending to Latin America. The current debt crisis in Latin America is the fifth one in the last 150 years, involving British creditors in a major way; in all cases, the crises have been harmful to both creditors and debtors. Perhaps, in future, it would be convenient for the UK government (jointly with other industrial governments) to monitor and supervise more closely any major expansion of private credit to developing countries in general and to Latin America in particular. Inevitably in a financially interdependent world, governments will be forced to intervene as 'lenders of last resort' and put up their taxpayers' resources when serious debt crises occur (because stability of the international financial system is an important 'public good'); as they face the likelihood of such future interventions, governments should also have influence over the private decisions which will determine whether debt crises can in future be avoided.

Notes

1 For a more detailed discussion see, for example, S. Griffith-Jones and O. Sunkel, *The Crisis of Debt and Development in Latin America* (Oxford: Oxford University Press, 1986).
2 For detailed evidence see, for example, S. Griffith-Jones, M. Marcel and G. Palma, *Third World Debt and British Banks* (Fabian Society Working Paper, London, May 1987).
3 See M. Marcel and G. Palma, 'Third World debt and its effects on the financial and real sides of the British economy', *Cambridge Journal of Economics*, 12:3 (September 1988).
4 Quoted by D. Lascelles in 'How Midland was struck by a Californian earthquake' (*Financial Times*, 25 January 1988).
5 See, for example, S. Griffith-Jones (ed.), *Managing World Debt* (Brighton: Wheatsheaf and St Martin's Press, USA, 1988) and D. Lomax, *The Developing Country Debt Crisis* (London: Macmillan, 1986) for different perspectives.
6 All-Party Parliamentary Group on Overseas Development, *Managing Third World Debt* (London: Overseas Development Institute, 1987).
7 For detailed data see, for example, A. Cornia, F. Stewart and R. Jolly, *Adjustment with a Human Face* (Oxford: Oxford University Press, 1987); Inter-American Development Bank, *Annual Report 1985* (Washington, DC); and Griffith-Jones and Sunkel, *Crisis of Debt and Development*.
8 See Griffith-Jones, Marcel and Palma, *Third World Debt*, p. 77.
9 *Ibid.*, pp. 78–9.
10 For details see the chapter by A. Gurria, 'Debt restructuring: Mexico as a case-study', in Griffith-Jones (ed.), *Managing World Debt*.
11 For a clear description and evaluation of their ideas, the reader is referred to a paper by B. Snoy, 'European perspectives on the Third World debt problem', presented at the Overseas Development Institute Conference on Economic Prospects for the Third World, Brussels, October 1987.
12 P. Leslie, 'Techniques of rescheduling: the latest lessons', *The Banker*, April 1983.

8 Britain and Latin America: oil and minerals

George Philip

'Latin America is the region of the future', goes the old joke, 'and always will be.' A similar idea is contained in the old description of Peru (or Bolivia or at other times even Mexico) as 'a beggar sitting on a throne of gold'. Latin America is almost the living proof of the proposition that resource wealth does not necessarily produce economic wealth. Meanwhile, at the same level of semi-caricature, Britain is in many ways a society which has lost interest in the Third World, focusing politically on NATO and Europe and commercially on 'sunrise' industries and financial services rather than 'metal bashing'. Inner cities count for more in official thinking than ex-colonies and ex-colonies for more than other parts of the Third World.

This relative lack of interest may change considerably in the medium term. As for the present, quantification of British interest is difficult. Figures on British oil and mineral imports from Latin America are set out below (see Table 8.1); they were, of course, compiled at a time of low prices for most minerals. Direct foreign investment figures are not readily available, but the picture is probably also one of slow increase from a very low base.

The history

Although Latin America in terms of minerals has rarely been as central to British concerns as the Middle East and Southern Africa, there have been important connections. During the Second World War, Venezuelan oil supplies to Britain were vital. During the First World War Mexican oil, if not perhaps quite so crucial, was still of great importance; Mexican oil also provided the basis of the Cowdray fortune. It is also true that mineral, and above all oil, wealth was the major focus of British foreign-policy interest in some of the South American republics up until the outbreak of the Second World War.

Early British interests were far more concerned with oil than with minerals. (Oil could not be found in sufficient quantity within the British Empire; there was no such problem with most minerals.) Weetman Pearson and the Royal Dutch Shell Company both entered Latin America, in Mexico and Venezuela respectively, before 1914. There was, in fact, considerable Anglo-US rivalry over Latin American oil up until the mid-1920s. This reflected in part British

Table 8.1. *British imports of oil and minerals from main Latin American countries,*
1985

	£ million
Venezuela	
Petroleum and petroleum products	210
Iron ore	22
Mexico[a]	
Petroleum and petroleum products	129
Non-ferrous metals	9
Metal ores and scrap	4
Peru	
Non-ferrous metals	79
Metal ores and scrap	13
Brazil	
Metal ores	59
Chile	
Non-ferrous metals	56
Metal ores and scrap	15
Panama	
Petroleum and petroleum products	10
Bolivia	
Non-ferrous metals	9
Metal ores and scrap	5
(Imports from Colombia, Cuba etc. are negligible.)	

[a] Figures for Mexico are for 1984.
Source: Lloyds Bank, *Economic Reports.*

efforts to keep the United States out of the Middle East and also, to a point, US fears of oil scarcity which were alleviated only by the East Texas discoveries of the mid-1920s. On the whole, the United States had the better of such conflict as there was; it encouraged various Latin American countries to keep out the Anglo-Persian Oil Company (which was vulnerable to this pressure because of the direct British-government shareholding) and also made it difficult for Pearson to extend his interests beyond Mexico; British Petroleum (BP), on the other hand, has never had a Latin American involvement in any way commensurate with its role in the Middle East, the North Sea or the United States. Yet, while their governments considered themselves involved in rivalry, the oil companies mostly did business; Lord Cowdray came close in 1916 to selling his entire Mexican holdings to Jersey Standard. Meanwhile, some smaller British companies (such as Anglo-Ecuadorian and Lobitos in Peru) carved out limited pockets for themselves in places where they were to have a long, if unspectacular, history (Clyde Petroleum, eventual heir to Anglo-Ecuadorian, still operates on the Ecuadorian coast).

As early as the mid-1920s many of the contours of the modern Latin American oil industry were already in place. Venezuela and Mexico had become the main exporters – although Mexican production was in decline from its first peak. Colombia, Peru and Ecuador had a limited export trade while Chile, Argentina and Brazil were substantial importers. There have, of course, been some important developments since then, although two of these (the huge discoveries in South-east Mexico in the 1970s and the significant offshore finds in Brazil) have been carried out by state companies.

In any case British capital was soon dwarfed by the magnitude of first US, and later Latin American state, capital. By 1939 Jersey Standard had overtaken Shell as the major investor in Venezuela and all foreign oil companies in Mexico had been expropriated. In the years after the Second World War, moreover, fresh British investment in Latin America (a dollar area) was discouraged and some existing holdings liquidated. Middle Eastern oil was in any case being developed on an increasing scale, eventually dwarfing supplies from Latin America. Middle Eastern oil also began to displace Venezuelan oil in British markets and by 1970 this process was virtually complete. In Latin America itself, state companies began to take an increasing part of the industry; Petrobras was formed in Brazil in 1953 and, as we shall see below, a series of nationalisations during the decade 1968–77 extended state control throughout the Latin American resource sector. The nationalisation of Shell in Venezuela at the end of 1975 removed the last great block of (at any rate part) British-owned capital from the Latin American oil industry.

Latin American resources, politics and policymaking

Although British interests in Latin American oil and mineral resources (referred to from now on just as 'resources') will never again approach the importance which they had during the years 1910–30, significant opportunities are once again opening up. It is scarcely in dispute that Latin America still has vast mineral potential. To take some examples, only around 5 per cent of Mexico's land mass has been properly prospected for minerals; Ecuador has barely been explored for minerals at all; Brazil, Venezuela and Bolivia have promising and barely prospected areas; Chile has around 40 per cent of the world's lithium reserves, barely tapped; Cuba has the world's largest reserves of nickel. Indeed, virtually every Latin American country has untapped mineral resources and, perhaps more important still, technological progress is likely to increase the viability of existing resources which now appear uneconomic.

Development of these resources has been held back by infrastructural limitations (some of which are now being overcome), by government suspicions of foreign companies, and, until recently, by a slump in world markets. As far as Britain has been concerned, Australia, North America and South Africa have tended to be more attractive locations for investment, although the need to insure against major upheaval in South Africa is now playing an increasing part in company calculations.

Energy resources are in a different category. High international prices during the years 1973–85 led to a revival in official and (to a lesser extent) company interest in Latin America. In the mid-1970s there was a considerable debate about the 'ultimately recoverable' reserves of oil and gas in Latin America. Several estimates indicated that around 15–20 per cent of Latin America's ultimately recoverable level of oil reserves had been discovered by the late 1970s (a figure which partly, but not fully, includes recent discoveries in Mexico). Latin American governments themselves invested heavily in various forms of energy development – including such imaginative, but high-cost, programmes as Brazilian alcohol which seemed a good idea at the time, but may appear in retrospect as a major drain on resources. (The same point may be made, *a fortiori*, about nuclear energy.) There has also been a major move, within the Latin American economies, into hydroelectricity. According to the Inter-American Development Bank (IDB), the share of petroleum in the total Latin American energy supply fell from 76 per cent in 1972 to 53 per cent in 1986.[1] Hydroelectric, coal and natural gas projects already under construction will ensure that this trend continues. Hydroelectricity has taken most of the space left by reduced dependence on petroleum, but the relative importance of natural gas has been increasing and this trend will continue. Technical advances in the field of producing electricity from gas would therefore have a very considerable impact in Latin America.

By far the main tradeable energy sector, however, is oil. Until 1981 it was possible for Latin American exporters to sell all of the oil they could produce; the heady atmosphere encouraged extensive exploration and development work with dramatic consequences for the Mexican oil industry and more limited increases in reserves in several other countries. (Colombia became a net exporter of oil during the 1960s; Peru and Ecuador, like Mexico, made the transition during the 1970s.) Later, however, the international market imposed its constraints; since 1983 the main exporters have been restricted by quotas either imposed by OPEC or self-imposed (although Ecuador, unlike Venezuela, has made no real effort to comply with its OPEC quota allocation) and since early 1986 low international prices have cut directly into the attractiveness of further oil investment. Certainly state oil companies, often carrying debt burdens or facing funding difficulties, have had to cut back exploration activity, although more slowly and by less than several ministries have wished; reductions in private sector activity have also been evident, although lower drilling costs have partly offset lower exploration budgets.

Within Latin America as a whole, exploration results have inevitably been mixed. On the one hand the Argentine offshore, once believed by some geologists to contain promise of vast discoveries, has not yielded much so far. On the other, exploration in Venezuela, Colombia, Ecuador and offshore Brazil has been very promising; only in the last of these cases is the development cost of new oil unlikely to exceed the international price level. It has also become clear that several Latin American countries have vast natural gas potential, although only Chile, with a methanol plant at Cabo Negro, has adopted expensive liquifying technology; almost all commercially used natural gas is carried by pipeline, which imposes obvious locational constraints. Another important recent development has been the apparent discovery by the Venezuelan authorities that a significant proportion of their Orinoco oil reserves can be extracted for use as fuel oil far more cheaply than had once been envisaged.

If resources are not much of a constraint on Latin American production, political factors have tended to be more serious. Many observers have commented on the generally negative attitudes of many political leaders toward direct foreign investment in resource industries. Although British companies have not had to put up with the specific hazard of anti-US feeling, the general political climate has tended to persuade most foreign companies to apply a heavy discount to their ventures in Latin America. Specifically, the 1968–76 period saw a great wave of resource nationalisations. It began with the attempted confiscation of the International Petroleum Company (IPC) in Peru (where the general unfriendliness of the Velasco government persuaded the British-owned Lobitos oil company to sell out in 1973), continued with the expropriation of Gulf Oil in Bolivia in 1969 and Allende's nationalisation of Chilean copper in 1971. There was then the partial oil nationalisation in Ecuador (with Gulf selling, but Texaco remaining), the takeovers of Cerro de Pasco and Marcona in Peru and the full-scale nationalisation of oil and iron ore in Venezuela in 1975–6.

Some of these nationalisations appeared surprising and irrational; others were long-expected and even anticipated. Cumulatively, however, they greatly reduced the amount of foreign investment in Latin American oil and minerals. Although this kind of expropriation is often seen as resulting from a kind of economically short-sighted and volatile populism, the impact of popular pressure can easily be exaggerated. Emotive attacks on foreign oil or mineral companies may have a nuisance value, but should not be taken too seriously. While economic nationalism is rarely actually unpopular, I see no reason to depart from my earlier conclusion that mass opinion played a very subordinate part in these events.[2] What was generally crucial was the desire of various Latin American governments for control over what they regarded as strategic resources and the arrival of an opportunity to exert this control at low or moderate cost. Once the foreign investment exceeds a certain threshold of size and the local state acquires a certain administrative competence, it is virtually certain that the state will make a serious effort to gain control. This does not necessarily rule out foreign investment in any absolute sense, but foreign companies in over-dominant positions are unlikely to be welcome. A low political profile is a great advantage to all foreign companies operating in Latin America. It should, however, be noted that many of the nationalisations referred to above were of companies which had been operating locally since the 1920s or even before; even the most successful foreign company is unlikely to be in a position to remain *in situ* for ever.

Of course, apart from what might be termed official political problems, resource companies, often operating in remote locations, have to contend with terrorist or ordinary kidnappings and other hazards. In Peru and Colombia, in particular, the situation if anything appears to be deteriorating and this must be a factor in company considerations. Nevertheless it is certainly possible to exaggerate the element of political risk in Latin America. There is nothing to compare with the dangers associated with Southern Africa or the Middle East. In any case, as various Latin American republics manage their transition toward full popular democracy, so the likelihood of major political upheaval or arbitrary policy change is reduced.

As an alternative to foreign investment, Latin American governments – particularly during the 1970s – tended to prefer packages of foreign finance and technology either put together by themselves or, more generally, on a turnkey basis. This has tended to lead to both over-investment and over-borrowing. IDB figures (from the 1987 annual report) suggest that energy-related investments in Latin America increased from 9 to 20 per cent as a proportion of gross domestic investment between 1974 and 1984; between 1974 and 1982 the increase, as a proportion of total public investment, was from 24 to 50 per cent. A major part of foreign debt increases in Brazil, Colombia and Guatemala can be accounted for by investment in electric power projects; the relationship between oil investment and debt in Venezuela and Mexico is apparent; state investment throughout the region in metal mining and processing was also considerable.

What has happened, in fact, is that giant state companies have established themselves in the main Latin American resource industries. In virtually every Latin American country with a significant resources sector, a state oil or mineral company is the largest business enterprise in the local economy; often the largest two or three companies are all state-owned resource-based firms. Moreover Pemex in Mexico, PDVSA in Venezuela and Petrobras in Brazil are huge companies by any international standard – each normally in the *Fortune* top fifty non-US companies. The existence of these companies has greatly changed the business environment in Latin America.

A third general feature of Latin American policy-making, until quite recently, has been a dislike of becoming too dependent on exports of primary products. Economic technocrats have instead tended to prefer the idea of industrial development geared to their home market with limited balance of payments savings from import substitution. In fact, between 1945 and the early 1980s, Latin America's share of world trade fell consistently; it would have fallen still more, had it not been for the increase in world oil prices in the 1970s and the re-emergence of Mexico as an oil exporter.

This pattern – state control, reliance on indirect 'packages' rather than direct foreign investment and a relative lack of interest in exports of primary products – did not prevent many Latin American countries from enjoying an apparently successful period of economic progress up until 1980. What was crucial was the ability of these various countries to run up considerable foreign debts. Foreign borrowing, which throughout the 1970s could be undertaken with few constraints and at negative real rates of interest in a generally inflationary environment, enabled Latin American governments to run current-account deficits, finance nationalisations, attract packages of foreign finance and technology, achieve reasonable or even rapid rates of growth and feel in control of their economic strategies. Although policy obviously varied considerably between countries, the availability of easy money offered temptations which were not generally resisted; only in hindsight did the pattern of growth chosen seem damaging.

It is not being suggested here that all, or even most, of the projects undertaken during this period were worthless or wasted, but recent Latin American experience has established a clear relationship between authoritarian government and a propensity to engage in giant, spectacular projects which rarely manage to come off as expected; a 'small is beautiful' reaction is long overdue in many Latin American countries. Moreover, at least some economists have concluded that the happier developmental experiences of most ASEAN countries by comparison with Latin America have much to do with the relative preference of the former for acquiring foreign exchange through exporting rather than borrowing, and with their relatively greater respect for competitive markets.

In any case, whatever conclusions may be drawn from history, it is now obvious that no strategy of 'development through borrowing' can work in Latin America for many years to come; new ideas, although at different speeds in different countries, are now being adopted. A general conclusion seems to be that Latin America's growth potential will, once more, be determined largely by the rate of growth of its exports. Even if one avoids the more pessimistic predictions about imminent slump, the outlook for world trade as a whole is not particularly encouraging. If it is to do even reasonably well, Latin America will have to increase its exports by more than the world average. Some of the things which it has to sell are minerals and hydrocarbons.

This change of direction is not likely to lead Latin American economies back to the *laissez-faire* days of the 1920s. What is happening instead is a much more subtle rebalancing of forces as governments seek to set their political obligations and constraints off against their economic strategies. Moreover, political constraints are more than usually unclear in that many South American countries are still facing the after-effects of a transition from military dictatorship to a more open pattern of politics.

Most pro-market Latin American political leaders appear to want *both* more private investment *and* a continuation of the power of state companies. This has sometimes (as recently in Brazil) led to some apparent inconsistencies in policy. In the longer term, what is likely to be important is that major sections of the Latin American bourgeoisie itself have swung heavily in favour of attracting foreign investment. Evidence of such investment will help give the local private sector some of the confidence which it will need if it is to invest on a significant scale itself.

There is little doubt that exporting as such is taking on a much higher priority with Latin American governments than it did before the debt crisis and there is much less interest in various forms of cartel agreement. Instead the Chilean copper industry, the Brazilian tin industry, the Venezuelan and Brazilian aluminium industries and the Brazilian iron and steel industry have moved aggressively into exporting, seeking to increase market share at a time of low world prices. Many of these are low-cost producers, who will stand to gain considerably if they can force their rivals to cut back. The Brazilian tin industry played a major part in the collapse of the International Tin Cartel and can still produce profitably at the lower world prices. Colombian coal has also been aggressively priced. The oil exporters have moved in a similar way. Mexico has relaxed its support for OPEC, Ecuador has more or less ended its co-operation with it and Venezuela, formally the most loyal, has looked for ways of bypassing it.

Also of great commercial importance is the fact that a number of Latin American state companies are moving downstream into international markets; PDVSA has so far been the most notable of the Latin American companies and has gone into direct equity-sharing ventures in West Germany, Sweden and the United States. Alcasa of Venezuela has also moved into the Belgian aluminium market. Pemex has moved downstream into a venture in Spain, while Petrobras is also extremely active internationally through its subsidiaries Braspetro and Interbras. No Latin American producer has yet been as audacious as Kuwait with its shareholding in BP, but the 'reversal of history', with resource-based state companies from the Third World (or ex-Third World) moving directly into consumer's markets, still has a great deal further to go. There are many implications here. Some senior executives in certain state companies have in fact expressed concern that excessive 'virility' (or at any rate nationalist) considerations might lead to inappropriate investment in the USA or Western Europe.[3] (By the same token, some European and US concerns have been keen to dispose of 'lame duck' industries in this way – much as Britain once sold the Argentine railways to Perón.) Behind this, two considerations spring immediately to mind. On the one hand, reciprocity considerations may give a degree of protection to British companies operating in Latin America since the British government is reasonably friendly to inward direct investment. On the other, foreign companies which in their own countries have worked against Venezuelan interests in ways of which some powerful Venezuelans have disapproved have been subjected to strong and at times irresponsible attack by Venezuelan politicians in Venezuela. There is not much redress.

A final consideration is that heavy investment in hydroelectric projects has given several Latin American countries – most obviously, but by no means only, Venezuela and Brazil – huge power-generating potential and therefore a considerable competitive advantage in metal-smelting industries. An obvious growth area during the 1990s will emerge from a combination of local raw material, cheap hydroelectricity and foreign loans tied, in many cases, to promised access to the market of an industrialised country.

British opportunities

As we have seen, British involvement with Latin American resources has been reduced by a number of considerations. Latin American nationalism, the conflict in the South Atlantic, the development of North Sea oil and the slump in mineral prices in the early 1980s were all factors. Here the contrast with Japan is instructive. Japan has been becoming more, rather than less, dependent on imported resources; it has also been the fastest-growing of the main industrialised countries. The Japanese have not had a history of large-scale direct investment in Latin America and have been willing to look more flexibly at different equity and financing packages than have Britain or the USA. With their own pollution problems and balance of payments surplus in mind, they have been very willing to invest in resource-transforming activities *in situ*. Moreover, their ability to co-ordinate the resources of their public and private sectors is legendary. All in all, their needs provide a much better 'fit' with what Latin American governments want than do Britain's.

On the other hand, Latin America may become more important to British interests than it has been in the recent past. Before the turn of the century, Britain is once again likely to become a significant importer of oil; with political conditions in the Middle East unlikely to become any easier, there may be value in assuring supplies from one or more of the Latin American exporters. An obvious way to do this is to encourage Pemex, PDVSA or by then perhaps even Ecopetrol in Ecuador to buy into a British-based refining and distribution network. Secondly, if violent revolution really does come to South Africa, Latin American countries will be in an obviously attractive position in respect of most (though not all) minerals currently supplied by South Africa.

Apart from these political contingencies, there are more commercial considerations. If we can find a way of encouraging Latin America to sell to us, there are a number of reciprocal advantages which we can expect. These relationships will necessarily be more complex than was the case in the past when wholly foreign-owned companies dealt at arm's length with a tax-collecting state and an unambitious local bourgeoisie.

The only way to prosper in Latin American markets is by working with, rather than against, the powerful state companies that dominate the main resource sectors. An example of co-operation that has proved successful in a small way is that between Britoil and Petrobras; Britoil (now BP) has a minority stake in an exploration bloc in Ecuador which Petrobras is operating. This connection surely helped Weir Pumps of Glasgow to develop a joint research project with Petrobras. Indeed a joint venture with one state company is often something of a passport into 'third' Latin American countries. Occidental Petroleum developed a lucrative partnership with Bridas of Argentina, which helped it to win a big secondary recovery contract in Peru in the late 1970s. Once a partnership has been developed, there may be a variety of interesting spin-offs. Moreover, with the most sophisticated Latin American companies, 'technology transfer' need not be considered necessarily as only one-way; British companies may have things to learn as well as teach.

Direct investment also provides its opportunities, although the most successful companies have needed to prove their ability to survive a hard time. Cowdray had a difficult time in Mexico – it almost bankrupted him – before he emerged triumphantly after 1915. More contemporary examples include Texaco, which held out during a difficult time in Ecuador (sufficiently difficult to prompt its partner, Gulf, to demand its own nationalisation at the end of 1976) and later found itself the chief beneficiary when the political tide turned away from oil nationalism. Occidental Petroleum has made a very good return from Peru despite having to deal with difficult political and geological conditions.

Occidental's success warrants a little more examination. Armand Hammer runs a secretive company; his executives are formally forbidden to make any kind of political statement when in his employ. A very low profile is therefore kept. Hammer himself is a master diplomat; he relishes political difficulty and makes a point of telling Third World nationalists that he once did business successfully with Lenin. In terms of bargaining strategy, Occidental in Peru has always been careful not to reject any government plan or initiative out of hand, always putting forward counter-proposals if it found existing measures unacceptable. Nothing negative found its way into the newspapers even when Occidental felt frustrated. Occidental also offered a range of services, some of which were plainly sweeteners for the Peruvian government. At the same time the company was careful to invest only the minimum and offered to re-invest (in a fanfare of publicity) only after it had amortised its existing investments. The Peruvian government was invited to build the infrastructure (including the pipelines to take Occidental's oil to the coast). Subsequently, when Occidental needed something, it offered to step up its investments if it was made worth the company's while. Armed with these tactics, Occidental entered Peru under Valesco, prospered under Morales Bermúdez and Belaúnde, and appears to have survived under Alan García (which another US-owned oil company, Belco Petroleum, has not).

Foreign companies can insure themselves in mineral ventures more easily than in oil exploration by tying themselves directly to local private capital. It is generally recognised that local capital offers a degree of political insurance and it can play an active part in all but very large ventures. Local capitalists generally react positively to this kind of venture and have a domestic political weight that foreigners obviously lack. Joint ventures of this kind are often required by law in Latin American countries; even when they are not obligatory, they are often to be recommended.

It is noteworthy that there is British interest in some of the most actively prospected ventures currently being undertaken in Latin America. Rio Tinto Zinc has a 30 per cent stake in the huge La Escondida copper development in Chile, where Northern Strip Mining has a share in developing the Pecket coal deposits. Shell is heavily involved in developing the Caño Limón field in

Colombia. British Petroleum has already achieved some exploration success behind the Ecuadorian Andes. Smaller British companies have also involved themselves in gold prospecting in Venezuela and there is a variety of British interests involved in the Brazilian mineral sector.

A word of caution is perhaps in order here. Foreign companies, notoriously, tend to hunt in packs. Typically there is a 'rush' into an area which has the effect of convincing the host government that it has more foreign investment than it needs (or that the original terms under which the companies came were too generous, or at any rate that it can afford to bargain more toughly in future). This leads to something of a backlash; the host government becomes more involved and demanding and the less motivated or less successful companies withdraw or at least scale down their operations. (Geological disappointment may also be a factor here.) Companies which then maintain a presence in the third stage (when some of their rivals have gone and the government begins to regret their departure) are the most likely to enjoy a worthwhile return.

There is a sense in which British companies may acquire interests in Latin America if not exactly in a fit of absent-mindedness then at least as a by-product of other activities. With the dollar weak and the US emerging as a major debtor, British companies have been busily extending their holdings of US concerns. Since US direct investment in Latin America is vastly greater than Britain's, the purchase of the one may involve expanding their investment in the other. Mineração in Brazil, one of BP's most profitable mineral operations in Latin America, was acquired along with Sohio. This kind of commitment can be expected to increase.

On the consortium/package side, British companies have tended to find Latin American projects unrewarding even when they appeared to have a chance of the contract. It is notable that BP decided not to bid seriously on either of the two important recent coal projects – El Cerrejón and Zulia. The Cerrejón project is particularly interesting both because of its size and because Colombia is generally regarded as one of the most open and least nationalist of all the larger Latin American countries. There are two points worth making here.[4] The first is that Exxon's success in north Cerrejón owed a great deal to its long tradition of operation within Colombia and the contacts which it had thereby built up. An outsider would have found it very hard to break in. The second is that north Cerrejón, since coming onstream in 1986, has been trading at a loss. (Central Cerrejón failed outright before coming to market after heavy losses were made at the development stage.) The main reason for this is that international energy prices are much lower than was projected in the late 1970s and early 1980s when the decision was taken to go ahead. However, in a competitive market with a variety of possibly interested companies, it is likely that at least one competitor will prove to be an optimist and will bid accordingly. There is no reason to undertake projects in Latin America merely for the sake of doing so.

Conclusion

In many ways, Britain's major role in developing Latin America's natural resources belongs to the past and not the future. Nevertheless, the pendulum has swung too far – from heavy involvement to excessive detachment. In the ordinary course of events, some increase is likely in British trade with and investment in (and also inward investment from) Latin America in the oil and mineral sectors.

One thing that needs to be considered is whether this 'natural' and limited increase in trade and investment is seriously sub-optimal from a national point of view. There are things which a British government could do to increase involvement in Latin American oil and minerals sectors; the question is, should it do them?

Oil and minerals probably do not, on their own, justify a greatly increased level of official concern; if countries other than Britain choose for security reasons to invest heavily in non-Middle Eastern oil and non-South African minerals, then so much the better for us. This may, however, be an area in which other problems could be dealt with; in particular the British government may usefully follow the Japanese in establishing a direct mechanism by which bankers with more exposure to Latin America than they would wish could be introduced to would-be direct investors in Latin America. There may even be some point in a limited official subsidy (if only to reduce the cost to the Exchequer of tax write-offs). If US and Japanese banks prove more successful in selling debt for equity than are British banks, then Britain's relative position will be more diifficult in a subsequent default. The really big direct investments are normally in oil and mineral ventures.

The main implications of this chapter, however, should perhaps be directed more to the private sector than to government. British companies thinking of buying US companies with Latin American holdings will need to acquire some expertise on Latin America unless they wish to be wholly at the mercy of their local US management. Companies dealing with Interbras, PDVSA or other Latin American foreign investors will also have to know something of the political climate in their respective countries and the political problems with which they have to deal. Companies involved in energy and minerals outside Latin America will need to consider to what extent changes in that area will have repercussions in world markets as a whole.

Notes

1 See Inter-American Development Bank, *Annual Report* (Washington, DC: 1987).
2 See George Philip, *Oil and Politics in Latin America: Nationalist Movements and State Companies* (Cambridge: Cambridge University Press, 1982), especially chapter 16.
3 This point was expressed by a top Pemex executive in discussion with me.
4 For a discussion of the Cerrejón project see H. Kline, *The Coal of El Cerrejón: Dependent Bargaining and Colombian Policy-Making* (University Park and London: Pennsylvania State University Press, 1987).

Part III
Sources of friction

9 Further forward thoughts on the Falklands

Malcolm Deas

A book on British relations with Latin America cannot avoid addressing the Falklands question directly. It may become wearisome to revisit themes that became over-familiar in 1982 and 1983, but we have to remind ourselves that this spectacular breakdown in our relations with a major Latin American republic came about in some small part through British failures and through a change in Britain's position in the region. The failures can be recalled by a simple list: the eyes not on the ball, 'Micawberism', the 'wrong signals', the reluctance of frontbenchers in the major parties to grasp a minor but thorny issue, the assumption that our order of priorities would somehow always prevail, a forgetfulness about anniversaries ... The best analysis that has been attempted since the war has been Michael Charlton's radio series, *Little Platoon*, which surely deserves to be published before general oblivion descends.[1] The change in Britain's position to which I refer is simply stated, though often overlooked. Though it was concerns of naval strategy and British naval supremacy that established us in the Islands in the first place, both briefly and partially in the years 1765–74, and finally in 1833, it was surely Britain's importance to Argentina (as trading-partner and investor) that played, along with the Royal Navy, a major role in ensuring that this peculiar and long-running dispute was for nearly 150 years peacefully conducted. It was not in Argentina's interest to sharpen it over-much. Since the Second World War those interests which weighed against the more forceful pressing of their claim were progressively weakened.

There is an additional consideration relevant here. Britain's 'historic presence' in Latin America since Independence was certainly sizeable, but it differed from our more directly imperial historic presence elsewhere in the world – in Africa, India and the Far East. It was more individual, unofficial, and the number of Britons involved even at the height of British influence was never large. It has left little official or corporate memory, no informal body of opinion, no informed sensibility behind in this country. This seems to me as true about Argentina, the republic where the old connections were closest, as it is about countries where our historic presence was much less evident. One *cri de cœur* of an Argentine negotiator comes back to mind: 'You wouldn't treat an African country like this.' There are, as far as I know, no African parallels to the Falklands issue, but one still has an idea what he meant: we have had African policies, African priorities;

we have been acutely aware of African sensibilities; African issues have concerned and still concern large numbers of people here, though their numbers have fallen and may fall further. Interest in Latin American issues is, in every sense of the word, thinner.

I would not of course argue that the Argentine invasion of the Islands was the inevitable result of the decline of the old relationship – it was the product of internal Argentine dynamics and miscalculations far more complex – but it would be hard to design an event that so clearly demonstrated the limitations of a certain sort of sentimentality. Its aftermath does pose a large problem for British policy in Latin America. Argentina must still be on any list of the half-dozen 'major' states of the region, and our relations with Argentina cannot be relegated to the status of a complicating factor in the future of British Antarctica or of fishing protection in the South Atlantic. We are in duty bound to attempt some forward thoughts on the Falklands/Malvinas question. This chapter does not attempt to explore every nuance of what has passed since 1982; what follows may be crude. It is perhaps none the worse for that, as the subject holds out many temptations towards unreal finessing. It will consider how British and Argentine policy and opinion have evolved since 1982, how they are likely to evolve in the foreseeable future and how much the Falklands/Malvinas may affect our relations with the rest of Latin America and with the United States. It will also speculate on developments in the Islands themselves.

We are all familiar with the evolution of British policy since 1982. Mrs Thatcher's government has reiterated its support for the principle of self-determination in the Islands: she has done so herself, so has the British Foreign Secretary, Sir Geoffrey Howe, and so have successive British representatives of the United Nations. It is salutary to remind oneself of this fact, repeatedly recorded in the *British Yearbook of International Law*'s résumé of the government's statements on matters of international law, when one is tempted down the superficially attractive solutions offered by Sir Ian Sinclair's rather awkward wrestlings with the Nootka Sound Convention of 1790, and other details of the Islands' history prior to 1833. Though it is still impossible in United Nations debates for our arguments to skate entirely over former territorial claims, the emphasis is now heavily on the 'inalienable right' of self-determination. Nothing much has changed in the contrast between British and Argentine arguments in the field of international law since in 1968 Professor H. S. Ferns pointed to the contrast between 'ignorance, patriotism and devotion to the dogma of self-determination on the part of the British' and 'legal pedantry' on the Argentine side.[2] Those who recall the arguments between the 'wishes' and the 'interests' of the Islanders at the time of the conflict in 1982 may care to note the ingenious amalgamation of the two made by Sir John Thompson, the British ambassador to the UN, in the UN debate that followed the war:

> Their interests are paramount and they are of course the best judges of their own interests. That is one reason why my government attaches so much importance to their wishes.[3]

Though some attention was drawn during the war to the history of the dispute – Yale University Press republished J. Goebel's 1927 study, *The Struggle for the Falkland Islands*, though Oxford University Press refused to republish V. Boyson's *The Falkland Islands* of 1924, still an indispensable work, and the House of Commons Committee on Foreign Affairs spent a day on the history too and reported itself puzzled[4] – it cannot be said that this had any marked effect on either official statements (which would be most unlikely, as no state ever expresses doubts about the solidity of its titles to territory) or on the writing of British 'publicists' for want of a better word, who continue to treat historical-legal arguments in a cavalier fashion.[5] A perhaps predictable feature of the war and its aftermath was the near-universal silence of British international lawyers on the matter of the conflicting claims to sovereignty, as if there was in the air some *sub judice* rule: for various reasons, they have to be very careful what they say. The British consequently remain almost as unfamiliar as before with the sort of legal arguments by which these disputes are conducted. The list of post-imperial territorial questions in which we are still involved is short; it is officially given as:

British Antarctic Territory
Belize
Indian Ocean Territory
Falkland Islands
Falkland Islands Dependencies
Hong Kong
Gibraltar.[6]

Belize is quiescent – for different reasons our presence is welcome there to almost everybody around – and the case of Hong Kong has been decided. The Indian Ocean Territory includes Diego Garcia, an island that figures in Falklands arguments, but is not of much pedagogic help. There is little chance that 'legal pedantry' will make greater inroads here: Argentina will continue to employ arguments of a type that are widely understood and command much support in Latin America and in countries of a similar international law tradition, but which will remain unfamiliar even to educated British minds. So much the worse for 'legal pedantry', which, though it is very much present in the origins of such disputes as this one, rarely has as much to contribute to their solution.

Be that as it may, British policy has based itself on self-determination and we have refused to discuss the question of sovereignty with Argentina. Judged from a fair distance, our diplomacy has been soft-spoken, low-key, skilful within this limitation. It was not the British who looked hasty or obstinate at the negotiations in Berne after the war, though they may have looked rigid; it was Dr Alfonsín who at his first UN appearance laid down a palpably unreasonable calendar of desired progress. On economic and financial matters in international fora we have been scrupulously co-operative. Stressing heavily the word 'interim', and even more heavily the word 'conservation', we have successfully established the fishing zone around the Islands. Some argued that it would have been more prudent, more desirable to work more patiently for a multilateral agreement under international auspices, and the move did produce a small storm in Buenos Aires and a declaration of disapproval in the Organization of American States (OAS) with which the United States concurred. But the small storm was weathered and the interim zone does not preclude future multilateral arrangements. In Washington, 'non-papers' have been exchanged between Britain and Argentina about fish. The issue of fish has been skilfully managed and this success has some further implications, but it is not clear that fish-management provides a model for anything else or that 'non-papers' are likely to be exchanged on other subjects.

We will uphold the right to self-determination of the Islanders. We will conserve fish and thereby increase the revenue of the Islands. We also intend to reduce the level of the garrison on the Islands. This was, of course, the object of Operation 'Fire-Focus' in 1988, which was used to practise the rapid deployment of British troops to the South Atlantic. The declaration of the fishing zone, long delayed and carefully worded, showed awareness of Argentine sensibilities. Operation 'Fire-Focus' showed no awareness of anyone's sensibilities and is a prime example of that pig-headed British refusal to imagine that anyone could conceivably doubt that our motives are exactly what we say they are – no more, no less. It is inevitable that troops will have exercises – the British army with its heavily paternalist traditions will go to any lengths to save the men from boredom and lassitude, which must be an ever-present threat in the Falklands now that there is not much bulldozing and building left to do – and it is no doubt necessary that the arrangements for a rapid reinforcement of the garrison should be tested. This could certainly have been done in a more suave fashion, however, and it would have been better done in a more suave fashion. The argument of Andrew McEwen in *The Times* (5 March 1988), on the contrary, favours maximum bluster:

> If the British government wants to be taken seriously in Buenos Aires, it is vital that it should not be put off by the extraordinary effort Latin America is making to get [Fire-Focus] cancelled, postponed or scaled down.

Once the military exercise had been announced, it was no doubt best to go ahead, but 'Fire-Focus diplomacy', as recommended by Mr McEwen, has costs that go beyond the cancellation (as happened in 1988) of a British junior minister's planned visit to Brazil. Better presented, the same operation could have been carried out and its intention better explained elsewhere in Latin America, while being less easily exploited in certain Argentine quarters.[7]

The issues of fish and defence may have been handled rather differently, but they have one thing in common: their needs are unpredictable. The technical reports hint at an element of uncertainty in the future of this fishery. Dr Peter Willett's *Fishing in the South West Atlantic* (South Atlantic Council Occasional Paper no. 4, March 1988) concludes that 'the current fishing zone provides an unsatisfactory answer to the conservation problems': he quotes the Food and Agriculture Organisation (FAO) study that it is not possible in any British fishing zone to guarantee effective conservation measures: 'an adequate management of the shortfin squid stock will require the collaboration and some kind of understanding with the states fishing in the adjacent area'. Squid are the most valuable catch, a 'hard currency' fish, but they come and go across maritime boundaries. This is not to deny their present importance as a source of revenue; they are also a new element of diplomatic leverage.

As for defence, the strategic significance of the Islands has been changed from near-zero by the construction of the airport, now a prominent feature on any strategist's map of the region. The defence of the Islands remains expensive, an inconvenient drain on resources that even Lord Shackleton's high prediction of fish-revenue – £50 million compared to actual receipts of £13.5 million in 1987 – would come nowhere near balancing. It is all the more necessary to reduce the garrison, since now there is less to do the posting is even less popular than immediately after the war. Given the needs of refit and relief, the naval commitment is a multiple of the ships on station. A succinct review of the defence position is given in General Sir Hugh Beach's *British Defence Policy and the South Atlantic* (South Atlantic Council Occasional Paper no. 2, May 1986). General Beach's dispassionate survey does not quarrel with the arrangements that have been made – 'the key to success is the capability for rapid reinforcement in an emergency, hugely improved by the new airfield and transport force' – but he goes on to say that

> quite a different perspective is opened up by the question of opportunity costs – the capabilities forgone (not least in the UK's commitment to NATO) in order to meet the Falklands commitment. In round figures the effect is startling. In the Report of the Defence Committee of the House of Commons, published on 23 May 1985, it was explained that the total Falklands costs over the period 1982 to 1994 will be some £4,650 million at 1983/4 prices; almost exactly half the programme cost of Trident on the same price base and over a rather longer period.

General Beach does examine the question of how much of this expenditure would be incurred one way or another anyway and his paper gives an introduction to those arguments.[8] It also discusses the naval aspects of the problem and notes that the Defence Committee expressed itself 'not completely satisfied' with Ministry of Defence arguments that an increase in ship numbers 'more than offset' reductions in the state of readiness of NATO-declared forces. (The role of the Admiralty in the whole history of the Falklands dispute is worth a monograph on its own, but that will have to await the opening of the archives.) General Beach seems to cover all the arguments – my only quibble would be that he is too polite about Lord Buxton's fantasies about new military perspectives opening with a possible closing of the Panama Canal. He concludes:

> So here is a dispute screaming for a solution. Both sides are being driven by it into forms of military investment which are needed, almost desperately, for other purposes.

The foreseeable costs are also predicted on the assumption that the situation remains stable, just as fishing revenues are predicted on certain assumptions about the behaviour of fish. The Argentines are unlikely to be convinced by the diplomatic equivalent of Morton's Fork ('If you have become democratic, then you approve of self-determination in the Islands and there is no need to raise the subject; if you do not approve of self-determination in the Islands, then that is proof that you have not become democratic and we therefore cannot discuss the matter': this formulation may come in useful in the next United Nations debate). How predictable will their actions be?

The reaction of members of the Argentine intelligentsia to any prospect of renewed action on the Falklands/Malvinas is to make sure immediately that their passports have not expired. There is no need, indeed it is undesirable, to be too respectful towards all forms of Argentine nationalism – more Argentines than ever are less than respectful about many of its manifestations themselves. Any serious student of the Falklands question can see where Argentina has a case and why no imaginable Argentine government will abandon the claim. Yet being too polite can send the 'wrong signals' to the 'wrong' Argentines, forgetting those who are resolutely opposed to any sort of heightening of tension in the dispute, as most – not all, but most – intellectual Argentines are. 'But what you must realise', as one (no doubt well-briefed) member of the British Interests Section of the Swiss Embassy in Buenos Aires said to a leading Argentine academic (now a Deputy in Congress), 'is that academics don't matter.' Their influence over the conduct of Argentine policy is perhaps greater than that of their British equivalents over British policy, but that is not saying much. Argentine policy may evolve in directions they would not wish.

There are many reasons why Dr Alfonsín did not find it convenient to take Falklands/Malvinas initiatives, many ways in which he shared with Mrs Thatcher a need to avoid the subject. For her it is a talisman, not to be touched by others. For Dr Alfonsín, it was best left alone. There have been costs – he may now think that it would have been better to have been more multilateral somehow on fish – and he can point to no gain apart from some unspectacular erosion of support for Great Britain in the UN and elsewhere, but initiatives might well have cost him more and this inertia, even perhaps his early unrealistic expectations as stated in the UN, must be seen in the light of his order of priorities and his relations with the armed forces. Criticisms which pointed out the dangers of doing nothing – the excuse provided to the British by the absence of any formal 'cessation of hostilities', the gradual emergence of new vested interests, the lack of adequate Argentine representation in Britain – had to be balanced against the dangers of re-opening the debate and of doing so with little prospect of British responses that would not begin with some diplomatic equivalent of 'what you must realise is . . .'

So the shock of the imposition of the fishing zone was weathered. Alerts were declared, and then undeclared. The Argentines themselves do not traditionally fish in that area. Care has been taken that incidents should not occur. Operation

'Fire-Focus' was more exploited by the Argentine government, though the fishing zone was itself the subject of an Organization of American States (OAS) resolution. The reinforcement exercise was the subject of loose adverse comment elsewhere in Latin America, Chile excepted, and it for a time fuelled presidential ambitions in Dr Caputo, the Argentine Foreign Minister, until they were effectively checked by Dr Alfonsín – something of a contrast to Dr Caputo's milder reaction at the time of the declaration of the fishing zone. What will follow in Argentina? There is no evidence that Mrs Thatcher has the slightest interest in this question, but it must interest the FCO and the Ministry of Defence. As an optimist, I would argue that there are certainly currents of a new realism present; though as usual change will take much longer than one feels it ought, there is a new realism about economic possibilities and policies and the rhetorical opposition to this has a half-hearted sound. Dr Terragno's drive towards greater economic rationality in the Argentine public sector may still have little to show in terms of practical achievement, but it is more likely in future that arguments will be about pace than direction, and that by the mid-1990s the country will not have been able to avoid some recovery. A pessimist of my acquaintance sees a Peronist victory in the 1989 presidential elections, followed by such a degree of misgovernment that in a couple of years an at present absent element, a large body of civilian opinion wanting the military back, will have returned in force. I have little confidence in the value of such long-range predictions.

Some pertinent developments in Argentina are easier to list. The Chilean frontier is a settled issue and there has been a *rapprochement* with Brazil. There is now no internal-security role for the armed forces: there is no threat and such a role is now unconstitutional. The subject of the Islands must occupy a larger place in military thinking than it did before the war, both from the interminable analyses of what went wrong – at this point I remember an observation put to the late Professor Hedley Bull after he had lectured on some theoretical aspects of the dispute and conflict in Buenos Aires: 'From what you say all we did wrong was lose the war' – and from the absence of other conspicuous concerns. General Beach's conclusion from his analysis of the Argentine military line-up in 1986 was that

> there would not appear to be a likelihood of a further invasion of the islands, even under an aggressive military regime in Argentina, but it would be possible to envisage a low intensity war of attrition which would be costly to Britain, and would require a massive increase in the UK commitment to the defence of the islands.

I am not sure what he means by 'a low intensity war of attrition'. It is possible to conceive of some sort of squid-war, though the diplomatic consequences of that are not so clearly in Argentina's favour. The non-exchange of 'non-papers' might precipitate an incident, and incidents could certainly have expensive consequences for us, as well as increasing the number of those applications for passport renewals in Buenos Aires. I do not think that such 'low intensity' operations would receive much sustained support from elsewhere in Latin America. There is certainly a general feeling, of 'low intensity' itself, that the British military presence is undesirable: it introduces an 'East–West' dimension in the South; it may be nuclear. Nonetheless there is still a deal of suspicion of Argentina that would revive if the level of intensity in this still essentially Anglo-Argentine dispute were raised above a certain point. Yet apart from fishing confrontations there may be other ways in which the now ever-vigilant British Ministry of Defence might be led to conclude that it would be prudent to increase our Falklands expenditure, if that depends on what Argentina has and where Argentina puts what she has got.

Another change in Argentina is worth mentioning, though it fits into no formal category, and may indeed be no more than a projection of feelings of my own. I detect a distinct decline of interest in 'informal contacts' of the sort that aroused much greater interest for a time after the war. The unofficial Anglo-Argentine *encuentros* of 1983 and 1984 did not get very far in any concrete sense, but they did attract the interest – at least on the Argentine side – of some weighty people. There is now little enthusiasm in Argentina for carrying on with this sort of meeting and interest will not revive until there is a closer prospect of real negotiation. This may make real negotiation all the harder. Argentine expectations of what is likely to result when real negotiations are resumed may grow to unreasonable heights.

Meanwhile, what of developments in the Islands? Mrs Thatcher in her Christmas Message from Chequers, 24 December 1985, referred to the opening of the airport at Mount Pleasant in May that year, and to 'better communication between the Falkland Islands and the rest of the world'. It is perhaps unfair to quibble at a Christmas Message, but for 'the rest of the world' one should read Great Britain, or at least the rest of the world via Great Britain. The communications of the Falklands with the rest of the world have not so obviously increased since 1982, even if one counts the sightings of foreign-flagged fishing vessels. Communications with the South American mainland have decreased, and it is nowadays the style (see Eduardo Crawley's review of Alexander Bett's *La verdad sobre las Malvinas – Mi tierra natal*, in *The Times Literary Supplement*, 25 March 1988) to minimise their role in the Islands' history. The new interested parties in the Islands can most of them see no obvious gain in closer relations with Argentina, though paradoxically the realisation of the value of the fishing has perhaps made a few Islanders aware of the importance of an agreement with Argentina on that subject, though they may not yet be fully aware how difficult such an agreement as they would like would be to reach. Securing the interim fishing conservation zone gave not only an access to wealth, but also a certain access to power – would it have been declared without strong Island pressure?

In the years since the war a number of new interests have emerged. Some of those in the speculative, volatile, so far scandal-free but subsidy-ridden world of fish do not look so deeply rooted, but they have brought a bonanza, and with that a louder voice, more officials and a public-relations agency. The Islands' economic problems are compounded, as well as to some small degree 'solved', as the disparity of incomes in Port Stanley and in 'the camp' increases, and more people shift to the Islands' capital. Falkland Islands history is extraordinarily repetitive: the current schemes for 'hydroponic gardens' in Port Stanley recall the plots of 'esculent vegetables' planted on Admiralty orders in 1765, and the prefabricated tourist lodge recently flown to West Falkland, by courtesy of the military, the original timber blockhouse that graced Port Egmont. It is not, to my mind, possible to discuss seriously the economic potential of these efforts of the 1980s, any more than it would be possible to analyse the investments of the 1760s. The exception is the fishery.

British public opinion appears to be realistic about this sort of thing. The quality press, on balance, favours some sort of deal, though not always – *The Times*, having changed its line after the war, now sometimes appears to shift its tack – and there is no clarity about what sort of deal. Polls show majorities for unobjectionable general propositions – as Sir Anthony Parsons (former UK representative to the UN) has remarked, hardly anyone is ever against 'negotiations'. The Labour Party is in favour of negotiations on all matters relating to the Islands, but remains in opposition. Will Mrs Thatcher's chosen successor, when she chooses her successor, be a fundamentalist on this issue as on the others?

Laurence Whitehead, writing on the likelihood of changes in US policy and their repercussions (see p. 97, above), singles out this question as one where the British could find themselves seriously isolated, since the Bush administration appears keen to improve US–Latin American relations and can be expected to resist identification with British rigidity over the Islands in order to avoid offending Argentine sensitivities. This fence-mending process has already begun and will proceed apace. The United States shilly-shallied about the Islands in the nineteenth century, but since 1908 has regarded them as disputed territory; it has required no changes in US policy to favour negotiations, though it is unlikely that Washington will wish to take any prominent role as an intermediary. Argentina does wish to buy arms from the USA – for a mixture of practical and symbolic reasons – and visits between the two countries' militaries have been exchanged at the highest level.

How high are the costs, besides those of defence and null relations with Argentina, of our being 'isolated and backward-looking' on this one point? Does this difference, which could be an agreed difference, affect our relations with the United States in other spheres? David Thomas has given his opinion (see pp. 81, above). I think much might depend on how strategically important the arms sales were and I would distinguish between the general British reaction and the reaction of the Prime Minister. Given a not too significant choice of arms, the last two might easily diverge.

What of indirect costs in the rest of Latin America? As we noticed at the time of the war, sensitivities vary and will continue to vary, the two extremes of sympathy with, and indifference towards, the Argentine claim being exemplified by Venezuela and Chile. Venezuela is (if one forgets Antarctic Chile) the other republic in South America that has a post-imperial claim on a (formerly) British territory, Guyana, and also memories of an undoubtedly imperialist *démarche* – the Anglo-German blockade of 1902–3. Her foremost defender then against the high-handed and confused attentions of Lord Lansdowne, the Kaiser, von Bülow and von Tirpitz was the Argentine Foreign Minister Luis M. Drago. Venezuela is a particularly frontier-conscious republic. It is now clear, however, that we do not any longer have any role in the Guyana frontier argument. Though our relations with Venezuela certainly worsened during the Falklands crisis, they have since improved, as has our trade. It is not, of course, always possible to detect indirect damage: a major contract lost may well go undetected and it is not impossible to imagine a Venezuelan government being hesitant to favour Britain through fear of a political reaction with a Falklands/Malvinas element in it, but the idea for many reasons looks far-fetched. 'Business as usual' based on more basic considerations is more likely to prevail; business at the moment is not such that the grand visible public contract is prominent. Is there any evidence that British business outside Argentina has suffered in Latin America because of the Falklands war? Such evidence may exist, but I have not come across any. In current circumstances I cannot see that it is likely that the attitudes of governments towards British investment and enterprise would be critically determined by this outstanding Anglo-Argentine dispute.

This does not seem to me to be any grounds for complacency. In many ways we are back where we were before the war at a far higher level of expense. It is no criticism of those who had to fight in 1982 to say that the Islands, to someone interested in our relations with Latin America, often seem to bring out all that is worst in the gamut of British attitudes: a preference for birds over people, out-dated fantasies of Antarctic 'policing', a real fear of anything foreign . . . That there has been some change in educated opinion should not lead one to be too sanguine. Opinion in the Islands has hardened and is now represented by some new and agile vested interests, together with that sizeable section of public and political opinion which regards the issue as now 'settled'. Against that, there is the stated intention of the Labour Party to negotiate on all aspects of the problem, including sovereignty.

Can one predict what such negotiations would be like? Changes of government commonly produce less change in foreign than in domestic policies and before 1982 Labour's record on the Falklands does not differ significantly from that of the Conservatives. No student of the war should need reminding that the Labour Party did not oppose sending the Task Force and the Islanders have a number of firm supporters in Labour ranks. The only obvious result in this country of the departure of Mrs Thatcher from Downing Street would be an end to the drought of serious discussion of the issue, a drought that in the Conservative Party is maintained by common prudence and elsewhere by the feeling that while she remains in power there is little practical point in detailed thinking about the future. What evidence there is about British public opinion does not get one far: 'A 1984 Harris survey indicated 46 per cent support for sovereignty negotiations, and 1984 and 1986 Gallup Polls suggested that only about 38 per cent (but 51 per cent among Conservative voters) favoured the Islands' retention as compared to 38–44 per cent support for a leaseback/condominium/UN-trusteeship solution, or 9–10 per cent in favour of abandonment.'[9] These indications are vague. The approach of negotiations 'on all aspects' of the Islands' future would revive interest in the quite numerous alternatives that have from time to time been mooted.[10]

Are the chances for any of these better or worse than before 1982? In contrast to the 'Micawberism', ignorance and timidity that characterised ministerial thinking in the two decades before the war, there is a general awareness that here is a problem of sizeable dimensions. There will for some time be a bloc of parliamentary, and national, opinion which thinks that, expensive though the solution was, the problem has now been solved; one would guess that most of that bloc, but not all, is Conservative. The Islands are no closer to being an Athenian-style democracy, where complex alternatives are discussed, than they were before the war; to use the old phrase once more, it is neither the wish nor in the interests of the Islanders that they should start to shoulder more responsibility. Most Islanders would probably like Mrs Thatcher to be Prime Minister until Kingdom come. Most want nothing to do with the mainland of South America. Perhaps the most important change since the war is that a few are now aware that the long-term future of the fishery does make an agreement with Argentina more attractive. There is just the hint of a hopeful paradox here: in so far as the Islanders can foresee an independently viable economic future, so much the more desirable is an agreement with Argentina that would guarantee it.

In 1989 a new government will be elected in Argentina. If it is a Peronist government, it will be seen in Britain as less reliable than the Radicals, closer to the military and therefore a less suitable interlocutor. Yet it is no less true for Argentina, notwithstanding the errors of the Galtieri junta, than for ourselves that changes in government produce less alteration in foreign than in domestic policies – Argentine diplomats might well argue that their own position in negotiations with us in the 1960s and 1970s was more consistent than ours, just as their negotiators changed less frequently. It is unlikely that any new government will prove significantly more accommodating, in part because they will feel that Mrs Thatcher's term of office will be that much nearer its end and a dialogue 'on all aspects' that much nearer.

Nobody should expect that that dialogue will be easy. Just as the Falklands question, as I have complained above, sometimes brings out those strains of Little Englandism in us, it brings out all that is worst in a gamut of Argentine attitudes as well, which it requires more political courage to face down. Our own more stolid and occasional prejudices are less threatening to politicians here and it is perhaps easier for us to imagine that something might even be gained by concession, that besides reductions in costs, an honourable settlement could do our relations with Latin America, and the general level of rationality in world affairs, some more positive good than an infinite number of repetitions of Operation 'Fire-Focus'. It is an inviting but a distant prospect. Adolfo Bioy Casares' *Breve diccionario del Argentino exquisito* contains two most pertinent entries:

Dialogar: Usase en lugar de las formas anticuadas conversar, discutir, reñir. 'Hoy lo vi al del 3°B con un ojo negro. Había dialogado con el encargado.'

Diálogo: Conversación entre enemigos. 'El funcionario nos declaró que su gobierno se muestra abierto al diálogo con los piratas.'

Clearly a prophetic work.[11]

Notes

1 Six broadcasts in the summer of 1987 (BBC Radio Three). See Peter Beck, *The Falkland Islands as an International Problem* (London and New York: Routledge, 1988). Lawrence Freedman provides an admirable short refresher course in *Britain and the Falklands War* (Oxford and New York: Blackwell, 1988). From the Argentine perspective, see Virginia Gamba, *The Falklands/Malvinas War: A Model for North–South Crisis Prevention* (London: Allen & Unwin, 1987).

2 H. S. Ferns, *Argentina* (London: Ernest Benn, 1969), p. 260; on pages 253–60 Ferns shows that at least one British commentator was capable of going to the heart of the dispute before 1982.

3 Speech in the UN General Assembly, 2 November 1982 (A/37/PV.51, 57–60), quoted in *British Yearbook of International Law* (1982), p. 378.

4 See House of Commons Foreign Affairs Committee, 1983–4, Fifth Report, *Falkland Islands*, vol. I (London: HMSO (HC 268 – I), 1984), p. xvi.

5 There is a reluctance to leave such arguments entirely alone, combined with a disposition – even in Lawrence Freedman – to find the history 'hazy' and 'confused'. See Sir John Thompson's 2 November 1982 speech in the UN referred to on p. 152, for a vain attempt to 'nail, once and for all, four persistent myths'. A recent summary of historical and other arguments is provided by Lowell S. Gustafson in *The Sovereignty Dispute over the Falkland (Malvinas) Islands* (New York and Oxford: Oxford University Press, 1988).

6 Minister of State at the FCO, Hansard (House of Commons Debates), vol. 25, Written Answers, col. 141: 10 June 1982, quoted in *British Yearbook of International Law* (1983), p. 433. The Dependencies were renamed South Georgia and South Sandwich Islands in 1985.

7 For the House of Commons debate on 'Fire-Focus', with Parliamentary Under-Secretary of State for Foreign and Commonwealth Affairs with responsibility for Latin America Mr Tim Eggar's defence of the exercise and its presentation, see Hansard, 31 March 1988, col. 1331ff.

8 Estimates vary, even within the same work. Lawrence Freedman gives the costs of the campaign, Operation 'Corporate', at 'about £1.5 billion', of which £720 million represents replacement of ships, stocks and stores lost, and garrison costs, including the new airfield, at £1,777 million. He concludes, 'the total cost of the Falkland War comes out at some £3.5 billion' (*Britain and the Falklands War*, pp. 88–9).

Elsewhere (p. 116) he gives '£780m on the campaign itself, £1200m on protecting the islands against a recurrence throughout the rest of the 1980s's', omitting the replacement costs.

The FCO estimate for the 'extra cost to the defence budget of establishing and maintaining the Falklands garrison, 1983–1990s', is £1777 million, the annual cost stabilising at somewhat over £100 million. The percentage of the defence budget represented by the Falklands (replacement costs and garrison) falls from 4.03% 1983–4 to 0.64% 1989–90. See Peter Beck, *The Falkland Islands*, p. 177. His tabulations are from *Government Expenditure Plans* 1987–9 to 1989–90, vol. II, Cmnd 56–11 (London: HMSO, 1987), pp. 43–4, and House of Commons Defence Committee, *Defence Commitments in the South Atlantic* (report published 1987), p. 3.

9 Peter Beck, *The Falkland Islands*, p. 179, citing Dr Peter Willetts, 'Public opinion in Britain and the Falklands', unpublished paper, conference on 'Anglo-Argentine Relations after the 1987 Elections', City University, London, 1987.

10 See Bruce George MP and Walter Little, *Options in the Falklands–Malvinas Dispute* (South Atlantic Council Occasional Paper no. 1, April 1985).

11 Buenos Aires: Emece, 1978. The entries translate into English as

    To dialogue: Used in place of antiquated expressions converse, discuss, quarrel. 'Today I saw the chap from 3B with a black eye. He had dialogued with the caretaker.'

    Dialogue: A conversation between enemies. 'The spokesman told us that his government is always open to a dialogue with the pirates.'

10 British relations with Latin America: the Antarctic dimension
Peter Beck

Antarctica covers some 14 million square kilometres (5.5 million square miles), or about 10 per cent of the world's land surface, and exceeds the combined extent of Argentina, Brazil, Chile, Peru and Uruguay. In 1912 Captain Robert Scott, standing at the South Pole, remarked that 'this is an awful place' and in this vein the cold and remote Antarctic region has often been dismissed as an insignificant 'Pole apart'. Nevertheless, certain countries – most notably, Argentina, Chile and Britain – possess a long history of involvement therein, culminating in their participation in the Antarctic Treaty System (ATS) over the past quarter of a century. Whether or not Antarctica constitutes anything other than a peripheral interest even for these countries remains questionable, but any appraisal needs to be considered in the light of the recent assertion of a study group (chaired by Sir Anthony Parsons, Britain's UN representative from 1979 to 1982) that, 'as a factor in international relations, it [Antarctica] cannot be ignored any longer'.[1]

The Antarctic scene

The ATS derived from the Antarctic Treaty, which was signed in December 1959 by the twelve governments – including Argentina, Britain, Chile, South Africa, the Soviet Union and the USA – involved in the region in 1957–8 during International Geophysical Year (IGY). This limited-purpose treaty came into effect in June 1961, and was designed to safeguard the peace and stability of Antarctica through international scientific co-operation, prohibitions upon military and nuclear activities and a freeze of the sovereignty question. In effect, the management of the area south of 60°S was vested in the original signatories, which are described as Consultative Parties (ATCPs) and meet biennially at Consultative Meetings (ATCMs) – the most recent ATCM assembled at Rio de Janeiro in October 1987 – in order to agree through consensus on recommendations designed to further the Treaty's objectives. The Antarctic Treaty, lacking any time limit, may last indefinitely, although there exist provisions for review during and after 1991.

During its lifetime the ATS has been characterised by increased international participation (thirty-eight parties (ATPs) by September 1988, including twenty-

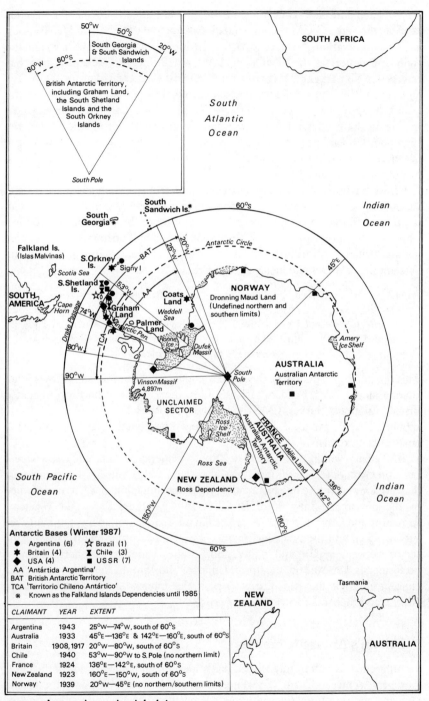

Antarctic Bases (Winter 1987)

●	Argentina (6)	☆	Brazil (1)
✳	Britain (4)	Ⅱ	Chile (3)
◆	USA (4)	■	USSR (7)

AA 'Antártida Argentina'
BAT British Antarctic Territory
TCA 'Territorio Chileno Antártico'
✳ Known as the Falkland Islands Dependencies until 1985

CLAIMANT	YEAR	EXTENT
Argentina	1943	25°W—74°W, south of 60°S
Australia	1933	45°E—136°E & 142°E—160°E, south of 60°S
Britain	1908, 1917	20°W—80°W, south of 60°S
Chile	1940	53°W—90°W to S. Pole (no northern limit)
France	1924	136°E—142°E, south of 60°S
New Zealand	1923	160°E—150°W, south of 60°S
Norway	1939	20°W—45°E (no northern/southern limits)

10.1 Antarctic territorial claims

two ATCPs) and the regime's accommodation of new situations and needs, for example through ATCM recommendations (164 to date), the 1980 Convention for the Conservation of Antarctic Marine Living Resources (CCAMLR) and the 1988 Convention for the Regulation of Antarctic Minerals.[2] Recently, there has emerged a Non-Aligned Movement in the UN-based campaign for the ATS's replacement by a more democratic and equitable international regime in the context of a growing perception of the region's resource potential; changing legal and political attitudes related to the New International Economic Order, the 'common heritage' principle and the 1982 UN Convention on the Law of the Sea; and the attempt to expel South Africa, an original ATCP, from the ATS as part of the anti-apartheid campaign.

British territorial claims, dating back to 1908 and 1917 and comprising some 1.2 million square kilometres (700,000 square miles) between 20°W and 80°W south of 60°S, have proved an established feature of the Antarctic scene for a long period (see Figure 10.1). The British Antarctic Territory (BAT), representing Britain's prime interest in the region, originated in 1962 from the Falkland Islands Dependencies (FID):

> The root of the United Kingdom's title ... lies in British acts of discovery between 1819 and 1843, accompanied by formal claims in the name of the British Crown ...formally confirmed and defined by the Crown in Letters Patent in 1908 (as amended in 1917). Since then there has been...a continuous display of British sovereignty and activity appropriate to the circumstances.[3]

This territory, possessing no permenent population, is administered by a High Commissioner (also Falkland Islands Governor), while officially designated British Antarctic Survey (BAS) scientific personnel based within BAT are appointed to perform legal, administrative and other functions appropriate to the on-the-spot exercise of sovereignty.

BAT falls within the so-called 'South American Antarctic', a concept reflecting Antarctica's traditional significance for Latin American governments; thus the long-standing involvement of Argentina and Chile has been reinforced by the developing interest of Brazil, Cuba, Ecuador, Peru and Uruguay. Argentine and Chilean claims, as defined in the 1940s, overlap most of BAT (see Figure 10.1), and the two governments, glossing over their own rivalry for the sector between 53°W and 74°W and seeking wider hemispheric support, performed a key role in the formulation of the 'South American Antarctic' concept through the Rio Treaty (1947), the Donoso–La Rosa Declaration (1948), and the Act of Puerto Montt (1978).

Britain's Antarctic interests

Antarctica is often interpreted as a peripheral concern for a NATO/European-centred Britain. To some extent one is forced back into the past in studying the question, since the current position can be understood only by reference to the historical perspective, according to which Britain's polar tradition forged strong vested interests in Antarctica. In 1983–4 the British government, recalling Captain Cook's search for *terra australis* and Bransfield's alleged discovery in 1820, reminded the UN that Britain, 'active in Antarctica since 1775', was 'the first state' to became involved there.[4] These polar activities, together with those of Scott, Shackleton, Fuchs and others, constitute not only an emotional, even heroic, chapter in British history, but also an influential framework for the formulation of current and future policies. Therefore, the historical dimension, albeit difficult to quantify in contemporary terms, explains why Britain remains in Antarctica in spite of the post-1945 retreat from a global role. In general, official policy statements have tended to lack both specificity and any evaluation of Antarctic priorities, although in 1983 a Foreign and Commonwealth Office (FCO) paper defined British national interests in Antarctica under four main headings: territorial, strategic, economic and scientific.[5] This policy framework was not elaborated, but such headings provide a useful basis for an evaluation of Britain's Antarctic interests, with special reference to Latin America.

At present, several question marks exist about the future of the ATS in general and of Britain's Antarctic role in particular. Will the ATS succeed in accommodating the UN-centred challenge regarding the most appropriate form of management for the continent? Will the ATS's co-operative qualities in the sphere of international relations survive any further increases in membership? Will the problem surrounding South Africa's continued participation in the regime become a serious point of discord between Britain and certain Latin American ATPs? Will the introduction of the Antarctic minerals regime bring latent points of tension over sovereignty to the surface, particularly in the light of suggestions that some of the most promising areas for exploitation are located in the sector claimed by Argentina, Britain and Chile? Will 1991, when the treaty may be reviewed, prove a crucial year, perhaps resulting in the ATS's demise? In this eventuality will Antarctica return to the instability characteristic of the pre-Antarctic Treaty scenario and will Britain be capable of upholding its rights to BAT against not only Argentina and Chile, but also those governments which refuse to recognise sovereignty and might emerge as territorial rivals (for example, the USA and USSR), other South American states advancing claims through the frontage concept (see below, p. 170) and the advocates of 'common heritage', among others? Does Britain possess any specific and significant national interests in Antarctica? In turn, are these interests satisfied best by either the maintenance of an allegedly divisive, unrealistic and anachronistic sovereign claim and/or support for the ATS? To what extent is Britain's position in Antarctica a function of its Falklands policy? What is the long-term realism of the post-1982 enhancement of the South Atlantic role of a European/NATO power like Britain?

Obviously, it is difficult to provide definitive answers, especially in a study concerned primarily with the Latin American dimension, but the following discussion will illuminate future policy possibilities in the context of the existing position. The nature of British interests will be analysed under the following headings:

(a) territorial/sovereignty interests
(b) strategic interests
(c) economic and resource interests
(d) scientific interests
(e) environmental/conservation interests
(f) the maintenance of the Antarctic Treaty System, and
(g) the 'Antarctic factor' in foreign policy.

(a) Territorial interests

The FCO reference in its 1983 paper to the desire 'to protect our sovereignty over BAT' offered only a sketchy indication of Britain's territorial interests. In fact, Britain advanced the first formal claims to Antarctic territory as part of the FID in 1908 and 1917, and, soon after (in 1920), the British government, stressing the priority, extent and nature of British activity, decided that 'the whole of the Antarctic should ultimately be included within the British Empire' through the pursuit of a gradualist annexationist strategy.[6] Although this objective was scaled down in the face of other claimants (for example, France and Norway), a serious problem arose during the early 1940s, when both Argentina and Chile defined their long-standing polar interests in a manner overlapping most of the FID and adding an Antarctic dimension to the Anglo-Argentine dispute over the Falkland Islands. Henceforth, Antarctica became a key element in the Anglo-Argentine-Chilean relationship, as is evidenced by the acrimonious tone of the diplomatic exchanges conducted on the subject between London, Buenos Aires and Santiago, the continuing effort to enhance the legal effectiveness of their respective Antarctic 'occupations' and the occurrence of occasional incidents, including the Hope Bay (February 1952) and Deception Island (1953) clashes.[7] Significantly, the basic emphasis was placed upon either the Anglo-Argentine or the Anglo-Chilean relationship, particularly as the emerging 'South American Antarctic' concept obscured Argentine-Chilean disagreements.

These developments typified the centrality of the Anglo-Argentine-Chilean dispute in the international politics of Antarctica. Indeed, during the late 1950s concern about the conflict potential of this rivalry for the same piece of Antarctic real estate, in conjunction with alarm regarding the possible consequence of growing US and Soviet involvement in the region, provided the impetus for the conclusion of the Antarctic Treaty. The twelve signatories, perceiving that they were – to quote Roberto Guyer, an Argentine participant – 'on the threshold of a conflict which could have had serious political consequences', welcomed the opportunity for a political and legal accommodation of their Antarctic interests designed to facilitate the stable development of international relations, such as through the creation of a zone of peace, the promotion of scientific collaboration and the suspension of the sovereignty problem.[8] The Antarctic Treaty pushed the sovereignty issue aside under the carpet provided by Article IV, which stipulated that legal positions could be neither improved nor prejudiced by activities taking place during the treaty's lifetime. In reality, this non-solution conceals a rather uncertain, even ambiguous, situation.

In 1982 the Report of the Shackleton Committee, set up by the British government immediately after the Falklands war and chaired by Lord Shackleton, warned about 'possible threats to the Antarctic Treaty' and BAT consequent upon the fact that Argentine governments interpret 'Antártida Argentina' as an integral part of national territory, wherein the country possesses a natural right to establish settlements, including family groups and schools.[9] Chile has adopted a similar approach, as was evidenced in 1984 when President Pinochet inaugurated a family settlement at Teniente Marsh in 'Territorio Chileno Antártico'. According to the Antarctic Treaty, these activities cannot affect the relative strength of claims and British governments, when confonted by such fears as those articulated by the 1982 Shackleton Report, have stressed 'the protection given by the Treaty to the United Kingdom's position in the British Antarctic Territory'.[10]

However, these reassurances failed to prevent the expression of anxieties about BAT's security at the time of the 1982 Falklands war, which represented the major threat to Britain's Antarctic interests in the recent period. Although the Falklands and Antarctic questions are separate historically, politically and legally, Argentina interprets the Falklands/Malvinas, South Georgia, the South Sandwich Islands and 'Antártida Argentina' as part of a single territorial claim. Against this background, during April 1982, certain parliamentary and media commentators speculated about a possible Antarctic dimension to the war, particularly as Argentine statements and writings tended to interpret the Falklands/Malvinas as the foundation for the enhancement of the country's Antarctic activities; thus President Galtieri stated that the islands' recapture represented 'merely the beginning of the reaffirmation of Argentina's right to assert territories'.[11] In the event, any fears proved groundless, partly because they reflected an underestimation – even ignorance – of the protective qualities of the Antarctic Treaty. Indeed, subsequently the latter became interpreted as a possible way out of the Falklands/Malvinas impasse, but the surface attractions of this proposal conceal a range of difficulties, including the risk of introducing a destabilising element into the ATS and the fact that a legal freeze fails to meet the basic Argentine demand for sovereignty over the islands.[12] Argentine, British and Chilean territorial claims, an established feature of the Antarctic scene in 1959, remain still an influential policy consideration, causing the three governments to maintain, support and protect their respective legal titles. Certainly, for Britain, the Argentine and Chilean challenge to BAT remains just

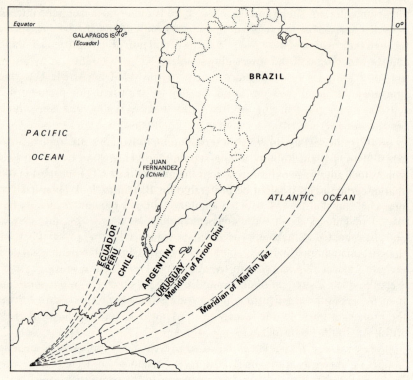

10.2 The 'frontage' concept

below – it has never been beyond – the horizon, particularly as both governments continue to treat Antarctica as a matter of fundamental importance and to act toward it in a relatively assertive manner.

More recently, a further complication has arisen from the emergence of alternative legal approaches to the region, including the 'common heritage' and 'frontage'(*defrontação*) concepts. In September 1985 Sir Geoffrey Howe, the British Foreign Secretary, informed the UN General Assembly that his govern-ment 'firmly' opposed any attempt to apply a 'common heritage' regime to Antarctica, since the area was subject already to legal claims.[13] In fact, this attitude is shared by Argentina and Chile, who have expressed strong opposition to any attempt to interpret Antarctica as the common heritage of mankind. The frontage principle, advocated by Brazilian writers to relate Antarctic rights to Latin American boundaries (see Figure 10.2), attracts a similar British critique. In general, Argentina and Chile have seconded British criticism of the 'frontage' concept – its application promised to reduce the extent of their claims – although recently Jack Child has detected a more moderate Argentine approach:

> There seems to be a growing realization that making good an Antarctic sovereignty claim is not very realistic and may alienate a number of important allies whose support

is needed on the *Malvinas* issue. Thus, there is cautious but intriguing discussion regarding the sharing of Antarctic sovereignty with other Latin American nations under Argentine leadership.[14]

To some extent, this conforms with the post-1985 enhancement of Argentina's scientific presence in the region as compared to the previous emphasis upon sovereignty secured through military personnel.

Over recent decades some observers have noted an ambiguous British stance on sovereignty. For example, during the 1960s Wilson's Labour government considered the scaling-down, even termination, of Britain's Antarctic activities, while in 1977 Brian Roberts, a long-standing influence upon British Antarctic policy, took advantage of his recent retirement from the FCO to suggest publicly that in certain cases it might be preferable for Britain to 'look upon itself as a non-claimant state'.[15] It was debatable how far this comment reflected official thinking, although occasionally government statements have indicated a moderate stance, such as in June 1982 when Arthur Watts, head of the British delegation at the minerals negotiations, stated that his government might be prepared 'in the common interest' to utilise 'certain powers at present vested in the United Kingdom . . . for the general good'.[16] Yet recently commentators have detected a contrary strand, most notably a more assertive stance developed in the wake of the Falklands war, which has prompted an enhancement of British visibility in both the Falklands and Antarctica. There have been occasional indications that a future Labour government might prove more sympathetic towards an alternative strategy based upon the 'common heritage' concept, but it seems more likely that pressures for continuity will predominate.

The ATS, providing a focus for co-operation, has helped to contain the conflict potential of the Antarctic territorial problem, even if sovereignty considerations have never disappeared from the Antarctic perceptions of policy-makers; in fact John Heap, head of the FCO's Polar Regions section, has observed that 'where sovereignty has been claimed, it is unlikely that any State, having claimed it, will give it up. And, indeed, the more it is attacked, the less likely it is to be given up.'[17] During the past decade or so the resource-management negotiations have stressed the sovereignty issue, thereby serving both to unite and divide Britain and Latin American ATPs. For instance, Argentina and Chile, although they are territorial rivals for BAT, found common cause with Britain in stipulating the need for any marine resources and minerals regime to recognise the special position of claimants, particularly as the experience of international regimes suggests that national sovereignty is capable of making a constructive contribution to the management process. In any case, a territorial claim provides an invaluable lever to strengthen a claimant's influence over any Antarctic discussions and clearly the sovereignty issue will continue to influence Britain and Latin American attitudes, policies and relationships in both co-operative and harmful ways. The continued operation of the ATS may moderate the impact of sovereignty considerations, while also indicating perhaps that the regime's maintenance is a more important policy goal than the pursuit of claims.

(*b*) Strategic interests

The FCO's assertion that Britain's strategic interest was 'to deny the use of Antarctica for military purposes' offered only an imprecise guide to the policy benefits arising from the Antarctic Treaty's demilitarisation and denuclearisation provisions. The effective transformation of Antarctica into a strategic irrelevance was accentuated by the manner in which the pre-1959 period was characterised by fears about the continent being drawn into either the Cold War, perhaps as a base for nuclear weapons and submarines, or an Anglo-Argentine-Chilean confrontation. In this sense, Antarctica's transformation into a zone of peace, including its insulation from external tensions, enhanced international stability in general, and proved beneficial to all countries, especially to those, like Britain, with global interests; thus the strategic value of Antarctica derived less from a concern to use it for military or nuclear purposes than from a desire to deny an advantage to a rival.[18] For governments either located in the southern hemisphere or, like Britain, possessing territory therein, specific strategic concerns derive from Antarctica's character as their 'Near South', as evidenced by pre-1959 fears that the continent might offer the Soviet Union a 'back door' through which to threaten territory and sea lanes. The 'continent for peace' aspect has been reinforced by the way in which the 1959 Treaty offered a model for regional disarmament and 'zone of peace' schemes, that is, an oft-forgotten precedent which was recognised by recent UN Studies on Antarctica (1984) and Conventional Disarmament (1985).[19] As a result, the Antarctic Treaty has proved both an inspiration and a boundary point for subsequent projects, including the Tlatelolco Treaty (1967), the South Pacific Zone of Peace (1985), and the 1986 proposals for a South Atlantic Zone of Peace.

Historically, Britain's imperial and world role prompted a strategic concern about Antarctica, but the post-1945 British retreat into Europe has raised question marks not only about the realism of a continuing role in the South Atlantic and Antarctica but also about the extent to which an Antarctic presence is linked to policy towards the Falkland Islands. These questions were posed in an acute form by the Falklands war of 1982. Subsequent developments have tended to enhance Britain's stake in the region, including the potential utility of the Islands as a gateway guarding – to quote Mrs Thatcher – 'the entrance to the Antarctic', while the new Mount Pleasant Airport means that Britain, like Argentina, Chile and the USA, possesses now a capability to project power in Antarctica, even if military, political, geographical, climatic and other factors prompt the conclusion that

> Continuous combat is virtually unimaginable ... neither Argentina, Chile nor the United Kingdom could effectively defend their overlapping claims ... Britain would be deluding itself if it believed that it could fight for its Antarctic claims. Thus it would be in the British interest to ensure that issues in Antarctica are resolved peacefully, and the continent remains demilitarised.[20]

Antarctica's neutralisation therefore possesses an obvious relevance to Britain as long as the Falkland Islands and the Dependencies of South Georgia and the South Sandwich Islands (FID until 1985) remain under British control.

Jack Child, pointing to the 'frontage' concept and Argentina's stress upon the Malvinas and Antarctica as one claim to 'Atlantártida', has asserted that 'A frequently overlooked source of Antarctic tension is the geopolitical thinking which has been the legacy of military regimes in southern South America over the past quarter century.'[21] South American geopolitics, though coloured by individual national preoccupations, has stressed the importance of national security and the projection of power in the maritime, aerospace and resource dimensions with special reference to the control of sea lanes and so-called 'choke points' (for example Drake Passage). In 1988 Child conceded that

> There are indications that the old chauvinistic, aggressive and nationalist geopolitical rhetoric of the past has been giving way to a current of cooperative and integrative geopolitical thinking. But even this current may lead to confrontations if it unites the South American or Latin American nations, but pits them against outside nations who also have an interest in the political and economic development of the frozen continent.[22]

Within this context, Britain, having been identified as responsible for so-called 'geopolitical aggression', may be confronted by a more concerted Latin American effort in support of a South American Antarctic.

Although commentators continue to speculate about Antarctica's future military potential, few clear answers have emerged. To date, the general view is that most military functions could be performed better elsewhere, especially as technological developments have reinforced Antarctica's strategic irrelevance – satellites, for example, have reduced the need for ground-tracking stations. In addition, the shared perception of ATPs that the termination of the Antarctic Treaty would remove the lid from a veritable Pandora's Box appears likely to ensure the preservation of Antartica as a zone of peace isolated from the strategic calculations of policy-makers.[23]

(c) Economic interests

Antarctica's perceived resource potential, in association with the global scramble for access to increasingly scarce resources, helps to explain contemporary international interest expressed through the UN and the Non-Aligned Movement. Although fish and krill are exploited on a limited scale already, most observers express a somewhat exaggerated 'treasure island' vision of future possibilities regarding krill, oil and natural gas. Reality falls far short of such optimism; thus, the annual fishing catch of between 0.3 and 0.6 million tons is well below statistical estimates in the range of 4 to 170 million tons, while so far geological research has failed to provide evidence supporting notions of tremendous Antarctic mineral riches. Indeed, most scientific and oil industry experts, treating Antarctic minerals as resources of the last resort, subscribe to the view that neither oil nor natural gas of economic value in the foreseeable future are known in the region. In addition, a range of technical, economic, environmental and other problems combines with market and supply forces to render debatable even the long-term prospects.

Britain's economic interests have been defined by the FCO as the need 'to secure an appropriate share of potential benefits from Antarctic resources'.[24] This raises a number of questions. For example, which resources, if any, are exploitable? Does this mean a 'share' in the management and/or benefits or resources? Historically, the prospect of resources linked to whaling served as a major cause of British interest, whereas at present the government's approach towards resources reflects a concern to secure not only the recognition of its rights in BAT, but also an ATS-based regime governed by responsible conservation and rational-use measures. Certainly, these considerations influenced the British approach towards the 1980 CCAMLR proposal (see p. 166), particularly as Britain had previously demonstrated little interest in exploiting the region's fishing resources. This seems unlikely to change in the future although the recent enhancement of fishing around the Falkland Islands, including the growing participation of British commercial interests (often as part of joint ventures with other nations), may provide a foundation for activity within the CCAMLR area. The British government, although pessimistic about mineral prospects and indicating minimal interest in exploitation, has supported the ongoing attempt to negotiate a minerals regime before deposits are actually discovered or exploited, especially as this procedure promises to strengthen the ATS, avoid the possibility of an unregulated scramble for resources and facilitate the adoption of sound environmental measures. Several writers, including Barbara Mitchell and Evan Luard, have mentioned the interest of British Petroleum (BP) in the area, whereas Geoffrey Larminie of BP has disclaimed any commercial interest in Antarctic minerals.[25] Possibly Antarctica will remain a low priority for the oil companies, who will continue nevertheless to keep open their future options.

Traditionally, the management of resource activities has assumed the clear identification of ownership. However, Antarctica lacks a definite legal framework, a situation exacerbated by the ATS's failure to cover resource matters until 1980, when CCAMLR was concluded to manage living marine resources upon the basis of the so-called 'bi-focal' formula – this enabled parties to interpret the same language according to their divergent legal positions. The sovereignty issue was raised in a more acute form after 1982 by the Antarctic minerals regime negotiations, providing the principal cause of the difficulties and delays. The British emphasis upon the need for any regime to allow an appropriate role for claimant states had to be qualified by a grasp of Antarctic realities:

> As our sovereignty over BAT is not recognised by many of our Treaty partners, and is contested by Argentina and Chile, we could expect difficulty in trying to be able to go it alone in Antarctica or to control and benefit from mineral activities there in the way we

do domestically. We therefore agreed to negotiate with our Treaty partners for a regime to control mineral resource activities.[26]

For both Britain and Latin American nations, the minerals negotiations of 1982–8 raised significant points liable to produce both co-operation and confrontation. At one level they focused attention upon the Anglo-Argentine-Chilean divide about their respective mining rights within the same sector of Antarctica, whereas at another level the three claimants were ranged against those ATPs, including Brazil, Ecuador, Peru, the Soviet Union, Uruguay and the USA, which refuse to recognise claims. In fact, this shared Anglo-Argentine-Chilean interest explained their participation in the separate, secret meetings held by the claimant nations in order to discuss a collective position for each negotiating session. The minerals convention was adopted at Wellington in June 1988, but several question marks remain about the future, as is conceded by Maarten de Wit, a geologist, when he suggests that the exploitation of the significant mineral potential of the Dufek complex and the Weddell Sea – located within the area of Anglo-Argentine-Chilean dispute – 'could put the Antarctic sovereignty issue to severe test and undermine the most delicate pivot of the present *modus operandi* of the Antarctic Treaty'.[27] Similarly, Christopher Joyner, admitting that an Anglo-Argentine 'resource war seems unlikely to occur', feared that 'the unraveling of Anglo-Argentine rivalry over Antarctic natural resources would not come as a great surprise'.[28] Regulatory committees will perform a prime role in the management of exploration and exploitation within specified areas. Argentina, Britain and Chile will be represented upon any committee responsible for a management scheme within the area of their respective claims, thereby providing scope for both co-operation and confrontation when, and if, exploitation takes place.

Although Antarctica's contemporary economic utility is minimal, one should not discount future economic possibilities, which may involve not only fish, krill, natural gas and oil, but also tourism and even the exploitation of icebergs for fresh water. It might be argued therefore that Britain, possessing a legal entitlement to share in the control and exploitation of any resources, should not close down its Antarctic options, a view reinforced by the recent enhancement of the economic prospects of the Falkland Islands (see chapter 9). Indeed, in certain quarters the 1982 war was interpreted incorrectly as being 'intimately connected to the future exploitation of Antarctica', while the subsequent period has been characterised by numerous references to Falklands–Antarctic interconnections, including the view that the Islands represented a 'latchkey to open the front door of a palace filled with riches beyond calculation' in Antarctica.[29] However, this 'gateway' argument, although possessing some substance, should not be pressed too far, since it has often been exploited in order to provide an Antarctic rationale for the large-scale post-war expenditure on the Falklands.

(d) Scientific interests

Prior to 1959 Antarctic science served not only to unveil the continent's mysteries but also to establish the 'occupation' required to support sovereignty. As a result, the principal emphasis was placed upon a national rather than an international approach and significantly the 1952 Hope Bay incident arose out of an Anglo-Argentine clash over the location of scientific bases. However, during 1957–8 the International Geophysical Year offered a multilateral framework for Antarctic science and the Antarctic Treaty, representing a means of perpetuating international scientific co-operation through the containment of sovereignty issues, enabled the transformation of Antarctica into a continent for science. Indeed, scientific data may remain Antarctica's chief export.

Britain has long-standing scientific interests in Antarctica, dating back to the explorations of Ross, Scott and Shackleton and the post-1920s research on whaling. During the 1940s Operation 'Tabarin', although prompted primarily by sovereignty and strategic considerations, established a permanent British scientific presence in Antarctica, which was taken over subsequently by the Falkland Islands Dependencies Survey until its re-designation as the British Antarctic Survey (BAS) in 1962. BAS, providing an on-the-spot presence, performs a major role in Antarctic science through the conducting of long-term, multidisciplinary research, particularly as Antarctica offers – to cite BAS's David Walton – 'a unique laboratory to research into many of the features of scientific significance to our understanding of the globe as a whole' in such spheres as the atmospheric sciences, tectonic processes and climatology.[30] Although the distinction between fundamental and applied research is blurred, BAS has moved gradually towards work in the marine and earth sciences in order to provide an informed background for British policy towards marine and mineral discussions. BAS's national emphasis has been qualified by its continuing involvement with the ATS's Scientific Committee on Antarctic Research (SCAR) and the exchange of scientists and information as well as its participation in various co-operative schemes, most notably the BIOMASS project on krill.

In 1982 Richard Laws, BAS's Director from 1973 to 1987, cited a forthcoming Anglo-Chilean mapping project as evidence that international scientific co-operation in Antarctica was 'extremely good', while one can quote existing examples of BAS-Chilean co-operation on South Shetlands geology; BAS-Brazilian paleobotanical research in the Hope Bay area; Argentine, Brazilian, British and Chilean collaboration in the multilateral BIOMASS project; and BAS's advisory role to such new ATPs as Ecuador and Peru.[31] Further linking aspects include BAS's use of such countries as Brazil and Uruguay during the course of its logistical support activities. In this manner Antarctic science has provided, and continues to provide, a practical framework for Britain's co-operation with its treaty partners and particularly with Latin American ATPs on account of their special interest in the BAT region and use of BAS's scientific

Table 10.1. *British Antarctic Survey (BAS) Funding*

	£million	
1973–4	2.1	
1976–7	3.76	
1980–1	6.19	
1981–2	6.3	
1982–3	6.7	(increased to 7.2 after Falklands war)
1983–4	10.2	
1984–5	11.5	
1985–6	12.17	
1986–7	12.6	
1987–8	14.9	
1988–9	23.8[a]	
1989–90	39.7[b]	
1990–1	23.6[c]	

[a] Extra amounts included for financing a new ship (£5.2 million) and plane (£2.14 million), Halley base rebuilding (£3 million) and Cambridge headquarters (£980,000).
[b] Allocation includes £14.4 million for a new ship and £1.39 million for rebuilding of Signy and Halley bases.
[c] Allocation includes further contribution towards the new ship and Signy rebuilding.
Source: British Antarctic Survey *Annual Report*, various years.

expertise. Naturally, it is difficult to assess to what extent such contacts might involve political consequences, but even the existing modest level of scientific co-operation offers an added and meaningful dimension to British relations with Latin American nations that is capable of further development. However, David Drewry, writing prior to his appointment in May 1987 as Director of BAS, detected evidence of decreased scientific co-ordination in certain quarters, in part because of the development of a 'distinctive South American axis' around Argentina, Brazil, Chile and Uruguay: 'One may liken the process to the Antarctic nations with their hands linked moving back progressively into their own corners.'[32]

BAS constitutes a productive, high-quality and cost-effective research body, even if this scientific emphasis cannot disguise its political role in terms of expressing national interests in Antarctica, providing a physical presence in BAT, underpinning Britain's ATCP status, and yielding an authoritative and informed British contribution on resource matters. In fact, British moves since the Falklands war offer a good contemporary example of the continuing interconnection of Antarctic politics and science and especially of the fact that any country's policy commitment therein is measurable through its level of scientific activity. In mid-1982 the British government, acting upon the personal initiative of the Prime Minister and following a decade or more characterised by a gradual contraction in BAS activities, decided not only to allocate extra funding to BAS, but also to reprieve HMS *Endurance*, whose Antarctic presence symbolised Britain's role in the wider region. The additional annual amounts (around £5 million) proved relatively small in contrast to those devoted to the Falkland Islands, but they represented a large proportionate increase (approximately 60 per cent) in BAS's budget, thereby providing the basis for the rapid escalation of British research activity and visibility in Antarctica (see Table 10.1).

In future, the scientific dimension will provide the most visible evidence of British interest in Antarctica, since the government, aware that science proves the currency of Antarctic law and politics, has reaffirmed that the national interest in Antarctica is defined to require the maintenance of a significant level of scientific activity therein. Within this policy milieu BAS is engaged in producing a position paper entitled *Strategy and Priorities for Antarctic Research into the Twenty-First Century*, and significantly, even in 1987–8 when other research bodies experienced severe fiscal constraints, BAS was allocated extra funding into the early 1990s in order to facilitate expensive logistical improvements, including base rebuilding (for example, at Halley and Signy), an additional aircraft and a replacement ship for the *John Biscoe* (see Table 10.1). In 1986 Drewry noted that Britain 'has remained relatively static offering few opportunities to other nations while maintaining a small number of existing contacts'; in future, however, both scientific and foreign policy benefits will derive from the adoption of an even more outgoing strategy alongside this enhanced national scientific programme.[33]

(e) Environmental interests

During the 1980s the emphasis upon Antarctica's supposed and actual resources has focused attention upon conservation on account of the alleged threat posed by exploitation to the world's last great wilderness. Nongovernmental Organisations (NGOs), like Greenpeace, have proved active as pressure groups, lobbying the ATS in general and individual ATPs about the need to protect the fragile polar environment through the strict enforcement controls and the declaration of Antarctica as a 'world park'. Although the preservation of Antarctica's 'wilderness' character possesses an intrinsic value, there are other benefits related, for example, to the fact that any activities undermining the stability of the Antarctic ice sheet would have serious consequences for world sea levels. In addition, Antarctica acts as an unique laboratory, as is highlighted by both the use of ice-cores for the long-term measurement of world pollution levels and the research relating to the depletion of the ozone layer which shields the earth from the sun's damaging ultra-violet rays. BAS data, most notably that collected at Halley base since the 1950s, have performed a prominent role in both identifying and monitoring the ozone hole over Antarctica, thereby serving not only to push the region to centre-stage in terms of governmental, media and popular interest, but also to highlight the global relevance of Antarctic scientific research. BAS's studies, in association with those conducted by other nations, provided the background in September 1987 for the signing by twenty-four nations (including Britain) of the Montreal Protocol, which was designed to control the use of the chlorofluorocarbons ('CFCs' used in aerosols and refrigeration systems) adjudged to be primarily responsible for the diminution of the ozone layer. Future improvements scheduled for Halley base (see Table 10.1), including the construction of an airstrip, should ensure that BAS retains its leading role in monitoring changes in the ozone layer.

The ATPs, though stressing the ATS's conservation responsibilities and good record on these matters (for example, the 1964 Agreed Measures making Antarctica a 'Special Conservation Area', the ecosystem approach of CCAMLR, the strict controls in the minerals convention), have favoured a strategy founded upon rational use and strict environmental protection in preference to a 'world park' approach. The British government, lacking any strong exploitation interest, has devoted a high priority to the preservation of the unique Antarctic environment, particularly in regard to the adoption of responsible conservation measures for the management of marine and mineral resources in the light of informed scientific advice. This environmental interest, building upon whaling conservation measures adopted since the early years of this century, has proved a long-standing British preoccupation, whose contemporary importance has been enhanced by the emergence of resource questions and the pressure exerted by environmental NGOs. In Britain, the limited press coverage of Antarctic questions has tended to concentrate upon the conservation interest at the expense of other factors, especially as environmental groups, recruiting such well-known names as Peter Scott and David Bellamy, have proved better at public relations than the ATS. Nevertheless, the British government continues to perform a prominent role on conservation matters, as is evidenced by its contributions not only to the drafting of the Agreed Measures and CCAMLR but also at the 1987 ATCM, where recommendation XIV-2 on 'Man's Impact on the Antarctic Environment' – which provided guidelines for environmental impact assessment – was derived from a British draft.

In future, the British government, lacking any substantial economic motives, will be in a strong position to articulate the environmental point of view in the face of growing exploitation pressures, even if conservation, like science, needs to be seen merely as part of the broader geopolitical milieu; thus, conservation might be sacrificed in the face of diplomatic and economic priorities. In addition, the British government, stressing the merits of the ATS regime, believes that pressures towards further internationalisation will do little to improve the prospects for acceptable environmental safeguards in Antarctica.

(f) The maintenance of the Antarctic Treaty System

The British government, regarding it as the most appropriate framework within which to pursue the above-mentioned national interests, has often asserted that 'we are satisfied with the operation of the Antarctic Treaty to date and will continue to support it'.[34] Successive governments have reaffirmed that British interests 'were best protected by the maintenance and observance of the

Antarctic Treaty system' through the pursuit of a political strategy based upon compromise, accommodation and the 'delicate balance' of interests rather than upon conflict. In particular, the ATS has facilitated the avoidance of sovereignty-related complications over BAT with Latin American and other governments, while providing Britain with an influential voice in the multilateral pursuit of common Antarctic interests in such spheres as peace, stability, resource management, research and conservation.

During the 1980s Britain and the Latin American ATPs came together to deny the existence of any Antarctic problem in the face of the UN-based critique of the ATS. The British government reiterated that it was 'not prepared in any way to countenance the dismantling of the Antarctic Treaty System', a view echoed by its Argentine, Brazilian, Chilean and Uruguayan counterparts.[35] Sir Geoffrey Howe, the Foreign Secretary, reminded the UN General Assembly that any alternative structure 'would upset this proven system, risk destabilising the region and jeopardise the present close international scientific collaboration'.[36] The fact that he chose to mention the oft-ignored Antarctic at all during the course of a wide-ranging survey of world affairs proved as significant as the message itself. Subsequently, Sir Anthony Parsons sketched out possible dangers:

> If the treaty were to collapse ... these claims ... would be re-activated in a much worse atmosphere than existed when the treaty was signed. After all we had a war with Argentina only four years ago ... I feel much more secure in this belief [about peace in Antarctica] with the treaty in existence and the claims frozen than if there was no international umbrella over the Antarctic continent and there was a resumption of the kind of free-for-all which was just beginning when the treaty was concluded.[37]

Naturally, the ATS's future prospects will prove a function of the extent to which it succeeds in securing an external accommodation with the wider international community, even if this point should not obscure the accompanying need for an internal accommodation of divergent interests within the system, such as between claimants and non-claimants, developed and less-developed countries, or Western- and Eastern-bloc members. Any assessment of the manner in which participation in, and support for, the ATS has united Britain and several Latin American nations should be qualified by an awareness of points of difference, including their varying legal approaches to Antarctica. The 1988 Minerals Convention provided the most recent instance of the ATS's ability to accommodate these differences within a co-operative framework, although South Africa's role within the ATS remains a source of friction. During 1986 and 1987 Argentina, Brazil, Cuba, Ecuador (which became an ATP in 1987) and Peru voted at the UN for the exclusion of South Africa, an original ATCP, from ATCMs, whereas Britain, Chile and Uruguay, like most ATPs, expressed opposition to UN interference in Antarctic matters by non-participation in the vote. The practical implications of these actions remain uncertain, but the ATCM held at Rio de Janeiro in October 1987 was seemingly unaffected by the problem: South Africa sat down at the same table as

Argentina and Brazil, whose UN votes possibly represent a manifestation of their membership of the Non-Aligned Movement.

(g) The Antarctic factor in foreign policy

The British government, welcoming 'a way of avoiding the unmanageable escalation of national interests at variance with each other',[38] believes that one of the key elements in the ATS's success has proved to be the 'Antarctic spirit', that is, the close links forged between ATPs through the regime's consensus procedures. A kind of osmotic effect has resulted in a range of unquantifiable benefits for Britain's bilateral relationships, particularly in the case of governments with which it possesses either little else in common or clear points of dispute.

Within this context, Britain's involvement in the ATS provides an additional basis for meaningful contacts with thirty-seven governments – these account for some 70 per cent of the world's population – including its European partners, former dominions (Australia, Canada, New Zealand and South Africa), and the USA as well as those governments enjoying a more distant relationship, like Latin American nations, China and the Soviet Union. In particular, the British government has come to value the extra dimension which the 'Antarctic factor' provides for the conduct of relations with Latin America, although the nature, extent and significance of any diplomatic benefits is dependent upon not only Latin America's role in British diplomacy, but also individual government's perceptions of British policy.

Although Latin American ATPs may share a feeling of hemispheric and Third World solidarity against Britain through the 'South American Antarctic' concept, they lack a coherent approach towards Antarctica because of traditional rivalries based on territorial, legal and other factors. Antarctic issues exert more potential influence upon British relations with Latin American ATCPs, which tend to perceive Britain variously as a claimant to the South American Antarctic, as a major force within the ATS and in Antarctic science and as more capable, as a developed industrial power, than they of exploiting Antarctic mineral resources. However, Argentina, Britain and Chile, having assumed a somewhat distant relationship within the ATS for the regulated management of their territorial dispute, have been forced increasingly to talk to each other at ATCMs in order to seek consensus on a wide range of questions, including those with sovereignty implications. Even *during* the 1982 Falklands war, Argentine and British delegates sat down together on three occasions to discuss Antarctic marine and mineral resource matters at Canberra, Hobart and Wellington and subsequently Antarctic questions have offered an invaluable point of Anglo-Argentine contact unaffected by the Falklands problem. Similarly, the ATS provides a regular channel for Anglo-Chilean dialogue unencumbered by human rights complications. It is difficult to quantify the diplomatic impact of such practical contacts, which are reinforced by the manner in which scientific and logistical co-operation represents another instrument for the expression of friendly sentiments; for instance, during the 1985-6 season BAS ships visited Montevideo, Rio de Janeiro and the Chilean Antarctic base at Teniente Marsh. Clearly, the pursuit of a series of common Antarctic goals will remain a factor of some significance in British relations with Argentina, Brazil, Chile and Uruguay.

The above-mentioned considerations apply with considerably less force to the Latin American non-ATCPs (Cuba, Ecuador and Peru), although the ATS's contribution in providing a forum for the discussion of shared interests with Britain should not be underestimated. In addition, Britain's reservoir of scientific expertise – this extends beyond BAS to include such bodies as the Scott Polar Research Institute at Cambridge – is valued by countries either commencing Antarctic research or moving towards the 'substantial research activity' required for ATCP status, as is demonstrated by the use made of BAS and SPRI by scientists from Brazil, Ecuador and Peru. On the surface Antarctica figures hardly at all in British relations with other Latin American nations, which have assumed little or no interest in the region, but may perceive Britain as a claimant to the 'South American Antarctic' and an apparent supporter of continued South African participation in the ATS. On the other hand, the past decade or so has been characterised by growing Latin American interest in Antarctica through a kind of 'domino effect' in the sense that Brazil (1975), Uruguay (1980), Peru (1981) and then Ecuador (1987) followed Argentina and Chile into the ATS. Colombia is rumoured to be a potential participant. Post-1983 UN debates on Antarctica have meant that even Latin American non-ATPs were forced to consider the topic, balancing Non-Aligned Movement pressures for the 'common heritage' approach against an appreciation of the issue's significance for other Latin American governments. Thus, certain Latin American governments, including those of Colombia, Costa Rica, Guatemala, Honduras, Nicaragua, Paraguay and Venezuela, have responded in UN votes to the lobbying of ATPs in support of the ATS.

Conclusions

The ATS, having been in force for over twenty-seven years, constitutes a well-established fact of international life and its success and durability will prove an important influence upon the Antarctic future of Britain and its Latin American partners. Although Antarctica is not a mainstream global issue, the polar dimension represents a possible source of both co-operation and confrontation in future British relations with Latin America, since the key South American nations are playing a leading part in the ATS. So far, the Antarctic experience, in contrast to the divisive features associated with the Falklands dispute, provides a practical and meaningful basis for the development and improvement of British relationships with Latin America – even with Argentina. A further policy consideration derives from emerging Latin American interest in the southern continent, as reflected by Ecuador's recent accession to the ATS and Peru's pursuit of ATCP status.

At first sight, Britain's Antarctic interest might seem somewhat nebulous. In reality, a series of territorial, strategic, resource, scientific, environmental and diplomatic factors can be identified alongside an appreciation of the ATS's value as the preferred milieu within which to maximise such interests. Obviously, there exists the alternative scenario of British withdrawal from Antarctica – this option was given serious consideration by the Wilson government in the mid-1960s – but this development would undermine Britain's presence in the nearby Falkland Islands, South Georgia and the South Sandwich Islands, hamper British efforts to prevent the power vacuum in Antarctica becoming a source of international friction, terminate BAS's prominent and long-term contribution to the unveiling of the continent's scientific mysteries, deprive Britain of an influential voice in the management and exploitation of Antarctic resources as well as in the protection of the continent's fragile environment and remove a significant point of contact with a range of other governments, including those in Latin America. Furthermore, any proposed withdrawal from BAT would prompt domestic political complications, while saving relatively little money, since annual BAS and related expenditure amounts to only £20 to £30 million.

Recently, the ATS has proved active in 'educating' the international community regarding the Antarctic scene and possibly this trend should be paralleled at the national level by an exercise designed to enable politicians, the media and society in Britain to gain a realistic and accurate appreciation of both this unknown region and British Antarctic interests, thereby illuminating the problems raised at the start of this chapter. In the meantime, Britain should remain in Antarctica, utilising its presence in BAT, BAS's research contribution and its ATCP status as the foundation for the performance at little cost of an influential role in the future of Antarctica. Indeed, the policy benefits of the relatively small Antarctic investment are substantial with improved relations with Latin America providing one of the possible yields.

Notes

1 See the Report of a Study Group chaired by Sir Anthony Parsons under the auspices of the David Davis Memorial Institute of International Studies (London), *Antarctica: the Next Decade* (Cambridge: Cambridge University Press 1987), p. 3; Peter J. Beck, 'The Antarctic Treaty System after 25 years', *The World Today*, 42:11 (1986), pp. 196–9; Peter J. Beck, *The International Politics of Antarctica* (London: Croom Helm, 1986), pp. 3–16.

2 The ATS has a two-tier membership: ATCPs, comprising the original twelve ATPs plus those adjudged to be 'active' in Antarctic research, perform the key role, whereas non-ATCPs merely accept the ATS's principles and have observer status at ATCM's.

3 FCO memorandum, House of Commons Foreign Affairs Committee, *Falkland Islands, Minutes of Evidence*, 10 November 1982, p. 3.

4 United Nations General Assembly Records (UNGA) A/C 1/38/PV44, pp. 16–18, 29 November 1983; UNGA A/39/583 (Part II)/Corr.1, p. 2, 30 May 1984; Hansard (House of Lords), vol. 426, col. 214, 16 December 1981; Peter J. Beck, 'Britain and Antarctica: the historical perspective', *Fram: Journal of Polar Studies*, 1:1 (1984), pp. 68–9, 80.

5 See Foreign Policy Document no. 98, *Antarctica – an Overview* (London: FCO, 1983), p. 6.

6 Beck, *International Politics of Antarctica*, pp. 28–30; Beck, *Britain and Antarctica*, pp. 78–9.

7 In the Hope Bay incident Argentine military personnel fired on British scientists attempting to land and rebuild British bases; in the Deception Island incident, Britain removed Argentine and Chilean base huts. See Peter J. Beck, 'A cold war: Britain, Argentina and the Antarctic', *History Today*, 37:6 (1987), pp. 16–17.

8 See Roberto E. Guyer, 'Antarctica's role in international relations', in F. O. Vicuna (ed.), *Antarctic Resources Policy: Scientific, Legal and Political Issues* (Cambridge: Cambridge University Press, 1983), p. 270; John A. Heap, 'Cooperation in the Antarctic: a quarter of a century's experience', in Vicuna (ed.), *Antarctic Resources Policy*, pp. 104–5.

9 Lord Shackleton, *Falkland Islands: Economic Study 1982* (Cmnd 8653, 1982), p. 3; Lord Shackleton, speaking on the BBC Radio Four *File on Four* programme: 'Antarctica as the last great wilderness', 2 December 1986.

10 See Beck, *International Politics of Antarctica*, p. 133.

11 See Jack Child, *Geopolitics and Conflict in South America: Quarrels among Neighbours* (New York: Praeger, 1985), p. 81; Jack Child, *Antarctica and South American Geopolitics: Frozen Lebensraum* (New York: Praeger, 1988), pp. 71–4.

12 See Peter J. Beck, *The Falkland Islands as an International Problem* (London: Routledge, 1988), pp. 148–9.

13 See UNGA A/40/PV9, p. 62, 25 September 1985.

14 Jack Child, 'Antarctica: arena for South American cooperation or conflict', paper presented at International Congress of Latin American Studies Association, New Orleans, March 1988, p. 9.

15 Brian Roberts, 'International cooperation for Antarctic development: the test for the Antarctic Treaty', *Polar Record*, 19:119 (1978), p. 112.

16 New Zealand Ministry of Foreign Affairs, *Note on Special Consultative Meeting on Antarctic Minerals 14 June 1982* (Wellington), p. 2 (A. Watts speaking).

17 Quoted in Rüdiger Wolfrum (ed.), *Antarctic Challenge* (Berlin: Duncker and Humblot, 1984), p. 58.

18 See Peter J. Beck, 'Antarctica as a strategic irrelevance', published in Portuguese in *Contexto Internacional* (Rio de Janeiro), 7:1 (Jan.–June, 1988).

19 United Nations, *Report of the Secretary-General on the Question of Antarctica*, UNGA A/39/583 (Part I) (New York, November 1984), pp. 44–6; and United Nations, Department of Disarmament Affairs, *Study on Conventional Disarmament* (New York, 1985), pp. 34–7.

20 Hansard (House of Commons), vol. 25, vol. 740, Thatcher, 15 June 1982; Parsons, *Antarctica: the next decade*, pp. 100–1.

21 Child, *Antarctica and South American Geopolitics*, p. vii (see also pp. 33, 37–44), and Child, *Geopolitics and Conflict in South America*, pp. 42–7.

22 'Antarctica: Arena for South American Cooperation', p. 18.

23 See Beck, *Antarctica as a Strategic Irrelevance.*
24 FCO, *Antarctica – An Overview*, p. 6.
25 See Beck, *International Politics of Antarctica*, pp. 242–3; F. G. Larminie, 'Antarctic mineral and maritime resources', in T. B. Millar (ed.), *Australia, Britain and Antarctica* (London: Australian Studies Centre, 1986), pp. 20–3.
26 FCO, *Antarctica – An Overview*, p. 6.
27 Maarten J. de Wit, *Minerals and Mining in Antarctica: Science and Technology, Economics and Politics* (Oxford: Oxford University Press, 1985), p. 68.
28 'Anglo-Argentine rivalry after the Falklands: on the road to Antarctica?', in A. R. Coll and A. C. Arend (eds.), *The Falklands War: Lessons for Strategy, Diplomacy and International Law* (London: Allen & Unwin, 1985), pp. 206–7.
29 Adrian Berry, 'The riches that lie beyond Antarctica', *Daily Telegraph*, 25 September 1984. See also 'Falkland Islands crisis: the politics of resources', *Eco*, 19:1 (May–June 1982), pp. 1–4; Lord Shackleton, 'Why the Falklands matter', *The Times*, 22 April 1985; BBC Radio *File on Four* programme, statement by Richard Laws (for details see n. 9, above).
30 BBC Radio *File on Four* programme (for details see n. 9, above); see also D. W. H. Walton (ed.), *Antarctic Science* (Cambridge: Cambridge University Press, 1987).
31 See House of Commons, Foreign Affairs Committee, *Falkland Islands, Minutes of Evidence*, 13 December 1982, p. 91, Richard Laws.
32 David Drewry, 'International scientific coordination in Antarctica', in Millar, *Australia, Britain and Antarctica*, pp. 32–3.
33 *Ibid.*, p. 33.
34 See FCO, *Antarctica – An Overview*, p. 6.
35 UNGA A/C 1/38/PV46, p. 2, 30 November 1983; UNGA A/C 1/39/PV53, pp. 11–12 and 16, 29 November 1984; UNGA A/C 1/40/PV50, pp. 22–3, 26 November 1985; see also FCO, *Background Brief – Antarctic Treaty: Twenty-fifth Anniversary* (London: 1984).
36 UNGA A/40/PV9, p. 62, 25 September 1985.
37 In the BBC Radio *File on Four* programme (for details see n. 9, above).
38 See FCO, *Background Brief – Antarctic Treaty*, p. 5.

11 The illicit drug trade
David Webb-Carter

The average citizen of the United Kingdom has only a superficial knowledge of the problems caused by illicit drugs and the writer was no different until a military posting to Central America (as Commander of the British forces in Belize) brought the difficulties home in a most vivid manner.* Across the world drugs have been smoked, chewed or sniffed for thousands of years. We have learnt how Helen of Troy offered Telemachus nepenthe in Homer's *Odyssey* and there is definitive evidence of the use of coca leaves as stimulants found on pottery and in wall-paintings of the Amerindians. The coca shrub enjoyed a pre-eminent position in the Inca Empire and it was regarded as a sacred manifestation of divinity, which was buried with the deceased to speed them on their way to another and better world.

Unlike tobacco and chocolate, coca was never exported to Europe from the Americas under Spanish rule, although the Moors are thought to have brought marijuana to Spain from Africa for use as a tranquilliser or pain-killer. Opiates from the East made their appearance in Britain largely through the successes of the great British trading companies. Clive of India was an addict for twenty years, before dying in a fit after a double dose of opium. Whilst the British East India Company's opium trade was finally curtailed towards the end of the nineteenth century, cocaine had by then begun to make its appearance in the Western world – first as a wonder-drug manufactured by the US pharmaceutical firm Parke-Davis. Shortly afterwards, in 1886, an unknown US pharmacist called John Pemberton invented a 'brain-tonic' elixir which he called 'Coca Kola'. This new drink was directed at the fast-growing temperance market in the United States. The coca element was continued in the drink until 1903, the kola element being drawn from the West African kola tree whose nuts contain caffeine. The name of the drink was changed to Coca Cola around the turn of the century.

More recently the illicit trade has expanded into an enormous market, perhaps second only to the arms trade in the world economy. This illicit trade has brought not only problems to the producer countries of Central and South America, but also a growing and serious crisis of addiction leading to crime in the Western world. The trade is so extensive, so powerful and so ruthless that any visitor to Latin America becomes rapidly aware of it, while its impact in the United Kingdom has grown significantly in recent years.

Illegal drugs

There is so much confusion about the definition of different drugs that it is necessary to describe briefly each category of illicit substance. The term 'narcotic' in its medical meaning refers to opium, opium derivatives and synthetic substitutes. Narcotics are fundamental to certain medical practices, not least the relief of intense pain, and are regularly used for cancer patients and others. Illegal users and addicts find that narcotics produce relief from anxiety and stress, whilst producing a temporary sense of comfort and well-being. Heroin is the most commonly abused narcotic.

Stimulants, on the other hand, give users a feeling of strength, superiority and self-possession. These effects are greatly intensified if the drug is injected intravenously; this produces a sudden sensation known as a 'flash' or a 'hit'. Cocaine is the most potent of the stimulants and, in its freebase form known as 'crack',[1] it is lethal. Because it is smoked rather than snorted, crack reaches the brain in seconds, resulting in a sudden, intense high. This reaction dissipates within minutes, leaving the user with an enormous craving to take more. Hallucinogens, which were so popular in the Flower Power days of the 1960s, are substances which distort the perception of the brain and users speak of seeing sounds and hearing colours. LSD (lysergic acid diethylamide) is the most common hallucinogen and the user normally experiences a 'trip' in which he or she sees a kaleidoscope of lights combined with fantastically vivid images. These substances have now slipped out of fashion.

The last category of substance is the depressant. Often prescribed by doctors to combat insomnia, depressants are mainly used as relief from depression and stress. However, a sinister development in the United States has given cause for further alarm: the arrival of 'designer' drugs, which are a chemical mixture of narcotics and depressants. Based on methodone, these analogues are a hundred times more potent than heroin. In one county of Los Angeles designer drugs caused eleven deaths during three months in 1988; particularly deadly is a substance known as 'ecstasy'.

Many would argue that at least cannabis or marijuana, which grows wild in most tropical and temperate regions, should be legalised. Advances continue to be made, however, in research into THC (tetrahydrocannobinol – Delta 9) which show long-term chemical effects in the human body – in particular on fertility. Individuals trying the substance find an altered sense of self-identity, a dulling of emotion and widely fluctuating images and emotions. One person in every six in the USA has tried marijuana and 40 per cent of those are regular users.[2] Given emerging medical evidence, there is no case for legalising marijuana in spite of the United States and Caribbean problems with domestic production. In the United Kingdom only the Green Party has proposed its legalisation and there is a strong body of opinion that legalisation of marijuana would lead to user escalation followed by the use of stronger and more addictive substances. *A fortiori*, the case for legalising other drugs, which have more serious side-effects, is even weaker.

The global trade in illicit drugs

The crisis in drug addiction has reached such dimensions that it occupies priority attention at the highest level in many countries. The trade in illicit drugs is estimated to have overtaken that in oil in cash terms and they are now the world's second most traded commodity after armaments, so that in value they amount to approximately 9 per cent of all international merchandise.[3] In the United States itself, marijuana is the second-largest cash crop – a distasteful fact which has been seized upon by many Third World leaders facing US pressure on drugs crop eradication.

South America and Asia are the two main areas of illicit cultivation, with many countries involved in the trade. Not only does internal cultivation lead to domestic misuse by the citizens of the country concerned, but the additional cash in circulation is regularly used to corrupt the government of the country itself. In Belize certain ministers of the People's United Party (PUP) administration (in power until 1984) were known to have been involved in trafficking and Mr Briceño, the former Natural Resources Minister, was convicted in South Carolina in 1985 and is currently under sentence.

The vast amounts of money involved have a totally disproportionate effect on ordinary people. Cash is the medium of exchange and substantial amounts are available to ensure that individuals co-operate with the drug barons' intentions. For example, two British army officers in Belize under my command were offered $250,000 each to turn a blind eye to a cocaine-trafficking exchange during a fishing competition. Fortunately, they declined to co-operate and reported the matter to the authorities. Many might not have been so high-minded.

Money-laundering is the process of changing the money gained from drugs operations from cash to a more manageable form whilst concealing its illicit origins. The use of 'shell' companies, numbered accounts and many other 'offshore' schemes are devices used by the drug barons to legalise their wealth. There is a lively trade in 'narcodollars' in the banking institutions of such offshore havens as the Cayman Islands, the Bahamas, British Virgin Islands, Panama, India, Pakistan, Luxembourg, Liechtenstein, Switzerland and the Channel Islands. Not surprisingly, the traffickers prefer a climate of political stability without exchange controls and with good bank secrecy in which to convert narcodollars to straight currency and legal transactions. Because of differing requirements, the money-laundering activities are kept well separate from growing and distribution operations. A recent example of the transfer of money into legal activities has been the significant moves by Colombians into the European hotel and restaurant trade. Although it is very hard to prove, police feel that this sort of activity is the ideal medium for laundering money which has been acquired through the trade in illicit drugs. No fewer than five large Colombian hotel and restaurant chains were operating in Europe in 1988 when five years previously there had been none.

The British Government has acted in a forthright manner with a 'Drug Trafficking Offences Act' (1986), which enables courts in England and Wales to impose a confiscation order in addition to any sentence.[4] Moreover, the Act also requires banks and individuals employed in banks to watch out for, and if necessary refuse to negotiate, any substantial unexplained sums of money. Similar legislation is in hand for Scotland, but for the time being both the Channel Islands and the Isle of Man remain open to narcodollars.

Ideally placed in the Caribbean Basin, some of the remaining British Dependencies continue to be easy prey for the vast amounts of cash in possession of the traffickers. The Prime Minister of the Turks and Caicos Islands, Norman Saunders, was a hero in his own country, even when under sentence for narcotics trafficking in the United States, because he had used much of the illegal money to finance social services for the local Islanders. The Turks and Caicos problem highlights the difficulty of richer nations imposing anti-drug legislation on poorer countries, whose inhabitants see the illicit trade as a windfall.

The drug–terrorism connection

The interdependence of drug trafficking and terrorism is a subject which generates considerable debate amongst informed observers. The extent of this relationship draws together the interests of not only the law-enforcement agencies of the Western world, but also their intelligence-gathering bodies. For some years, it has become gradually apparent that many terrorist organisations have formed ties with the drug traffickers. Whether it is merely the armed protection of the coca fields in Latin America, the laundering of the money, protection racketeering or general illicit drug trading to generate funding, terrorist organisations have found the temptation of the rich pickings of the illicit trade too tempting to resist in spite of ideological differences between themselves and the traffickers (many of whom have pronounced right-wing views).

Colombia

The most obvious example of such an interdependence exists in Colombia. It is not the function of this chapter to list a series of drug-related acts of terrorism, but the continual attempts by guerrilla and terrorist groups to shape both political and judicial attitudes cannot have escaped the notice of the rest of the world. Whilst political violence has been a problem in Colombia since the 1940s, the relatively recent conversion of the country to being the main refinement and transshipment centre for cocaine has made the country's politicians a target for the activities of the drug barons of the region. The illicit drug traffickers have not hesitated to follow up their threats with violence and their aims have increasingly coincided with the aims of the terrorist movements.

The Revolutionary Armed Forces of Colombia – or FARC as they are more commonly known – have been one of the most regularly mentioned terrorist groups with close connections and interdependence with the drug trade. The FARC is the oldest, largest, best-armed and best-disciplined terrorist group in Colombia and arguably in South America. It operates through numerous fronts and ideologically it is the armed wing of the Colombian Communist Party. The FARC may cultivate some coca, but it mainly acquires its funds by collecting protection money from growers and traffickers. From time to time the traffickers may provide arms and ammunition in return for services, such as FARC's protection of drug-growing areas and of airfields and the provision of warning networks for the traffickers. The FARC is a rurally based movement and consequently operates in the same areas as the growers. In early 1984, when Colombian soldiers and police mounted an operation against cocaine laboratories in 'Tranquilandia', they were opposed by a well-organised and armed group of thirty men in jungle fatigue-type uniforms: after the security forces had seized some ten tons of cocaine, follow-up operations in the eastern *llanos* led them to a FARC camp which was located near a further laboratory. There can be little doubt that, when operating in the same area, the FARC and the traffickers form co-operative agreements for movement, trade and defence against attack.

The United States Drug Enforcement Administration (DEA) ran a prolonged operation against a well-known Colombian drug trafficker and cartel leader, Jaime Guillot Lara, who was of interest to the intelligence authorities because of his connections with Cuba. It appeared that Guillot had made arrangements with certain Cubans in influential positions for his trafficking ships to be given safe haven in return for payment. He also agreed that his ships would occasionally carry arms to the M-19 Movement in Colombia on their return journey. The 19th April Movement (M-19) is a guerrilla and terrorist organisation which first came to world notice when in 1980 it took over the Dominican Embassy in Bogotá and held eighteen diplomats hostage for several weeks. Like the FARC, the M-19 has extensive interdependence with the drug trade. The organisation derived considerable benefit in the early 1980s from the close association of its leader Jaime Bateman Cayón with Guillot, whose Cuban connections proved invaluable.

The Colombian authorities can contain but cannot eradicate these movements. Drug money has continued to flow through the country using long established illegal networks and, although the relationship is unstable and at times antagonistic, there is a persistent symbiosis between the drug trafficker and the guerrilla.

Peru

The 'Sendero Luminoso', or Shining Path, guerrilla movement – a fundamentalist neo-Marxist movement – has been trying to destabilise the Peruvian
government since 1980. The fighting has caused more than four thousand
deaths and has certainly affected the country's tourist industry. Although
there is little real evidence, a number of Peruvian officials including President
García have stated that the Sendero Luminoso derives much of its funding
from illicit drug-trading activities. As a mainly rural group, Sendero Luminoso also operates in the same areas as the coca growers and, although
ideologically at odds, they would doubtless combine to meet any threat from
the security forces. Moreover, they have moved to portray US eradication
efforts as a further extension of 'Yankee Imperialism'. Their stated aim is to
rid the Peruvian Indian population of 'foreign' influences.

The 'Movimiento Revolucionario Tupac Amarú' (MRTA) group is an
amalgamation of three or four small older guerrilla movements. It has fought
bitterly with Sendero Luminoso in order to try and gain control of the Alto
Huallaga area where some of the best-quality cocaine paste is produced. The
reason for the fighting is only too clear, for the illicit drug trade in the region
is worth millions of dollars annually to the victor.

European terrorist movements

There is little evidence of an interdependence between drug traffickers and
European terrorist groups. Whilst there have been a few instances of Italian
terrorists being connected with Bulgarian heroin traffickers (and IRA rack-
eteers continue to dabble with heroin and cannabis in Belfast), no formalised
links appear to have yet been established with Latin American traffickers. The
ethnic Armenian terrorist organisation, called the Justice Commandos of the
Armenian Genocide, have carried out acts of terrorism against Turkish
installations in Europe, the United States and Australia and one of its leaders,
Nouban Sofoyan, is an alleged cocaine trafficker who has so far escaped
extradition to the United States and is currently on parole to the Lebanese
government. The arrest of the known IRA activist J.J. McCann in 1988 with
members of the Marks syndicate in Majorca suggests that the IRA too is
involved in the classic drugs–money–arms cycle. There is also evidence that
the Bulgarian import–export agency Kintex is involved in this sort of
exchange. There can be little doubt that interested agencies are alert for any
moves which might suggest a cocaine/marijuana connection between European terrorists and Latin American organisations. However, no evidence is yet
available.

Narcoterrorism

The United States has tried to use extradition as a means of enforcing its anti-narcotics policies. To an extent this scheme has backfired in Latin America, as it is seen by many as a further manifestation of 'Yankee Imperialism' and consequently plays into the hands of the terrorist movements. A member of the Colombian Medellín cartel, Carlos Lehder, when interviewed on Spanish television in January 1985, stated that if extradition of Colombians to the United States was not stopped, he would arrange for five hundred US citizens to be killed. He went on to say that he had established contacts with the M-19, as well as with elements of the army and the police, to form a force of half a million which would defend national sovereignty. Moreover, the Medellín cartel offered the government $2.4 billion to reduce the public external debt, so strongly did it oppose the extradition treaty agreed with the USA. The offer was declined. Shortly afterwards, in 1984 the Colombian Minister of Justice, Rodrigo Lara Bonilla, was assassinated in Bogotá. No fewer than fifteen judges and magistrates were killed violently in 1985 and after a short lull, during which another former Justice Minister was shot and wounded in Budapest where he was Colombian ambassador, further narco-related political violence erupted in early 1988. The Attorney General, Carlos Hoyos, was assassinated while investigating the strange release from prison of one of the leaders of the Medellín cocaine cartel, Jorge Luis Ochoa. The traffickers had waged a violent campaign against the US–Colombian extradition treaty and it was finally declared 'unconstitutional' by the Colombian Supreme Court in 1987. Thus, it was unlikely that Ochoa would have been extradited; indeed, it was said, the police had only wished to interview him in connection with the illegal importation of bulls and had chanced to arrest him after he had driven his Porsche through a speed-trap at 110 miles per hour.

Recently the former United States Commander-in-Chief in Panama, General Gorman, stated before a congressional committee that 'the very survival of democracy in certain countries which have long been friends and allies is threatened by the Colombian cartel which is so wealthy it can literally buy governments and destabilise whole societies'. There is no doubt much truth in such statements, for junior officials with low salaries are given the simple option: death or a suitcase of cash, the equivalent of years of salary. In turn, untainted officials feel a sense of hopelessness as the cocaine cartel's tentacles reach far into the upper echelons of government. The approach is known as 'plomo o plata' – 'lead or silver'. The relationship between the Colombian government and the cocaine cartel has been discussed above. It was therefore unsurprising when a new Colombian Justice Minister, Alfredo Gutierrez, recently suggested that his government should negotiate with the cartel with a possible view to decriminalising the cocaine trade. He was quoted as saying that 'the fight against drug dealing is useless'.

The present United States–Panama crisis in mutual relations can also be easily traced to illicit drug trafficking. Panama is ideally placed as an interface between North and South America. It had superb banking facilities and a world-famous duty-free area in Colón. The military strongman General Manuel Noriega has long been the target of international speculation on his involvement not only in electoral fraud and espionage, but also in drug trafficking. Efforts by the Reagan administration to remove him from power failed and fuelled to a certain extent further anti-US sentiment throughout Latin America. Whilst the General vehemently denied charges levelled at him by Grand Juries in the United States, he has tenaciously hung on to his position. The extent of official US involvement with Noriega is still unclear – the Central Intelligence Agency (CIA) may have used him as a vehicle for some of its more nefarious Central American adventures, particularly in support of the Nicaraguan Contras. Recent revelations have also pointed to extensive drug involvement among the US military stationed in Panama.

In the Caribbean, the former Turks and Caicos Prime Minister, Norman Saunders, was in 1988 serving a prison sentence for illicit drug trafficking and rumours continue to abound that other Caribbean political leaders are also involved. The emerging trend of using drug trafficking to support political ends represents a change in historical and ideological patterns. Previously drug traffickers were solely interested in profits and viewed the activities of the security forces and police as part of the cost of the operation. Direct confrontation with government was avoided as it was likely to be counter-productive. In the face of increasing pressure from the United States, some Latin American governments have attempted to introduce more effective drug-control measures. The interests of guerrillas and traffickers can then coincide, although it should always be remembered that guerrilla leaders and traffickers are usually at opposite ends of the political spectrum so that any co-operation is most likely to be only a marriage of convenience.

Economic implications

The trade in cocaine and marijuana has stimulated the economies of producer countries, particularly so in countries with few other prospects. Depending on the country, the growth in economic activity has varied according to the prevention measures carried out by respective governments. At the same time, the rapid increase in domestic drug abuse has concentrated the minds of politicians. Naturally, it is the United States which has brought the most pressure to bear, although the United States has increasingly tried to assist in crop alternatives through its overseas development agency (USAID).

Many people, most notably former President Belaúnde of Peru, have believed that the jungle areas where the coca is grown could become a fertile region to provide vegetables, meat and other food materials at affordable prices to the people of the region. Yet thousands of peasants in Colombia, Brazil, Peru and Bolivia grow the coca because of its high cocaine yield: it is a true cash crop. As demand in the Western world has increased, so has the number of peasants involved in production in the remote jungle areas. Many poor people, frightened by the intimidation of the drug barons and their followers, have joined the general migration to the cities. For those who remain and for those who join them from other areas, their smallholdings can become highly cash-productive with an acre producing possibly as much as $12,000 a year. In Belize, where rice is priced at fifteen cents a pound, marijuana can be sold for as much as fifty dollars a pound. The economics are only too simple.

In Bolivia it is estimated that 5 per cent of the population is involved in the drug economy, the highest percentage of any country in the world. From the production areas in the *yungas* and the east, through a distribution process including aircraft and motor transport, to the laboratories which employ many elementary chemists, a whole economy has developed. The export revenue from cocaine far exceeds any other for Bolivia, including that from tin. For a country such as Bolivia, the illicit trade has produced an injection of hard cash into an ailing economy, which will make it almost impossible for the government to introduce hard measures against the traffickers on anything but a short-term basis. Even the much-vaunted 'Blast Furnace' operation by US forces in 1985 against the traffickers in Bolivia was a failure – not least because it was announced in Washington some twelve hours before the troops were due to move.

Whilst many peasants are employed in the growing of cocaine in Peru and Bolivia, the same does not at present apply in Colombia since production is so much cheaper in the former countries. Colombia is more concerned with the chemical processing of the drug, as well as providing the entrepreneurial skills for distributing the illicit product to the USA and Europe. Nevertheless, the trade is worth considerably less to Colombia than its street value. A young Briton recently convicted in the United States claimed his cargo of 500 kilos was worth $5 million – yet the street value in the United States would have been nearer $20 million.

Against what is perceived as a foreign threat to its national interest, the United States' solution is to use its economic and political strength to influence local governments. In particular, eradication programmes have been funded for almost every country in the region, using aerial spraying. Trade penalties and political pressure are difficult for poor countries to resist, but with the increasing domestic abuse and the gradual decline of the rule of law, nearly every producer country is now seeking a way out of the illicit-drugs vortex.

A significant effect of the US pressure to eradicate illicit drug growing is, nevertheless, an increase of anti-'yankee' feeling among many Latin Americans who resent the apparent arrogance of their northern neighbour. Yet whatever policies are introduced, it is hard to see that anything will prevent such a lucrative trade. Those involved have no lack of enterprise and there can be little doubt that, as one route or means of production is blocked, another will be discovered.

The marijuana and cocaine trade has a significant influence on the poor economies of the Caribbean. The Bahamas, Jamaica, the Turks and Caicos and many others have proved to be vital refuelling and transshipment bases for the traffickers. The pay-offs for poor economies have been significant, but – as the Islands are closer to the United States – it has been easier to monitor these small nation-states. The success of US enforcement policies has again fuelled anti-US sentiment.

The present British policy, promulgated by the Overseas Development Administration (ODA), is to provide crop-substitution programmes on a limited basis. Without spending considerable sums of money, this programme has been successful and locally popular. Some limited police training assistance is also being given, but the British government is perhaps a little reluctant to extend that particular aspect, given the poor reputation of some Latin American police forces and the cultural and language difficulties.

From a European point of view, the Caribbean and Latin American production of marijuana is not significant because the crop is almost all for domestic consumption or export to the United States and Canada. In recent years the availability has also diminished because of the relative success of crop-eradication campaigns in Colombia, Mexico, Jamaica and Belize.

However, as quickly as the crops diminished elsewhere, the Brazilian marijuana industry moved into a higher gear. The crop is now cultivated in fourteen out of twenty-three states and territories and, whilst previously it was thought to be mostly for internal consumption, it is now a very large export operation and a small, but steadily increasing, flow is now reaching Europe. During the severe drought in North Eastern Brazil, which ended in 1984, there was a large-scale migration to the cities, but many farmers who remained began to cultivate marijuana on a far larger scale than before. Profits now exceed income from legitimate crops or livestock and up-to-date reports talk of traffickers able to supply up to fifteen-ton consignments of marijuana at a time. Following hard on the trail of the production boom, incidences of robbery and murder have also multiplied. The area is the most lawless in the whole of Brazil, and the State of Bahia has the highest murder rate. With this backdrop of lawlessness, law-abiding farmers avoid confrontations with the traffickers and will not co-operate with the police or armed forces for fear of reprisals.

Wholesale prices of marijuana in Brazil vary from state to state, but at embarkation point they range from $50 to $60 a kilo, whilst at point of cultivation it will sell for $35 a kilo. At the same time, Colombian marijuana sold for about $4 a kilo at point of cultivation and $14 at embarkation. Whilst the Brazilian crop is expensive compared to the Colombian, it compares with prices in Belize at around $50 and Jamaica at $45 a kilo.

For the most part Latin American marijuana is traded with the United States and not with Europe, which is already supplied from elsewhere. However, cocaine is the commodity which has found a ready clientele. The map in Figure 11.1 describes the networks in general terms against a world-wide trade. The United Kingdom has an almost unique advantage in this context, because as it is

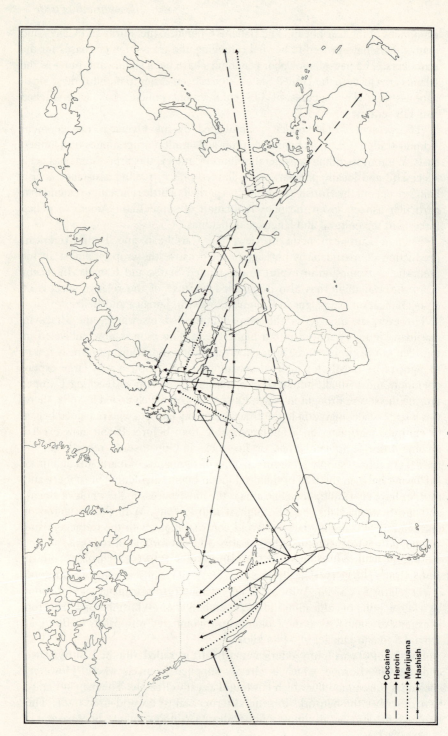

11.1 Main world drug-trafficking networks in the 1980s

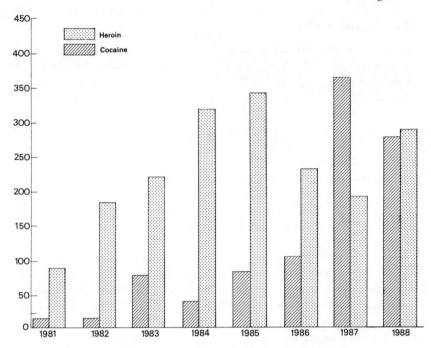

11.2 HM Customs heroin and cocaine seizures, 1981–8 (1981–6 figures based on Home Office Statistical Bulletin 40/86; figures for 1987 and 1988 reported in *The Independent*, 19 January 1989, p. 3)

an island, its Customs and Excise is able to scan almost every visitor if it so wishes.

It seems that cocaine is brought to the United Kingdom by a number of means, but mainly through air traffic, containers and other sea routes from Europe and occasionally by private yacht. In late 1987, Customs at Southampton uncovered the biggest haul of cocaine from Colombia yet to come to light in this country. The seizure (discovered in a container) was more than half the previous year's total haul. The sinister increase in cocaine seizures (see Figure 11.2) shows clearly the increasing threat.

In the early 1980s cocaine was the prerogative of the better-off illicit drug user. Now, with prices dropping to between £40 and £50 a gram, it is no longer in the expensive category; with the US market at near-saturation point, the traffickers are seeking new markets. UK Home Office bulletins demonstrate the readiness of the market to take on the new and increasing trade with an estimated 500 new cocaine addicts recorded each year. Although cultural and historic links make Spain and Portugal the natural entry points for Latin American illicit drugs, Customs officers all over Europe are now paying particular attention to all shipping and flights from South America, Central America and Miami.

The British scene

Whilst the present British government has made some energetic and timely commitments in increasing the resources available to combat the importation and distribution of drugs, there is still much to be done. The extent and pattern of drug misuse is still not fully apparent in the United Kingdom because of the largely covert nature of the practice. Home Office research has suggested that possibly only one in five addicts is registered, whilst a survey in Glasgow indicated the figure was as low as one in ten. The 1960s popular image of a typical hard-drug user was that of a disaffected young registered heroin addict living within an alternative sub-culture in the inner-city area, supporting his habit through prescription from certain well-known general practitioners. Hard-drug users today share few of these characteristics. The National Association of Probation Officers (who are in regular contact with illicit drug users) has recorded frequent changes in pattern by the users. The black market has expanded and heroin, or the equally dangerous methodone, have become easily available in powder form. Heroin is now inhaled or smoked rather than injected; it is a tragic consequence of the government AIDS awareness campaign that the use of syringes is now seen as dangerous in itself and addicts have the mistaken belief that inhalation or smoking is a less dangerous practice.

Illicit drugs follow distinct fashion phases; in the 1960s and 1970s LSD was a popular hallucinogen, but it is now rarely found and rather expensive. In the late seventies barbiturates became popular, but have now slipped back with changes in prescribing regulations. Solvent abuse reached almost epidemic proportions at the beginning of the 1980s. Different drugs, it is argued, have different cultural contexts; as unemployment reached hitherto unknown heights in the mid-1980s, it was opiates such as heroin which attracted young people who were experiencing a sense of hopelessness. Now as the economy has gained in strength, a new fashion is emerging. A desire for rapid stimulation is coinciding with a dramatic increase in the cocaine trade from Latin America. The unfortunate confessions of popular media personalities and rumours of quick stimulation to enhance the ability of money dealers in the City of London are no help in the campaign to combat addiction. The concept of cocaine as a fashionable and non-dangerous drug needs to be actively fought. Yet, whilst cocaine is the fashion of today, it may well be that the nineties will herald the 'designer drug' age with substances with exotic names like 'ecstasy' moving into the limelight.

Evidence is slowly emerging of the strong connection between drug abuse and crime. Whilst no figures are available for the United Kingdom, Figure 11.3 demonstrates the US problems in this field. Users in their need to support their habit have turned to robbery, prostitution, mugging and murder. It probably costs around £400 a week to support a heroin addict and that sort of money is not found from social security payments. According to the Metropolitan Police, users barter stolen property for more drugs and the pushers are increasingly associated with the 'fencing' of stolen goods. In Madrid it is

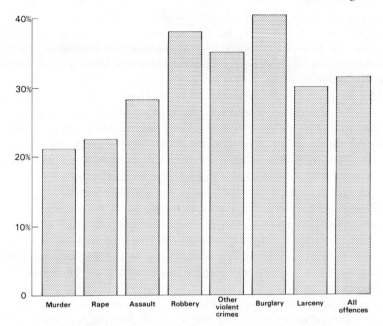

11.3 Drug-connected crime in the United States (based on US Department of Justice report, *Drug Enforcement Administration – A Profile* (Washington, DC, 1984))

reported that about 2,000 heroin addicts are committing 90 per cent of crime. Senior officials in the city have recently announced statistics which show that 5 per cent of the capital's 4 million people were victims of drug-related crime in 1987. Madrid police believe that drug addiction is almost solely responsible for the 60 per cent expansion in crime during the last year.

In the United States, the advent of 'crack' has heralded 'territorial' wars among rival drug-trading groups because of the huge amounts of cash involved. Dealers try to increase their profits by offering free samples to potential customers and, as they increase their business and attempt to expand, they meet similar groups which are also expanding. Firearms and knife offences are thus on the increase. The low cost of cocaine by-products such as 'crack' has alarming implications: aggressive sales procedures such as free samples, low introductory prices, brand names and attractive packaging are now the order of the day.

As far as Britain and other European nations are concerned, education against the menace of illicit drugs is perhaps the only effective direct action which can be taken since the main producer countries are far away and for the most part have little connection with Britain. The government has tended to work through the Health Education Council in order to convince the country at large of the dangers inherent in illicit drug-taking. However, given the experience of the AIDS awareness campaign in early 1987, new concepts are being developed to reach those most likely to be vulnerable. While previously a national campaign seemed to be the solution, it now appears that publicity schemes are more successful if applied locally; such campaigns are highly dependent upon local cultures and the resources and structures which already exist.

Moreover, it is vital that any campaign reaches the relevant groups in the community. In particular teachers, social workers, doctors and clergymen are in the forefront of the problem; many are completely unskilled in the procedures to deal with the drug sub-culture. It is these key professionals who can use the necessary information obtained from those they encounter. It is sad, but true, that surveys by independent bodies have discovered that many general practitioners are completely unskilled in dealing with the human and emotional problems which are occurring. For example, one doctor told a distressed mother whose son had become an addict that none of the problems would have occurred had the family stayed in 'the ways of the Lord'. Equally, drug-taking is endemic in some schools; an eleven-year-old girl was introduced to heroin by her thirteen-year-old sister during morning break in one case which came before one survey.[5]

In recognition of the huge illegal market, it is often suggested that some form of legalisation of the so-called 'soft drugs' should be supported. The experience of alcohol prohibition in the United States is cited as a first-class example of the emptiness of the present policy. In brief, legalisation would remove the prospect of profits from the illegal traffic operation, sleazy pushers could no longer find a reasonable trade and the prisons would be emptied of the unfortunate illicit drug consumers. In a leading article in 1988 the much-respected journal *The Economist* argued for such a policy, extending it to include the controlled registering of hard-drug users also. Key figures in United States society, including the three black mayors of Baltimore, Minneapolis and Washington, DC, have also called for legalisation.

In my description of each type of illicit substance earlier, the problems of the unknown long-term medical effects of cannabis were discussed. It has been said that cannabis is no more dangerous than tobacco and indeed, if introduced today, tobacco would also probably be illegal. It seems a curious argument that, as so-called civilised governments try to restrict the numbers of people with diseases related to cigarette smoking, a move should be made to introduce a further problem legally. The analogy with alcohol can also be made, as again civilised society is increasingly concerned about alcohol-related traffic accidents.

Apparently something like a society in which cocaine was legal existed on Norman's Cay in the Bahamas during the heyday of Colombian Carlos Lehder's trafficking operations. Whilst not necessarily connected, it is a fact that cocaine-related admissions to the only psychiatric clinic in Nassau increased from nil to 300 in the three years of Lehder's operation.

However, groups which have a considerable insight into the United Kingdom's national problem continue to advocate some legitimacy – particularly for users as against illicit suppliers. For example, the National Association of Probation Officers has called for the abolition of possession of cannabis as a criminal offence and for the investigation of a legalised means of supply.[6] The Association continues to stand against the present government's view that the social use of cannabis should be considered dangerous. It is often argued that the majority of hard-drug users have started on cannabis, although the Association claims there is no real evidence of a natural escalation from cannabis to hard drugs. On the other hand, the illegality of cannabis exposes users to a vibrant black market where the suppliers are only too anxious to introduce their clients to supposedly more exotic, and definitely more expensive, substances.

It is against this backdrop of debate over cannabis legislation that a new flood of cocaine is starting to arrive from South America. Whilst there seems little doubt in anyone's mind on the undesirability of legalising cocaine, the cannabis argument tends to obscure the issue. However, given the current government's views on 'Victorian values', it seems most unlikely that cannabis will be legalised in the near future. In the meantime it would seem that imprisonment is a particularly inappropriate way of dealing with drug-related offences which are not connected with other crimes.

Conclusions

The issues of illicit drug growing, money-laundering, trading and consumption are complicated and require sophisticated reactions from responsible governments. Producer-country governments are unlikely to be able to take effective action against the producers. The cartels and gangs are very powerful and the money generated has done much to stimulate local economies. The greatest incentive to take action is in countries where abuse is at its most serious.

The present United States eradication methods have provided an easy target for the anti-US forces in Latin America. The United States is shown as imperialist, arrogant and hypocritical. European governments, and Britain in particular, should stay well clear of eradication programmes, but there is a number of crop-substitution programmes which can make a useful contribution. Experience has shown these are popular and they are certainly not controversial. Police training is a vital aid gift, particularly in the Caribbean where language and culture have much more connection with the United Kingdom. The present British policy of sympathetic assistance and encouragement should be continued in the drugs field, which should not be allowed to overshadow other relationships.

The difficulties of tracing the large amounts of money generated by drugs has already been discussed. Legislation is gradually being introduced which will make it harder and harder for large sums to be moved around the world until they become 'clean'. However, this is an area where more international co-operation is required.

At present it would seem that there is widespread lack of knowledge of the extent and character of the illicit drugs problem. More knowledge in government circles would do much to clarify how the problem should be treated in the context of our relations with the Latin American countries involved. At the very least, however, international and local banking controls in Britain and its remaining dependencies should be strengthened and should continue to focus on money-laundering activities.

It is on the demand rather than the supply side that our major effort should be concentrated. Education programmes can be very effective, but they need to be carefully directed and researched. In particular, groups with direct contact with drug abusers and the young should be targeted for special education campaigns. Education techniques could be shared with producer countries, who themselves are beginning to face serious consumer problems. It is only by sensible and careful education that the demand can be reduced and therefore the illicit trade diminished. This will be a long road and will require considerable persistence and money – far more than has been spent hitherto. The Home Office figures for 1987 and 1988, which show a dramatic increase in cocaine seizures over 1986 (see Figure 11.2), demonstrate that there is no time to be lost.

Notes

* The views expressed in this chapter are those of the author alone and do not necessarily express those of the Army or Her Majesty's Government.
1 'Freebasing' is the fastest-growing form of cocaine use in the United States (where it is called 'crack') and the Caribbean (where it is referred to as 'rocks'). It is the most efficient way of delivering a potent form of cocaine to the brain in a very short time. The high addiction potential of this method is possibly a marketing strategy by the traffickers to increase demand. The 'freebase' form involves dissolving the white cocaine hydrochloride powder in warm water and adding an alkali-like sodium bicarbonate. This creates cocaine crystals (hence 'rocks' or 'crack').
2 See US Department of Justice, *Drugs of Abuse* (Washington, DC, 1985).
3 See B. Whittaker, *The Global Connection* (London: Jonathan Cape, 1987), pp. xvii and xix.
4 See Home Office, *Tackling Drug Misuse* (London: HMSO, 1986).
5 See Health Education Council, *Young People and Heroin* (Research Report no. 8) (London: HMSO, November 1988).
6 Memorandum of the Association of Chief Probation Officers, House of Commons Social Services Committee, April 1985.

Part IV
Conclusions

12 British relations with Latin America into the 1990s

Victor Bulmer-Thomas

The 1990s will be an opportunity for several European countries to re-examine their relations with Latin America. The quincentenary of Columbus' voyage, to be celebrated in 1992, will remind the British in particular of past associations and former glories; the golden age of this relationship (see chapter 1, by Leslie Bethell) ended many years ago, leaving a legacy which is visible in family names (for example, that of President Alfonsín Foulkes), company titles (for example, the Banco Anglo-Colombiano) and imposing architecture. Yet this legacy is of questionable value for rebuilding British–Latin American relations in view of the long decline in British influence over the last sixty years. If Britain is to establish closer relations with Latin America in the future, there will need to be a *rediscovery* of the continent rather than merely raking over the coals of the fire lit last century.

Although past associations have left a feeling of goodwill towards Britain in many Latin American republics, it is not an easily negotiable asset. Relations between states have always responded to more hard-nosed criteria and British–Latin American relations are no exception. It is contemporary and future trends within Britain and the republics, together with the broader international situation, which will determine future relations. In the 1990s, six themes are likely to be of primordial importance:

(1) The structure and strength of the United Kingdom and Latin American economies,
(2) The consolidation of the European Domestic Market, to be completed by 1992, and the commitment (or lack of it) by Britain to the European ideal,
(3) The scope and scale of UK priorities towards other regions (for example, North America, the Commonwealth, the Pacific Rim countries),
(4) The extent of autonomy in the foreign policy of the major Latin American republics and the commitment to regional integration,
(5) The pace of multilateral trade negotiations (for example, the General Agreement on Tariffs and Trade (GATT) Uruguay Round), and
(6) The scale of détente between the United States and the Soviet Union.

If the future of British–Latin American relations is to be determined by these 'objective' criteria, what role – if any – is left for policy? Policy, as we shall see, does have an important role to play, but it also has its limitations. Since 1945, Britain has followed a policy towards Latin America which has emphasised commercial relations to the exclusion of almost everything else; yet, ironically, our share of Latin American trade has gone steadily down (see chapter 6). Policy cannot of itself, therefore, reverse trends which are determined by more fundamental forces, but it can play a crucial reinforcing role if it is consciously fashioned in accordance with those trends, as the example of West German–Latin American relations testifies. In the case of British–Latin American relations, which have fallen so badly into disrepair, policy will certainly be needed if both sides are to take advantage of the opportunities which undoubtedly exist and which have been identified at various points in this book.

Economic relations

Throughout the post-Independence period, and indeed for much of the eighteenth century, British–Latin American relations have been dominated by commercial considerations. The 'British century', from Independence to the First World War, witnessed an exchange of goods in international trade according to the Ricardian law of comparative advantage; Britain's apparently insatiable appetite for food and raw materials was met in large part by new supplies from Latin America, while the foreign exchange earned permitted Latin America to import those manufactured goods which Britain alone supplied for much of the nineteenth century.

This complementarity between the two sets of economies came to an abrupt halt in the 1929 depression,[1] as Britain turned to Imperial Preference at the expense of Latin America's primary-product exports and Latin America turned to import-substituting industrialisation (ISI) at the expense of British manufactured exports. The absence of complementarity became even more marked after the Second World War, as Latin America shifted resources away from traditional exports and Britain appeared to lose its comparative advantage in manufacturing, while being sucked almost against her will into the European conduit.[2]

In the last decade, however, the basis for a potential new complementarity has emerged almost imperceptibly. The British economy has lost its tag as the 'sick man of Europe', becoming internationally competitive in sophisticated manufactures and a broad range of services, while the Latin American republics have started to shift resources back towards the export sector. This time the focus of their attention is non-traditional exports (manufactures and agro-industrial products) rather than traditional primary products, although even the latter (as George Philip makes clear in chapter 8 of this volume) have received some attention. Thus, there is the potential (as yet virtually unrealised) of an exchange of products according to the new revealed comparative advantage between the two regions.

The need for a re-evaluation of export-led growth in Latin America has been

Table 12.1. *Value of non-traditional exports^a for main Latin American countries ($ million; figures in brackets represent share of non-traditionals in total exports (%))*

	1978	1982	1986
Argentina	4,366 (68.2)	5,025 (65.9)	4,862 (71.0)
Brazil	7,940 (62.7)	14,010 (69.4)	16,978 (75.8)
Chile	1,127 (45.5)	1,975 (53.3)	2,428 (57.8)
Colombia	885 (29.5)	1,258 (40.4)	1,922 (35.8)
Ecuador	379 (24.3)	430 (18.5)	703 (32.2)
Mexico	3,602 (60.5)	3,707 (17.5)	8,653 (54.0)
Peru	1,084 (55.8)	1,114 (33.8)	1,055 (42.0)
Venezuela	448 (4.9)	708 (4.3)	1,936 (22.4)
Latin America^b	22,298 (44.7)	33,273 (38.0)	43,497 (56.0)

^a Non-traditional exports defined as all exports other than those listed as main exports by the International Monetary Fund in *International Financial Statistics*. The main exports by country are: Argentina – meat, corn, wheat, hides and skins, wool; Brazil – coffee, soybeans and products, sugar, iron ore; Chile–copper; Colombia – coffee, fuel oil; Ecuador – crude petroleum, bananas, coffee, cocoa paste, cocoa butter; Mexico – petroleum, coffee, shrimp; Peru – copper, crude petroleum, petroleum products, fishmeal, iron ore; Venezuela – petroleum.
^b Excludes Cuba.
Source: Derived from International Monetary Fund, *International Financial Statistics*, various issues.

emphasised by the debt crisis, with a premium now attached to earnings of foreign exchange, but the new realism predates the debt crisis in most countries. Mindful of the success of the Newly Industrialising Countries (NICs) in South-East Asia, a variety of Latin American republics experimented in the 1970s with policies to promote non-traditional exports. By 1980, Brazil was exporting more manufactured goods than any other upper-middle-income country except the 'Gang of Four'[3] while Argentina, Mexico, Colombia, Chile, Peru and Uruguay had recorded notable increases since the 1960s.

This trend towards non-traditional exports has been obscured in the 1980s by the poor performance of primary products, which has dragged down overall export earnings. Yet as Table 12.1 makes clear, the trend is still there for many countries and has been reinforced by policies adopted in the 1980s, at the prodding of international agencies, designed to create a trade surplus from which debt can be serviced. Indeed, there are now few countries (as Table 12.2 shows) where manufactured exports to the USA alone do not account for a significant share of export earnings. Provided that Latin America continues to have access to foreign markets, this trend towards non-traditional exports will continue into the 1990s with Latin American companies and multinationals based in Latin America seeking outlets in all the major industrialised countries.

The importance of access to foreign markets cannot be stressed too much. The growth of non-traditional exports in the first half of the 1980s was heavily dependent on the US market and was made possible by the rapid growth of the

Table 12.2. *Exports of manufactures to USA from main Latin American countries*

| | 1982 | | 1987 | |
	$ million	% of total exports	$ million	% of total exports
Argentina	522	7.3	679	11.0
Brazil	1,977	10.4	5,220	19.9
Chile	434	12.4	502	9.6
Colombia	174	5.9	356	7.0
Ecuador	12	0.5	28	1.4
Mexico	5,331	26.6	13,861	67.1
Peru	378	12.2	303	11.6
Venezuela	112	0.7	424	3.3
Latin America[a]	10,114	11.6	23,654	26.5[b]

[a] Excludes Cuba.
[b] Based on estimated total exports of $91.2 million.
Source: US Department of Commerce, quoted in *Latin American Weekly Report*, 23 June 1988, p.6.

US trade deficit. This deficit started to shrink in 1988 and Latin American exporters of non-traditional goods cannot expect such ease of access in future: other markets, however, including the British, remain virtually untouched for these kinds of commodities and geographical diversification of trade will become a high priority.

Because of their weight in the structure of exports, Latin America's primary products continue to exercise a dominant influence on overall foreign-exchange earnings. However, the dismal performance in the first half of the 1980s is unlikely to be repeated; the strong US dollar, which has a depressing effect on Latin America's commodity prices, could well be a thing of the past and the deep world recession of 1980–2 is now over. There are even opportunities for some increase in volumes, as chapter 8 makes clear, while more companies are likely to follow the Venezuelan state oil company PDVSA's example of buying into downstream operations in industrial countries.[4] Thus, Latin America's export earnings – having marked time for most of the 1980s – should grow steadily in the 1990s and even the cautious IMF is predicting volume growth in the early 1990s of 4.4 per cent per annum.[5]

The growth of export earnings will provide opportunities for an increase in imports from their current depressed level. Although the scale of imports will depend on the terms agreed for debt servicing, it is already apparent that Latin American priorities have shifted from prompt payment of external obligations to import recovery and economic growth. Thus, imports have already increased sharply from the trough of just over $60 billion recorded in each year between 1983 and 1986 and, assuming net investment income continues to require the same absolute amount of foreign exchange in the 1990s as in the late 1980s (around $30 billion per year), should double by the year 2000 even at constant prices. This pace of growth could clearly accelerate further if measures were adopted to reduce the burden of debt service payments (see chapter 7).

The debt crisis has prompted a reappraisal of direct foreign investment (see chapter 6), as Latin American governments have come to recognise the advantages of a capital inflow where the rate of return is linked to the ability to pay. Irrespective of how the debt crisis unfolds, however, the new realism towards direct foreign investment (DFI) is likely to continue, notwithstanding the nationalist drum beaten from time to time by the noisy, but ineffective, Brazilian Congress. The reasons are threefold: first, Latin America will need DFI in the non-traditional export sector as part of its strategy for winning market shares in industrialised countries; secondly, joint ventures between state companies and DFI are likely to become more common in the fuel and minerals sector, as part of the strategy to achieve vertical integration through the control of downstream operations; thirdly, and more controversially, the privatisation programme under way almost everywhere in Latin America will require the participation of DFI, as local capital is likely to be both unable and unwilling to take on board, without foreign participation, the large state companies whose sale is now being contemplated from Mexico to Argentina.

All these changes will create opportunities for British firms, many of whom have shown no previous interest in the Latin American market. On the other hand, the UK financial institutions which lent so disproportionately to Latin America in the 1970s (see chapter 7) are unlikely to be impressed by talk of future opportunities and will continue to scale down their commitments whenever possible. London, now re-established as an international financial centre of the first order following the abolition of exchange control in 1979, might well be used by Latin American governments (or even companies) to float new capital issues as voluntary lending resumes, but the UK banks are unlikely to seek more than commissions on any such issues. The 'collective unconscious' among bankers, first identified by Charles Kindleberger, takes at least twenty-five years to operate so that full amnesia will not be re-established until the next century. Yet it should not be forgotten that the existence of over $30 billion of Latin American debt in the hands of UK-based banks does give aggressive British firms a wonderful opportunity for debt–equity swaps in the Latin American market, taking advantage of low debt quotations in the secondary market and attractive terms offered by many Latin American governments.

British arms manufacturers would also do well to take a jaundiced view of the Latin American market in the 1990s. Since the Falklands/Malvinas war their successes have been few,[6] although this may not be cause and effect; a greater challenge has come from the growth of the Latin American arms industry (notably in Argentina and Brazil), which has provided the opportunity for regional ISI coupled with savings of scarce foreign exchange.[7] Furthermore, the fledgling democratic governments in many Latin American republics, although anxious to appease the military over pay and conditions, can be expected to cast a critical eye over any major plans for equipment expansion (see chapter 6).

The fact that opportunities will open up for British companies in the Latin American market in the fields of both exports and DFI does not, of course, mean that British capital will necessarily take advantage of such opportunities. We have seen in the past how in other regions British companies have fallen behind their international competitors, when market opportunities have presented themselves. Yet the British economy has changed in the last decade in a way that may make comparisons with the past misleading.

The first change involves North Sea oil. Britain's move from net importer to net exporter of oil at the end of the 1970s contributed to the massive real appreciation of sterling at the start of the 1980s which – coupled with a tight monetary policy and high interest rates – cut a huge swath through the British manufacturing sector. Those firms that survived did so only by cutting costs and raising productivity dramatically, leaving them in a much stronger position to withstand international competition. As North Sea oil exports decline in the 1990s, bringing in their wake a depreciation of the exchange rate, the manufacturing sector will be called upon to increase its export earnings.[8] British manufacturing firms simply cannot afford to ignore a Latin American market expected to exceed 500 million people by the end of the 1990s, where imports even at current depressed levels are greater than the value of all UK finished manufactured exports.[9]

The second major change is also indirectly related to North Sea oil. Following the abolition of exchange control in 1979, British capital (portfolio and direct) has left the United Kingdom in unprecedented quantities, taking advantage of the oil-induced strength of the balance of payments and favourable exchange rates. The net external-asset position of the United Kingdom rose from 4.9 per cent of GNP in 1980 to an extraordinary 28.9 per cent in 1986, the highest proportion in the industrialised world.[10] This stock of assets provides a regular source of investment income which will undoubtedly cushion the impact on the UK economy and the balance of payments of the decline in North Sea oil. Although most of these assets are represented by portfolio capital, an important contribution has been made by DFI which has taken advantage of the ending of nearly four decades of discrimination against investment in US dollar assets. Thus a new class of British companies has been established with a global view of their operations, to be added to the small group of such companies (ICI, for example) which already functioned on a world scale.[11] Since few UK companies are likely to be attracted exclusively to the Latin American market, the broadening of the list of companies with a world-wide vision increases the chances that British capital will take advantage of any opportunities Latin America might offer. With many Latin American currencies depreciated in real terms against the US dollar and with the US dollar having depreciated against sterling since 1984, DFI by UK companies – whether through privatisation, debt swaps or new investments – does have its attractions.[12]

At present, little attention is given to the Latin American market as a source of opportunities for British capital. Instead, the focus is on the completion of the European Domestic Market (EDM) within the European Community (EC) by 1992. There is no doubt that this will create opportunities for those UK firms with a strong presence in the EC market where restrictions on trading are currently irksome;[13] it will also increase the opportunities open to many firms in the service sectors, where Britain's international comparative advantage has long been established. The move towards the EDM, and the subsequent inevitable complaints about market disruption, are likely to occupy the energy and resources of many public functionaries and corporate planners and there is a danger that, for a time, the UK will become absorbed in the EDM to the exclusion of other regions. This temptation must be resisted since – apart from other considerations – our European, Asian and North American competitors can be expected to respond aggressively to any new opportunities offered by other markets including those in Latin America.[14]

European 'hype' regarding the EDM has fought shy of spelling out the Community's external trade policy.[15] There are two aspects of that policy which remain of critical importance to regions such as Latin America. The first is access to the EC for manufactured exports, currently governed by the Generalised System of Preferences (GSP), the Lomé Convention, the Multi-Fibre Arrangement (MFA) as well as the Community's Common External Tariff (CET). The second involves access to the EC for agricultural exports, currently governed by the Common Agricultural Policy (CAP) and subject to discussion under GATT's Uruguay Round of negotiations. In both these areas, the British negotiating position is closer to that of Latin America than it is to many of our Community partners; certainly, both Britain and Latin America have a keen mutual interest in the reform of the CAP[16] and British consumers at least would benefit from the reform of the GSP, MFA and so on to permit greater access to the EC for Latin American manufacturers. Progress is not likely to be spectacular in either of these areas, but if and when Britain commits herself more fully to the European ideal and pursues a leading role, to which she is now entitled, progress could be faster. Furthermore, if Britain helps to move the EC in these directions, it would help to undermine Latin American resistance to the British (and US) preference for freeing trade in international services under the GATT Uruguay Round – a move that would almost certainly create new opportunities for UK companies in Latin America.

The changes in the economies of both Britain and many Latin American republics over the last decade are sufficiently profound to suggest they are permanent. There *is* now emerging the basis for a new complementarity between the two regions quite different from that which existed in the past. Whether the potential will be realised depends on a number of factors.

First, the UK economy must maintain its growth momentum which has been exceptionally strong since 1982; in six out of the seven years from 1982 through 1988, UK growth exceeded the OECD average. This welcome trend, after years if not decades of sluggish performance, has enabled the UK to resist the protectionist threat which has afflicted both the United States and the rest of the EC.

Secondly, there must be no backsliding by the Latin American economies towards a further round of inward-looking ISI, uncompetitive exchange rates and public-sector expansion. There are reasons for confidence here, since governments from Mexico to Chile of very different complexions have shown a broad commitment to the new policies under very difficult circumstances. The greatest threat comes from the resistance of new democratically elected governments to the maintenance of policies which – in the short run at least – appear to depress real wages, increase unemployment and cause social discontent. Yet rhetoric must be distinguished from reality and governments are unlikely to abandon policies just as they begin to reap dividends in the form of faster growth. The other threat comes from the acceleration of inflation, which is not unconnected to the adoption of the new policies (particularly the competitive exchange rate) and which has so far resisted both orthodox and heterodox stabilisation programmes. Even with inflation, however, it is notable how adjustment programmes of very different types have been adopted, while leaving the new trade policies broadly unchanged.

Political relations

Despite the secular decline in British–Latin American relations since 1945, political relations were generally satisfactory until the war with Argentina over the Falkland/Malvinas Islands in 1982. There were – and still are – points of friction, but the fact that neither side had major interests to defend prevented these from spilling over into confrontation. Before the Falklands/Malvinas war, the most serious dispute was with Guatemala over Belize, but a shrewd diplomatic effort involving our Caribbean partners in the Commonwealth had left Guatemala isolated by the 1980s even within Latin America.[17] Britain had resisted US pressure to join the blockade against Cuba after 1960 and enjoyed correct formal relations with the island's Marxist government even during the most turbulent of the Castro years (see chapter 4).

The Falklands/Malvinas war has not destroyed our generally good political relationship with Latin America, but it has had indirect political costs in addition to the direct damage done to our relationship with Argentina. It is fashionable to emphasise how 'normal' our relations with the rest of Latin America have remained despite the war and despite the subsequent diplomatic effort by Argentina to isolate Britain on the question of negotiations; this is undeniable and much of the talk after 1982 about sanctions against British companies has proved to be rather wild. Yet we should not be lulled into a sense of false complacency; the Falklands/Malvinas remain a major source of friction with many opportunities for an escalation in tension (see chapter 9) and Britain's isolation in the United Nations and other international fora over the question of negotiations is unlikely to be ended.

Just as in the case of commercial relations, our political relationship with Latin America will be primarily determined by trends within the two regions over the next decade. Both sides are going through a period of realignment in international relations in which the British–Latin American relationship *per se* is not a primary concern. Yet our relationship with the countries of Latin America, and theirs with the United Kingdom, is likely to be significantly affected by the new realignments in the 1990s.

On the Latin American side, there are many reasons to believe that the new mood of nationalism and greater autonomy in foreign policy – which has been a strong feature of the 1980s – will continue into the 1990s. In retrospect, the post-war hegemony enjoyed by the United States in Latin America can be seen to have rested on a series of pillars (such as the US surplus of capital, the weakness and divisions of Europe, the eclipse of Japan), which were bound to be temporary in character. The efforts of the Reagan administration to re-establish the moral and political authority of the United States in Latin America have failed and the effort has paradoxically hardened the tendency towards greater autonomy in foreign policy which began before that administration came to power.

The most visible manifestation of this greater autonomy has been the formation of the Contadora Group in 1983, the addition of a Support Group in 1986 and their metamorphosis into the Group of Eight at the Acapulco Summit in November 1987[18] (the first American summit to which the United States was not invited). Furthermore, with the subsequent suspension of Panama, the Group could claim (with a little economising on the truth) to represent the democratic wave sweeping the sub-continent. The transition to, and subsequent consolidation of, democracy in a large number of Latin American republics in the last decade is, alas, not an irreversible process, but the signs are encouraging. It is a trend which is bound to have an important bearing on the region's international relations; this is made perfectly clear by the example of Argentina, whose new treaties with Spain and Italy (involving in principle a substantial increase in trade and investment) are contingent upon the continuation of democracy.

The Contadora process and the Cartagena Group,[19] both culminating in the Group of Eight, and the Esquipulas conferences in Central America[20] have all produced an unprecedented level of contacts among Latin American states, most of it outside the orbit of the Organization of American States (OAS). These contacts, at all levels of government, have produced many fine words and rather fewer deeds, but it would be quite wrong to dismiss the whole exercise as an example of rhetorical summitry. There *is* a new interest in regional co-operation in the broadest sense and the recent trade agreements between Brazil, Argentina and Uruguay have laid the basis for a different kind of regional integration.

The commercial links between Latin American states, however, remain fragile and have suffered severely as a consequence of the debt crisis. It will take many years to restore them to the level of 1980, yet alone increase them. Consequently, there is a keen interest throughout Latin America in establishing closer relations with the European Community. The commercial interest in the EC is also intertwined with the desire by many Latin American states to diversify their political relationships and establish closer ties with Western Europe (a process described as 're-linking' by Laurence Whitehead in chapter 5). This interest, underpinned in several countries by the close party-to-party relationships which exist through the three Internationals[21] as well as trade-union and other links, finds its expression in the repeated call by Latin American heads of state for greater EC involvement in the region and requests for EC support for Latin American initiatives.

As Laurence Whitehead makes clear in chapter 5, the relationship between Latin America and the EC is likely to be a recurring theme in the 1990s. The outcome of this relationship is bound to affect British–Latin American relations, but Britain – as a leading, if reluctant, member of the EC – can also affect the outcome. As in the 1980s, we can anticipate advances and setbacks with EC trade policy likely to remain a source of friction and EC support for democratic and non-military solutions to regional conflicts an area of harmony.

The EC is one of the world's largest and richest regions and its trade policies have ramifications which were not properly understood when the Treaty of Rome was signed in 1956. The Common Agricultural Policy has caused trade diversion at the expense of Latin America, led to dumping of surpluses and the depression of world prices for commodities produced by Latin America and increased prices in the EC for goods still purchased from Latin America through variable levies. The Lomé Convention has added insult to injury by discriminating against Latin America in favour of an array of small African, Caribbean and Pacific countries, most of whom are ex-British or ex-French colonies. At the same time, the EC's size as a consumer gives it a big stake in all negotiations involving international commodity agreements and a New International Economic Order. The EC is also a powerful voice in the General Agreement on Tariffs and Trade, the Generalised System of Preferences and the Multi-Fibre Arrangement.

While Britain is unlikely to be easily persuaded of the desirability of a united EC political approach to Latin America, she is relatively well placed to press for changes in EC trade policy which conflict with Latin American interests. As I have stressed earlier, there are points of convergence between Britain and Latin America over commercial policy and these should be emphasised to both sides' mutual advantage. While a common EC foreign policy remains a long-term ambition, the political interests of the twelve member-states are sufficiently heterogeneous to suggest that agreement over Latin America will be reached only over rather uncontroversial matters. If it is going to be difficult to make significant progress in the areas of potential harmony, there is all the more reason for pressing hard to reduce the areas of conflict.

The 1990s are also likely to see the consolidation of the most important Latin American republics (particularly Brazil and Mexico) as regional and perhaps even world powers. The San José Agreement (under which Mexico and Venezuela supply many countries in the Caribbean Basin with oil on concessional terms) and the Contadora process saw the major republics emerge as regional powers in the 1980s and policies have been maintained despite frequent differences with the United States. This ability to maintain foreign policy in the face of US opposition – a feature found only in Mexico among the major countries in earlier years – is likely to continue with Central America, Panama, drugs, trade and debt all possible sources of friction between the regional powers and the United States. Furthermore, Brazil (and more recently Mexico) has become more active in world trade negotiations (for example, the GATT Uruguay Round) and the Brazilian position in particular is one to which major trading countries, such as Britain, should be attuned. Domestic political considerations may obscure in the short term the qualitative changes taking place in the projection of Brazilian and Mexican power, but Britain should not delay the cultivation of closer relations with these emerging powers.

So far, we have indicated the path Latin America is likely to follow in the 1990s. Further de-linking from the USA can be expected, particularly if the thaw in the US–USSR relations persuades the Bush administration to take a more relaxed view of its strategic interests in Latin America, regional co-operation will expand at all levels and high expectations will continue to be placed in relations with Western Europe. Britain can play a part in fostering that relation, as we have seen, but this will depend on her commitment to Europe, which in turn is affected by the other claims on British loyalties.

It is these competing claims (EC, USA, Commonwealth for example) which are partly responsible for the inconsistencies and uncertainties in British–Latin American relations. The 'special relationship' with the United States (see chapter 4, by David Thomas), reasserted during the Reagan–Thatcher years following a period of quiescence, leads us to a *de facto* policy in Central America which is in conflict with the EC position we support officially. Our former imperial responsibilities leave us giving more aid to Belize and the Falklands (with a total population of less than 200,000) than to all of Latin America, excluding Costa Rica, despite the fact that the subcontinent has a population of nearly 400 million. Our dispute with Argentina over the Falklands/Malvinas obliges us to remain on friendly terms with Pinochet's Chile at a time when the EC is under pressure to promote democratisation in its relations with Latin America. Our political relations with Latin America are a residual after all other commitments have been addressed; inevitably, the result is sometimes confusing and unsatisfactory.

The different directions in which Britain is pulled over Latin America are reflected in inconsistencies between different government departments. The Ministry of Defence (MoD) sees the Falklands/Malvinas in strategic terms and plans its military exercises (such as Operation 'Fire-Focus') accordingly; the Foreign and Commonwealth Office (FCO) sees the Islands mainly in political terms, but cannot convey to the MoD the need for sensitivity in its handling of the issue. The Department of Trade and Industry (DTI) would like to foster commercial links with Latin America, but is hampered by restrictions on export credit cover – a Treasury responsibility. The Treasury accepts that African debt is a 'special case' and takes the initiative over a passive reluctant US government, but is content to follow the US lead on Latin American debt provided it has no serious budgetary implications (see chapter 3). All governments suffer from these inter-departmental rivalries and inconsistencies, but they become particularly acute when there is no overall regional strategy. Furthermore, far too much of the scarce Whitehall resources devoted to Latin America have been devoted to the Falklands/Malvinas issue in the last few years.

Because of its imperial past, Britain acquired responsibilities in the western hemisphere which represent potential sources of friction (Antarctica, the Falklands/Malvinas, Belize, Guyana, the Caribbean). Because of its role as a member of the EC, a wealthy club of industrialised nations, Britain is now a market for drugs originating in Latin America and remains close to the centre of world trade policies – both further potential sources of friction. With the exception of the Falklands/Malvinas, the record of disengagement from imperial responsibilities has been good and further progress can be expected in the 1990s. The Antarctic Treaty System (ATS), as Peter Beck makes clear in chapter 10, has smoothed away the irritating territorial dispute with Chile and Argentina in the polar region and should be renewed in 1991 without much difficulty. Guatemala looks set to recognise the independence of Belize, the last obstacle to Belize occupying its privileged position as a member of both the Latin American and Caribbean clubs. The British responsibility for drawing the boundary at the root of the Venezuelan–Guyanese territorial dispute has been largely overtaken by events; although this dispute is not likely to be settled in the 1990s, it is not expected to be resolved by force and Britain is not expected to play any part in the proceedings. Britain's residual Caribbean responsibilities (Montserrat, Turks and Caicos, Virgin Islands, Cayman Islands and Anguilla) have acquired an unsavoury role in the drugs trade and their 'dependent territory' status appears to be an unsatisfactory compromise between independence and annexation, but the resolution of these questions is not expected to impinge on British–Latin American relations in the 1990s.

The sources of friction expected to dominate the 1990s are trade policy, drugs and the Falklands/Malvinas. Trade policy has already been discussed and will be raised again in the final section of this chapter. The drugs problem is more serious, if only because the more successful the anti-drugs programme in the United States, the more likely it is that the drug traffickers will target Western Europe (and Britain) as an alternative market (see chapter 11 by David Webb-Carter). Yet the British response so far has been sensible, even if the material resources needed to fight the drugs problem have not so far been forthcoming in sufficient quantities. The British authorities have emphasised demand restraint over supply reduction, crop substitution over crop eradication, and have shown a commendable sympathy for the dilemmas faced by governments in drug-producing countries. The Latin American Study Group was adamant that relations between Britain and individual republics should not be conditional on progress against drugs, although the British government should obviously respond enthusiastically to any request for help from the government of a drug-afflicted country.

In view of the success achieved in handling these potential sources of friction, the continuation of the dispute with Argentina over the Falklands/ Malvinas stands out like a sore thumb. British–Latin American relations may be able to survive the continuation of the dispute, but they are hardly likely to be brilliant. Given the low level of the current relationship, it is argued by some that the costs of a further deterioration are small while the benefits from a resolution of the dispute are uncertain and must be set against the alleged high costs of media opposition, parliamentary revolt and charges of betrayal by the Islanders. This, it must be stressed, is a very short-sighted view; the Study Group had no illusions about the complexity of the issue (see chapter 9, by Malcolm Deas), but there was also a general recognition that any major improvement in British–Latin American relations will be seriously impeded by failure to make progress and progress, in turn, depends on dialogue with Argentina. Although it would be unrealistic to expect the present British Prime Minister to drop her objections to a dialogue involving sovereignty, future governments cannot afford to adopt so stubborn an attitude and policy-makers need to consider *now* how future discussions might be handled to our best advantage.

The 'special relationship' with the United States rested, it has already been said, in no small part on the personalities of Mr Reagan and Mrs Thatcher. With the Reagan administration now over, it is unrealistic to expect the relationship to continue in its present form. South Africa, the Falklands/ Malvinas and even Chile could conceivably drive a wedge in the 'special relationship' in the future, while trade disputes (particularly over agriculture) and defence policy may force Britain to line up with her European partners. The Anglo-US relationship will survive, but it is not expected to be such a dominant theme in Britain's overall political relations. Just as the Bush administration will formulate its policies towards Latin America with little attention to British sensitivities, so Britain must shape its own policies towards the region without undue consideration for the Anglo-US relationship.

It would no doubt be convenient if Britain, having followed the United States in the past on so many aspects of Latin American policy, could now switch to following EC initiatives towards the same region. This is not, however, realistic in the medium term; the commercial rivalry between EC states, the inter-party links through the three Internationals and Britain's residual responsibilities all ensure that on many important issues no Western European consensus will emerge. Britain should do what it can to build such a consensus, and we should all remind ourselves of the goodwill earned for the EC by the Central American initiative,[22] but Britain cannot abdicate responsibility for formulating its own policies towards Latin America in the last analysis.

Cultural relations

There is a marked contrast between our cultural relations with Latin America at the formal/official level and at the informal/unofficial level. Official cultural relations are maintained on a shoestring through a skeletal British Council presence, reduced BBC External Service broadcasts and minimal vernacular broadcasting services, with all three areas subject to cuts and constant threats of further cuts (see chapter 2). The FCO and the Overseas Development Administration (ODA), through an expanded scholarships programme, have gone some way towards limiting the damage caused by the raising of overseas student fees, but the number of Latin Americans studying in Britain is well below the level of ten years ago.

At the unofficial level, by contrast, cultural relations are quite healthy. The activities of Nongovernmental Organisations (NGOs) in the region are steadily increasing (see chapter 3, by Robert Graham). The churches are active and that activity is not confined exclusively to the Catholic Church and its related organisations (such as the Catholic Institute for International Relations). The number of British tourists going to Latin America is rising, despite the poor air links between the UK and Latin America, while the demand for Latin American novels and films is growing rapidly. Press and media coverage are greater than at any time since the Second World War, if not before, and each side's appreciation of the other's popular culture (for example, football, dance, music) is widespread.

Why is there this contrast between official and unofficial cultural relations? British–Latin American relations are not, of course, unique in this respect, but with other regions (Africa, for example) the contrast if anything runs the other way – much greater official than unofficial interest. The Study Group offered several answers by way of explanation (see chapter 2, by Gerald Martin), including the absence of colonial ties, the language barrier and US influence; there is a grain of truth in all these explanations, yet the one that perhaps comes closest is that of the generation gap. The interest expressed unofficially in Latin America is overwhelmingly by the young, whose impressions of the region have not been coloured by the decline of British influence in the past; officialdom, by contrast, is made up of men (and a few women) whose attitudes were shaped by the Second World War and the vital Anglo-US relationship, by the formation of the EC and the emergence of Western Europe as a potential superpower and by Britain's transition from colonial master to Commonwealth partner. The oldest generation of all, which had interests in Latin America and was therefore – as Gerald Martin says – interested, has now ceased to play a significant role and its demise was signalled in 1988 by the decision of the Council of Foreign Bondholders, headquartered in London, to disband and cease publication of its annual report.[23]

If the generation gap is an important explanation of the different weight attached to Latin American relations by government and 'the people' in Britain, it will not be true forever that there are 'no votes' in Latin America. Latin America is an electoral issue, albeit a minor one, in elections in several Western European countries (for example, West Germany, Sweden and Spain) and it would not be altogether surprising if Britain eventually followed suit. This is likely to be a long-term process, however, and in the shorter term there are reasons for deep concern at the gap between official and unofficial social and cultural relations.

First, as Gerald Martin again points out in chapter 2, the 'movers and shakers' at the unofficial level are usually out of sympathy with government policies, not just on Latin America, and cultivate an image of Latin America – no doubt for the best of motives – which is often very negative. Inasmuch as there *is* a popular image of Latin America, far too much of it is dominated by visions of nasty military dictators, drug trafficking, death squads, guerrillas, corruption and violence. All members of the Study Group know these things exist, but it is as false to base one's picture of Latin America on them as to judge Britain by football hooligans, London's Underground and the IRA. Fortunately for Britain, many avenues exist for promoting a more favourable – and more balanced – view of the country abroad. In the case of Latin America, however, such channels have virtually dried up and the field has been left to the media, the solidarity campaigns, the single-issue pressure groups and (dare one say it?) the novelists, all of whom have perfectly legitimate vested interests in emphasising the negative. We cannot ask the leopard to change his spots, but we can ask that he should not be the only spokesman on British–Latin American relations.

It is worth emphasising this point, because it stands in marked contrast to the earlier period when British influence was still strong. In the 1920s, many of the negative factors of contemporary Latin America were still visible: ugly dictatorships, US invasions, guerrillas, civil wars and so on. Yet the image of Latin America in this country was generally favourable and was propagated by a huge volume of books and articles (some commissioned by Latin American governments) emphasising the positive side; there was also an important English-speaking community in each of the main Latin American countries, promoting a positive image of Britain as well as feeding Britain with a more balanced view of Latin America itself. This community still exists, but it is a shadow of its former self, suffers from an identity crisis and cannot be expected to play a dynamic role in rebuilding British–Latin American relations.[24] Furthermore, unlike the Japanese community in Brazil used as a beachhead to the Latin American market by Japanese commercial interests, the English-speaking communities appear to lack the technological and other skills that would make them a useful adjunct of an increased British commercial presence.

The second problem with the low level of official cultural relations is the contrast with our main competitors, who take cultural diplomacy more seriously and are willing to pay for it. Our minimalist approach to cultural diplomacy in Latin America may be consistent with our tiny market share, but it is hardly conducive to an increase in the strength of British commercial and political relations with Latin America. Some would argue, as Under-Secretary of State Tim Eggar did before the Foreign Affairs Committee on Cultural Diplomacy, that 'a good performance by Britain economically does more for Britain's image abroad than additional expenditure on cultural activities' (see chapter 2, p. 41). Our competitors are not so sanguine. Japan and West Germany, both countries with an outstanding post-war economic performance, see cultural diplomacy partly as a way of informing the world about their domestic achievements and partly as a way of building market share. They also, along with France and other competitors, see cultural diplomacy as an end in itself: an opportunity to promote the values they would like their country to be associated with in the outside world. With the negative image from which Britain now suffers as a result of a minority of its tourists and football fans, this is an argument that needs to be heard loud and clear. We may not be very good at talking and thinking about culture, as Gerald Martin reminds us, but we still do it very well and members of the Study Group have drawn attention to the branches of excellence in British culture (such as theatre and opera) which are still virtually unknown in Latin America.

The FCO, the Central Office of Information and the British Council, to their credit, do what they can, within extremely limited resources, to bring Latin American leaders and expected future leaders to Britain. The result is a small elite, who have generally formed a favourable impression of this country and whose goodwill we have earned. The FCO claims, sincerely, that it would like to do more of the same. It is to be hoped that they succeed, yet it is a rather one-sided approach at present; the Latin American elites are far more knowledgeable about Britain, and fluent in their language, than is the British elite about Latin America. Some imbalance is inevitable, but it is surely not too much to ask that the British Foreign Secretary should be able to name correctly the capital of a Latin American country whose Vice-President recently visited us officially;[25] we also have over thirty MPs with great knowledge of the Falklands/ Malvinas, but only four who can speak Spanish. The FCO, alas, cannot give language courses to the British elite, but it can fight to prevent the study of Spanish and Portuguese dwindling in our state schools (see chapter 2) and it can encourage more of our economic and political leaders to visit the region.

A new policy for Latin America

Britain's loss of influence, and interest, in Latin America since the Second World War is not in doubt. To some extent, as the Study Group has shown, the decline was inevitable given the different paths that both Britain and Latin America have followed, but it has gone too far. Table 12.3 presents in summary form our share of various world variables and our share of the equivalent Latin American total. The difference is striking with Britain 'under-represented' across the board. These statistics, however crude they may be, suggest that the decline was due not only to 'objective' factors, about which little can be done, but

Table 12.3. *UK shares of world and Latin American totals (1983–4)*

	World %	Latin America %
Imports	5.3	1.8
Exports	5.0	2.9
Direct foreign investment	22.0	12.1
Official development assistance	4.5	1.3

Source: Department of Trade and Industry, *UK Overseas Trade Statistics* (London: HMSO, 1987); Business Monitor M4, *Overseas Transactions* (London: HMSO), various editions; Overseas Development Administration, *British Aid Statistics 1982–6* (London: HMSO, 1987).

also to 'subjective' factors among which British policy towards Latin America is the most important.

There was general agreement in the Study Group that British policy towards Latin America left much to be desired. Some took the view (see chapter 3, by Robert Graham) that there has been a policy, but it has not been implemented effectively so that the ends of British policy have not been supported by adequate means – making it impossible to fulfil the ends. Others took the view that British policy has been based on ends which are now redundant and irrelevant; the five factors identified by Victor Perowne in his famous 1945 paper, which Robert Graham claims still 'continue to form the core of official policy towards the region', were Latin America's supply of raw materials, the extent of British investments, the potential of Latin America as an export market, the significance of the region to US strategic interests and the potential influence of the Latin American bloc of nations in international fora. The first two of these reasons for paying attention to Latin America are now far less important than in 1945; the fourth reason is still valid, but the Anglo-US relationship has changed so much since 1945 that this in itself is not a reason for giving priority to Latin America; the last reason was overtaken by events, when decolonisation produced a flood of new members (including many that joined the Commonwealth) in international organisations. That left the third reason (export potential) and over the years British policy came to focus almost exclusively on this commercial consideration at a time when Latin America was turning away from international trade and Britain was increasingly uncompetitive in world markets for manufactured goods. Inevitably, the result was deeply disappointing – so much so that some members of the Study Group have felt able to claim that Britain has had *no* policy towards Latin America.

We have, of course, had a policy on the Falklands/Malvinas, on Belize, on drugs, on immigration and on decolonisation in the Caribbean, but – as Laurence Whitehead points out in chapter 5 – this does not add up to a policy towards Latin America as a region. Indeed, in one's more unkind moments, one could refer to an '1,800 policy' with policy towards the southern republics guided by 1,800 Islanders in the Falklands/Malvinas and policy towards the northern republics unduly influenced by 1,800 British troops in Belize!

Does the UK need a new policy for Latin America? I shall answer in the affirmative for both positive and negative reasons. The positive reasons have already been hinted at in this chapter: there are new commercial opportunities opening up, which need to be reflected in British policy; it is in Britain's interest to promote the consolidation of democracy in association with our EC partners; some of the Latin American countries, notably Brazil and Mexico, have already become regional powers and their influence could soon extend outside the western hemisphere; it should never be forgotten that Brazil and Mexico already have the eighth- and ninth-largest economies respectively in the non-Communist world and must eventually acquire an influence in foreign affairs commensurate with their economic strength – Britain simply cannot afford to ignore such changes.

There are negative reasons, also, for adopting a new policy for Latin America. The unprecedented 'unofficial' interest in Latin America in recent years has not helped to counter the negative image of Latin America as an unstable region of debt-ridden poverty, corrupt officials, human-rights abuse and short-lived dictatorships – indeed, it could be argued that this unofficial interest has exacerbated the image problem. It is exceedingly difficult to persuade British business to take a fresh look at the region when the dominant image is so negative. Yet, as I have argued above, it is not realistic to expect those responsible for the new unofficial interest to start emphasising the positive. Britain therefore needs an official policy towards Latin America which gives due weight to the region's positive side and emphasises the economic, political, social and cultural achievements in many republics.

A second negative reason for adopting a new, and coherent, policy is to avoid the fragmentation of existing policy. Britain's relationship with the region has evolved so that some interests or concerns have declined in importance (such as Guyana), others have remained (Belize, for example) and new ones have emerged (such as drugs). Each of these interests or concerns may involve different government departments – the Department of Trade and Industry in the case of trade, the Treasury and the Bank of England in the case of debt, the Ministry of Defence in the case of Belize and the Falklands, the Home Office and Customs and Excise in the case of drugs. If there is no overall, coherent policy towards the region, departmental clashes are inevitable (as happened over the Operation 'Fire-Focus' exercises in the South Atlantic – see chapter 9) and Britain's credibility suffers. We need only look at the much more serious problem in Washington, where the lack of a unified Central American policy under the Reagan administration left individual departments making up policy as they went along, to realise just how important coherent regional policies are.

If departmental clashes are to be avoided, there has to be some ministry with overall responsibility for formulating policy. In the case of Latin America, there is no question that this ought to be the Foreign and Commonwealth Office. Only the FCO of the interested parties can take an overall view, although the FCO must take on board the views and opinions not only of other government departments, but also of the other groups with a special interest in and expertise on Latin America. It is therefore up to the FCO to strengthen the machinery of co-ordination within Whitehall and open a permanent dialogue with other interested parties (see chapters 2 and 6), but its task will be made easier if there exists a coherent policy, which reflects Britain's new and emerging interests in the region.

One would have to be very naive not to recognise the obstacles that lie in the path of those seeking to formulate a new British policy towards Latin America. At the highest levels of governments, there has not been for several decades major interest in or knowledge of Latin America. This is reflected, as we all know, in the paucity of visits by senior British officials to Latin America (see chapter 3), a position which compares most unfavourably in the past with our European partners and now, it would seem, with the Soviet Union[26] and Japan. There is also the 'Thatcher factor' which is nevertheless a double-edged sword; while it *is* true that the present Prime Minister's refusal to countenance a dialogue with Argentina over the Falklands/Malvinas on the basis of an open agenda is an obstacle to improving our relations with Latin America, it is also true that many Latin Americans (including in private their leaders) admire Mrs Thatcher and believe that she has helped to reverse the decline of Britain as an economic and political power. Sadly, the Prime Minister has not shown any interest in exploiting the respect she has earned to further British–Latin American relations.

One should not, however, exaggerate the obstacles associated with lack of interest by senior officials and politicians. The importance assigned to different regions is not immutable; if the case for giving greater priority to Latin America is valid and if it is argued intelligently, officialdom will eventually listen. Indeed, this is the whole rationale for this Study Group which has had the comparative luxury of surveying the whole range of British–Latin American relations in a relatively unhurried fashion. Furthermore, among younger politicians there *is* more awareness of Latin America with at least two opposition leaders (Neil Kinnock and David Owen) having visited Central America in recent years.

The sources of friction already identified (for example, the Falklands/ Malvinas, Antarctica, drugs) are also potential obstacles to the formulation of a new, coherent policy towards Latin America. Yet, as I have already stated, they are much less of an obstacle than might at first appear; Antarctica, through the Treaty System, has become an area of co-operation rather than confrontation with several Latin American states (including Argentina); the drugs problem has also yielded co-operation with some republics with points of confrontation limited to our own Dependencies in the Caribbean. The Falklands/Malvinas issue is, of course, the most worrying; so far, other Latin American republics have not turned words of support for Argentina into deeds, but it would be very foolish for Britain to be complacent about the potential damage this issue could do us in the future.

The obstacles in the path of formulating a coherent new policy are therefore not overwhelming, but what should be the content of such a policy? Here it is a question of bringing together the strands with which this and other chapters have been concerned. I will begin with commercial relations, since these will continue to play the largest part in Britain's policy towards Latin America.

New opportunities for British companies will open up in the 1990s, but some of these will be missed if greater co-ordination is not achieved (see chapter 6, by David Atkinson) among the UK agencies responsible for trade and investment in the region. We all welcome the new sectoral trade missions pioneered by the Latin American Trade Advisory Group (LATAG), but the benefits will not be maximised if Export Credits Guarantee Department cover is not restored for exports to countries with debt problems. At a more basic level, the air links between Britain and Latin America need to be substantially improved and it is encouraging to see the newly privatised British Airways expressing an interest in purchasing part of the equity of Lan Chile as a way of promoting more direct connections.

Several chapters emphasised the obstacles to economic recovery in Latin America (and by implication to commercial relations with Britain) that have arisen from the debt crisis. All members of the Study Group were agreed on the need to reduce the negative net resource transfer from the region, but members divided on the question of whether this could best be achieved by debt relief (involving, inevitably, government decisions on tax relief for loan-loss provisions) or through direct negotiations between the commercial creditors and the debtor governments. Since the negative resource transfer is starting to decline, a reasonable compromise is that governments (including the British) should take a following, rather than leading, role on *commercial* debt and place as few obstacles as possible in the path of a flexible response by creditor banks to the ever-widening menu being proposed by debtors. With *official* debt, however, whether multilateral or bilateral, governments (including the British) could be accused of dragging their feet. The main multilateral organisations lending to Latin America, to all of which Britain belongs, have failed to rise to the challenge of increasing transfers to the region, while at the bilateral level Britain's absence from the co-ordinating committees under formation for each Central American republic is inexcusable.[27]

On the aid front, the distribution of Britain's limited effort (down again in real terms in 1987)[28] still owes far too much to former colonial responsibilities. Latin American countries are not poor, but there are many poor within the Latin American countries. Furthermore, within Latin America our aid has often gone to the richest countries (56 per cent to Mexico in 1982, for example). Since 1979, our aid to Nicaragua has never risen above £130,000 even though there are many projects which could be administered by British voluntary organisations (such as Oxfam) without the need to channel funds through the

Sandinistas. Aid is now an indispensable weapon both in the fight against drugs (as in police training), in the consolidation of democracy (for example, with the Central American parliament) and in the winning of market shares (for example, with aid and trade provisions). Britain needs to be more actively involved in all these areas as part of a strategy for improving relations with Latin America.

Within the EC Britain must continue to press for trade policies which will create greater opportunities for Latin American exports of agricultural and manufactured goods. It is generally in Britain's interests to do so, as we have seen, but Britain should not be afraid to advertise the common ground it shares with Latin America on many matters of trade policy. Other EC countries, notably France and Spain, have made much capital out of their common platform with Latin America on many political issues. We should not hesitate to do the same on trade issues. Furthermore, we should use our position as a major commodity trading centre and participant in the main International Commodity Agreements to press for more favourable treatment for Latin American commodity exports. It is a low-cost policy for us with large potential benefits for Latin America.

The development of the political side of a new policy towards Latin America is complicated by the need to work in harmony, as far as possible, with our EC partners. This will not be easy, but the example of the EC initiative for Central America – supported by Britain – shows what can be done. In the past Britain has followed, rather than led, the EC on Latin America; yet if the EC is to evolve a common position on support for democratisation, human rights, the battle against drugs and so on, the British voice will need to be heard at an early stage if our interests are to be reflected in the final policy.

Britain's former and current imperial responsibilities in the western hemisphere mean that some aspects of British policy towards the region must be conducted outside the EC framework. The crackdown on drugs abuse and money-laundering in the dependent territories is a British responsibility, while the resolution of the dispute between Belize and Guatemala may require a little pressure by Britain in the final analysis.[29] The dispute with Argentina over the Falklands/Malvinas is also a British responsibility, but we can expect in turn to come under some pressure from the United States and our EC partners to pursue negotiations. We should be wary of ignoring these pressures, since – as Spain and Italy have already shown – commercial and political links with Argentina could be important. No one is arguing that the Islanders should be abandoned for the sake of a few million dollars' worth of trade with Argentina, but Britain cannot allow her foreign policy towards a sovereign state to be dictated by fewer than 2,000 inhabitants of a dependent territory. It should not be beyond the wit of the Argentine and British governments, once discussions start, to safeguard the interests of the Islanders, while satisfying Argentine honour. What is abundantly clear from the chapter by Malcolm Deas (chapter 9) is that the Falklands/Malvinas issue, despite the wishful thinking of many in Britain, has not been resolved.

Cultural relations with Latin America are also primarily a British responsibility, which cannot be shared with our EC partners. British policy towards the region must start to reflect the importance of cultural diplomacy as an end in itself (see chapter 2). This is one of the most effective ways to counter the negative image which Britain has in some quarters and, if done well, can yield substantial commercial and political benefits. And we *can* do it well. The individualistic nature of the British character makes for excellence in a whole range of performing arts and sports, where our achievements are virtually unknown in Latin America. Cultural diplomacy is still an extraordinarily cheap way of promoting a country, but we have let our representation in Latin America fall to dangerously low levels. It should be a matter of priority to reverse this trend – not merely to state that Britain 'would not want to see any decline in the general level of activity'.[30] We are fortunate, as Gerald Martin makes clear in chapter 2, to have in Britain an excellent academic infrastructure for the study of Latin America; we should use that infrastructure to further cultural relations at the broadest level rather than watch helplessly while the best academics join the brain drain to the USA in frustration at the lack of national recognition of their achievements.

So far, all the emphasis has been put on Britain's role in improving British–Latin American relations. Yet Latin American governments and institutions have an important role to play as well. They have a strong, vested interest in reversing the negative image of their own subcontinent in Britain and can help in many ways. Students can be encouraged to study in Britain, British leaders – not just government officials – should be invited to visit Latin America. The London embassies of the Latin American republics should be far more active in hosting functions and holding conferences and their official representatives should be less reluctant to speak to and write for a wider audience. When distinguished citizens come from their countries, the event should be advertised as widely as possible and the British institutes concerned with Latin America should respond in kind. The commercial opportunities now opening up in Latin America, including debt–equity swaps and privatisation, should be given as wide a publicity as possible; Latin American governments should take a leaf out of the books of administrations earlier this century, which did *not* hesitate to promote a positive image of their countries in peacetime.

In a speech at Canning House in December 1988, addressing the subject of the significance of 1992 for relations between Britain and Latin America, the British Foreign Secretary, Sir Geoffrey Howe, said:

> Drake and Vernon were after plunder, but subsequently and indeed well into the early part of this century, Britain was by far the largest foreign investor in Latin America. It was British capital that developed agriculture and industry across Latin America.
>
> And the question I always asked myself is what happened? What took place to diminish that relationship? The shock of the Great Depression, forced disinvestment during Two World Wars, the allure of the Commonwealth and Europe, and – it must

be said – more recently Britain's own relative decline – all of these things had combined to erode our traditional links with Latin America.

Now we can say, without any fear of contradiction, that the period of neglect is over.[31]

The Foreign Secretary may have been a little hasty in reaching such a conclusion, but it is to be hoped that the events of the next decade prove him to have been right.

Notes

1 It had begun to fade even earlier, but the 1929 depression accelerated the process dramatically (see chapter 1).

2 Britain only joined the EC in 1972, but – as David Atkinson makes clear in chapter 6 of this volume – the reorientation of British trade towards Europe started long before.

3 The 'Gang of Four' consists of Hong Kong, Singapore, South Korea and Taiwan. In 1980 Brazil's manufactured exports were $7,770 million compared with $15,722 million, for example, for South Korea (see World Bank, *World Development Report* (Washington, DC, 1983), Table 13).

4 PDVSA has bought distributional outlets in both North America and Western Europe (but not in Britain). See chapter 8.

5 See IMF, *World Economic Outlook* (Washington DC, April 1988), Table A.55. Assuming Latin American exports recover to $100 billion by 1990, a rate of growth of 4.4% per annum – if maintained throughout the decade – would imply exports of over $150 billion by the year 2000 at constant 1990 prices.

6 See Latin American Bureau, *The Thatcher Years – Britain and Latin America* (London, 1988), pp. 79–80.

7 Many of these arms deals made by Argentina and Brazil involve countertrade and therefore do not require foreign currency.

8 See Charles Bean, 'The impact of North Sea oil', in R. Dornbusch and R. Layard (eds.), *The Performance of the British Economy* (Oxford: Oxford University Press, 1987).

9 In 1987, Latin America's imports were $71.1 million, while UK finished manufactured exports were $62.6 million.

10 See IMF, *World Economic Outlook* (Washington, DC, April 1988), Table 32, p. 89. The stock of net external assets fell in 1988, following a huge increase in the UK current account deficit, but the stock remains the third-largest in the world (after those of Japan and West Germany).

11 It is no accident that UK banks are disproportionately represented in Latin America's external debt profile, since they have for many years taken a global view of their operations.

12 Net outward direct investment by UK companies in Latin America has in fact been quite buoyant in the last few years. In 1982, it stood at $226 million (4.2% of all DFI in Latin America), but in 1986 a flow of $539 million was recorded. In 1984, UK DFI represented 16.3% of all DFI in Latin America and the Caribbean. See Business Monitor M4, *Overseas Transactions* (London: HMSO), various editions.

13 See J. Pelkmans and A. Winters, *Europe's Domestic Market* (London: Routledge, 1987).

14 This is particularly true of Japan, which appears to be on the verge of a major increase in its economic relations with Latin America.

15 In a major study of the impact of 1992 (see *European Economy*, special issue *The Economics of 1992*, no. 35, March 1988) the EC made virtually no mention of external trade policy.

16 Britain is not a member of the Cairns Group, set up in 1986 by countries with non-subsidised agricultural sectors and including five Latin American countries. The UK position, however, is closer to that of the Cairns Group than many of our EC partners. See Michael Kain, 'Recent trends in world agricultural trade', *National Westminster Bank Quarterly Review*, May 1988.

17 Not one Latin American country voted with Guatemala when Belize applied to join the United Nations on its achieving independence in 1981.

18 The Contadora Group consists of Colombia, Mexico, Panama and Venezuela, the Support Group of Argentina, Brazil, Peru and Uruguay and the two groups together now constitute the Group of Eight.

19 The Cartagena Group was formed by Latin America's principal debtors in 1984 in an effort to seek common ground on the external debt question.

20 The first Esquipulas Conference, involving the five Central American presidents, was held in Guatemala in May 1986. 'Esquipulas' is now the name given to the peace initiative for Central America launched by President Oscar Arias Sánchez of Costa Rica in February 1987 and which earned him the Nobel Peace Prize.

21 The three Internationals represent Social Democrat, Christian Democrat and Liberal Parties throughout the world with Latin American political parties well represented in all three organisations. There is also the International Democratic Union (IDU), which links Conservative parties around the world, in which Latin American political parties are rather less well represented.

22 By attending the San José Conference in 1984 and signing a Co-operation Agreement with Central America in 1985, the EC has earned itself a great deal of goodwill in Latin America at a very modest cost.

23 This annual report, first published in the 1860s, was prepared by country committees composed – in the case of the Latin American republics – of British capitalists and *rentiers* with Latin American interests. Its country studies are an invaluable source of statistics, as well as a fascinating guide to British commercial interests in Latin America.

24 Eduardo Crawley examined these communities – the most important of which (30,000-strong) is in Argentina – in a seminar given to the Study Group.

25 In the incident to which I refer the country was Guatemala and its capital (Guatemala City) was named by Sir Geoffrey Howe, in the presence of the Guatemalan Vice-President, as Tegucigalpa. See *The Independent*, 11 March 1988, p. 13.

26 The visit of Mikhail Gorbachev to mainland Latin America announced in 1988 will be the first by a Soviet leader. The Soviet Foreign Secretary, Eduard Shevardnadze, has already paid a visit.

27 The first such committee, formed to help Costa Rica, met in Paris on 27 June 1988. All the main European countries were represented except Britain.

28 The OECD's Development Assistant Committee reported that the real value of aid fell by 2 per cent in 1987 and 'major declines were noted in assistance from the United States, Italy, West Germany and Britain'. See *International Herald Tribune*, 23 June 1988, p. 17.

29 It is often forgotten that expenditure on the British troops, trivial for Britain, rivals the Belize national budget in size. The Belize government does have an incentive to drag its heels on this issue, since the presence of British troops is a major source of employment.

30 See House of Commons, Foreign Affairs Committee, *Cultural Diplomacy* (London: HMSO, 1987), p. 233. The decision, announced in 1988, to increase the grant given to the British Council in Mexico and Brazil is a welcome change of policy after many years of cuts.

31 See Central Office of Information, London Press Service, Verbatim Service, VS106/88, p. 1.

Index

Acapulco Summit (1987), 213
Adenauer Foundation, 89
ADLAF (German Association for Research on Latin America), 89, 90
agricultural exports, Latin America, 5, 91, 211
aid to Latin America, 93–4; British, 59, 63, 65, 118–19, 125, 215, 224–5; US, 93, 124, 125, 126
AIDS, 198, 199–200
air links between Europe and Latin America, 52, 113, 224
Alcasa company of Venezuela, 143
Alexandra agricultural colony, Argentina, 11
Alfonsín, President Raúl, 89, 96, 153, 156, 157, 205
Allen, John H., 15
Allende, Salvador, 63, 71, 72, 73, 140
Alliance for Progress, 31, 58, 73, 74
Alliance Française, 39, 42
aluminium industries, 143
American Express, 132
Amnesty International, 62, 63
Anglo-Argentine Society, 64
Anglo-Argentine Tramways Co., 8
Anglo-Ecuadorian oil company, 137
Anglo-Persian oil company, 137
Anglo South American Bank, 14
Anguilla, 216
Antarctic Treaty (1959), 164, 168–9, 172, 173, 176; Consultative Parties (ATCPs), 164, 166
Antarctic Treaty Consultative Meetings (ATCMs), 164, 166, 180, 181
Antarctic Treaty System (ATS), 164–6, 167–8, 169, 171, 174, 178–83 passim, 216
Antarctica, 83, 164–83, 216, 223; economic interests, 173–5; minerals,

167, 173–5; scientific and environmental interests, 176–9; strategic interests, 172–3; territorial claims, 56, 165, 166, 168–71, 173, 181, 182
Arbenz, President Jacobo, 71, 73, 74
Argentina, 13, 31, 42, 53, 58, 59, 64; and Antarctica, 164–77 passim, 180–2 passim; arms industry, 91, 112, 209; British community in, 4–5, 11–12; British diplomatic representation in, 60; British trade and investment, 6–10 passim, 15–20 passim, 55, 69, 103–6 passim, 110, 113–14, 117; economy, 117, 118, 138, 144, 207; and European Community, 88, 89, 98; external debt, 17, 71, 129, 133; and Falkland Islands/Malvinas issue, 3, 55, 66, 76–8, 87, 151–62 passim, 169, 212; historical links with Britain, 1, 2, 4–8 passim, 14; meat exports, 10, 14, 17, 18; railways, 7–8, 10, 19–20, 62; restoration of democracy, 77, 213; and United States, 14, 16, 17, 18, 21, 76–8, 81, 208
Arias Sánchez, President Oscar, peace plan, 79; see also Esquipulas peace agreement
Armenian terrorists, 191
arms trade, 63, 65, 69, 90–1, 112, 209
art exhibitions, Latin America, 32
Assunguy British colony, Paraná, 11
Australia, 114, 116, 181

Bahamas, 188, 195
Bahia, State of, 195
Baker, James A., 96, 129
Balfour, Arthur James, 13
Balfour Williamson, firm of, 5
Balmaceda, President José, 9